晕

Disoriented:

*Two Strange Years in China
as Unexpected Expats*

Howard Goodman
and Ellen Goodman

*Produced by OverWater Books
Delray Beach, Florida*

Cover photo: At breakfast, first dazed day in Shanghai

All photos by Howard and Ellen Goodman, unless otherwise noted

For color versions of the photos in this book, and more, please go
online to
bit.ly/disorientedbook

THIS IS the story of an American couple who, at an age that used to signal retirement, had their middle-class security rattled by the economic upheavals of 2008 and responded by seizing an opportunity to work and live on the other side of the world.

The two of us learned a great deal about China in our two years there. But anyone looking for an authoritative study of the Chinese people or their history, economics, politics, geography, media or language, be warned. This isn't that book.

This account got its start with a blog, "Shanghaied: Our Year in China," and its sequel, "Re-oriented: A Year in Hong Kong." Our posts were like letters home, our attempt to describe the amazing and puzzling things we were encountering in a country that was becoming increasingly important to America, but which was very much a mystery to most Americans. This is what we saw and felt and experienced.

Our thanks to the many people who enjoyed reading about our exploits and urged us to keep on writing.

This is what happened when we listened to you.

Ellen and Howard Goodman
Delray Beach, Florida
May 2014

In fond memory of Don Scarborough — who helped send us off on this adventure, and would have loved hearing every word about it.

Where to experience the next great expat city? Those with an eye to the future might consider Shanghai. With the inexorable rise of the Chinese economy, Shanghai is a good bet to become the financial capital of the 21st century.

— William Moss Wilson, "5 Best Places to Live Overseas for 2008"

Once a playground for foreign adventurers and socialites, the one-time whore of the Orient is now where home-grown tycoons build soaring monuments to capitalism and the locals party all night. But despite a past as evocative as it is notorious, Shanghai has dispensed with the rear-view mirror, pushed the pedal to the floor and is roaring towards its imagined future so fast that keeping up is almost impossible.

— Lonelyplanet.com

Just as New York City exemplified the strengths and aspirations of emerging America in the 20th century, Shanghai, perhaps more than any old or emerging rival, will personify the capabilities and dreams of rising Asia in the 21st century.

— Dr. Dan Steinbock, research director of international business at the India, China and America Institute

1
Take Care of Tumble

IT WAS not love at first sight.

That first morning in Shanghai, Ellen and I looked through our room's grimy window onto a thicket of high-rises — wall upon wall of boxy concrete against a hazy sky. We were staring at a dense metropolis of new buildings that looked prematurely old. We wanted to drink in the sight of the first great city of the twenty-first century, but something was ruining the Tomorrowland effect. Hanging from a lot of those buildings was drying laundry.

We'd had 20 hours of air travel before arriving at Pudong

International Airport, so new and gleaming it seemed unwrapped from a gift box. The terminal was open, sweeping, modern. But all those bright red flags with little yellow stars were a jolt. I felt a stab of great foreignness. We'd been brought up to loathe and fear the colors of the Red Chinese enemy, yet now times had changed and we had to readjust. The flags represented something else — not an enemy any longer, but could we say a friend?

A driver had picked us up and taken us through a bigger and busier city than we had even imagined. At our hotel, bored girls with minimal English and matching blue blazers had checked us in over a cluttered front desk blurred by cigarette smoke, or maybe our lack of sleep. We'd hauled our six overstuffed suitcases — our worldly goods for the next year — into our upper-floor room. And immediately slept away most of the next 12 hours.

Now we got up, half-awake, half-numb, and looked out that badly smudged window. As far as we could see were concrete and glass and steel and cars in motion. And somewhere out there we would have to find our home for the next 12 months.

Our room in the La Residence serviced-apartment hotel — that name gave us our first laugh, the misplaced stab at classiness — was gray and reeked of old cigarettes. The bathroom bore a warning sign to guests in Chinglish, the ineptly translated English we would see repeatedly in Shanghai.

"Take care of tumble," it said.

Meaning what?

Don't lose our balance by what we find in China? Don't get knocked over by the wicked curveballs that life had been throwing at us? Don't toss things down the toilet? Don't slip on the wet floor?

Yeah, probably that.

We went out to find some breakfast and were accosted by wonders: Streets crowded with bicycles, motorbikes and cars swerving in and out of lanes — a near-accident every few seconds. Bus stops with six-foot advertisements for Levis and Coca Cola, featuring young Asians playing electric guitars and beaming over plates of unrecognizable food, the familiar brand logos popping out from incomprehensible strokes of Mandarin. A Lamborghini dealership displaying super-expensive cars in the windows while dozens of beat-up bicycles, left by commuters, were parked in a dense row on the sidewalk in front. A swarm of pedestrians, everyone seemingly handed the same head of hair: black, straight, shiny. Ellen and I had thick, wavy locks — hers red, mine silver. Nobody was going to have any trouble picking us out in this country of 1.3 billion.

We walked directionless down a double-decker road called Yan'An Lu — named, we would learn, after the city that was Mao's Communist Party base after his Long March of the 1930s, one of history's most determined strategic retreats. Now Yan'An was a two-tier answer to urban congestion. It was like something from old science fiction. The upstairs was an expressway. Down below, where we were walking, it was a perfectly normal city street with sidewalks and greenery and store entrances. I knew of no equivalent in the United States, where an overpass usually creates a graffiti-streaked dead zone, cleaving previously well-functioning cities in two. Score one for Shanghai.

We were illiterate. Storefronts and street signs were impossible to read. Almost none used English — not even Pinyin, the written Chinese that uses English lettering. We found a restaurant. No one spoke English. So we weren't just illiterate. We were mute, too.

But by pointing to pictures on the menu, we succeeded in being served a breakfast of scrambled eggs with garlic, and fried rice with eggs and pork. We paid with yuan: unfamiliar bills printed in the colors of Monopoly money and on paper that seemed nearly as cheap. Chairman Mao's face stared at us from each and every denomination. The old dictator gave us a benevolent smile, as fatherly as George Washington.

Ellen and I sat across from one another at a small table by the window, and gave each other a look. I don't remember if we spoke the question out loud, but it was so clearly on our minds that we wouldn't have had to. It was written all over our jet-lagged, shell-shocked faces.

What the fuck were we doing here?

THE ANSWER was simple. We had been hit by the Great Recession of 2008-'09 in every way we could have been hit by a Great Recession.

I was laid off from my job. Our retirement savings lost a quarter to a third of their value, invested as they were in the stock market. Our one brave investment in local real estate, a rental property, went south. The value of our own house plummeted, but our monthly payments stayed as high as ever. And the prospects for Ellen's career as a Realtor were looking none too healthy. We were living in South Florida, a region that was one of the worst for the wheeler-dealer mortgage and banking abuses that crashed the economy.

When the opportunity came to escape the pitiful American economy by working for a year in China, we grabbed it.

I am a newspaper journalist. Ellen is a teacher turned Realtor. We each enjoyed long careers in our fields, proud of the work we did. But newspapers — which I'd loved and idealized ever since I was a kid, watching the wise-cracking movie heroes in fedoras who humbled the powerful by hacking at clattering Underwoods; spreading each day's *Chicago Daily News* all over the dining room floor to soak up Mike Royko's tough-tender prose while my mother made dinner; writing and illustrating my own mimeographed "newspaper" and selling it door-to-door as a suburban sixth-grader; editing my high school paper — that industry had been endangered for years.

I learned how to be a reporter in Oregon and Kansas City, just after Woodward and Bernstein exposed a corrupt presidency, the time when newspaper journalism was never more idealistic. For almost 15 years I was a staff writer at the Philadelphia Inquirer, a wonderful newspaper in what now seems a golden age for the rolling presses. I'd won prizes for beat reporting and feature writing, been nominated for the Pulitzer Prize for unearthing a massive Wall Street scam. I helped free a man serving a life sentence on an unjust murder conviction and wrote features that were pure fun. The work was a joy.

But it didn't last. The *Inquirer* fell victim to sharply falling circulation, periodic staff cutbacks and buyouts, diminished morale. In 2000, after an uncomfortable stint at Bloomberg News, I migrated to the *South Florida Sun Sentinel*, based in Fort Lauderdale, to be an editor. Two years later, I was a columnist, a dream job of the profession.

Newspaper circulation was still growing in South Florida, thanks to its older customer base: New Jerseyans and Long Islanders who brought the newspaper-reading habit down with them. The retirees staved off the forces that were killing print journalism in America almost everywhere else: the Internet, and newspapers' fatal decision to put their content online for free; the rise of free classifieds on Craigslist, which sapped newspapers of essential income from want ads; the squeeze on Americans' time as more families became two-worker households over a decade of stagnant incomes.

Staved off those forces for a time, that is. By 2007 or 2008, even South Florida newspapers were lashed by the same harsh winds. It was unusual to find anyone younger than 40 who bought a newspaper to get the news. The headlines popped up for free on their computer screens — until even that convenience was supplanted by mobile phones.

In short order, the *Sun Sentinel* and its parent Tribune Co. saw their profits slip. And as the losses mounted, it became clear that while we writers and editors had thought of ourselves as the newspaper's heart and soul, the executives calculated our value rather less sentimentally. We were an operating expense. A drain. The layoffs soon followed.

I was an old-timer, but I was no dinosaur. In 2008 my editors abruptly pulled me off the metro column I'd been writing for five years to make me the *Sun Sentinel*'s first-ever blogs editor. I gamely dove in to the brave new Internet world, figuring I should seize the opportunity to learn an additional set of marketable skills for myself while helping the paper. I must say, I did some good. I developed a slew of new features for the paper's online edition and taught several dozen print journalists how to get their footing on the Web.

Yet even with those successes and adaptations, it took only another year to feel the air leaking out of my *Sun Sentinel* career. My situation was all too evident: Several veteran journalists with distinguished credentials had already been let go. I was making good money by this newsroom's standard. I was 59 years old, and I had seen my column taken away in a flash. I was clearly expendable. I could feel the target on my back every day that I went to work.

Yet as prepared as I was for the ax to fall, the moment of my dismissal came as a complete surprise. The day was normal. I was reporting a story. I was making phone calls seeking interviews. I was expecting people to call me back.

I had returned to reporting because after a year and a half as blogs editor, the paper's infatuation with blogging had faded as staff members were laid off, the ranks thinning in every department. Fewer staffers meant fewer bloggers. There was less and less for me to do. I suggested a transfer back to reporting, and my request was readily approved. Too readily. It was one more sign of my expendability.

I was expecting the phone to ring. And it rang. But it was not any of the sources I had called for the story I was researching.

"Howard, this is Philip. How are you?"

Philip Ward, the newspaper's deputy managing editor for news. The man who had told me, almost two years earlier, that the paper wanted me to drop my column and run the blogs. The man who had told me, about two months before, that I could return to reporting.

"I'm fine, thanks. And you?" I said automatically, thinking, gee, maybe Philip has another interesting assignment he'd like me to take on.

"Well, I need to talk to you. I'm downstairs."

Downstairs? That didn't compute. Philip didn't work in our bureau's building in Deerfield Beach. He worked in the paper's main newsroom in Fort Lauderdale.

"And come right away," he said. "Leave everything up there. But bring your car keys."

"My car keys?" I still wasn't catching on.

"Yes, you won't be coming back upstairs."

Oh damn.

My stomach knew it before I did. It did a somersault while my mind was still forming the words: This is it. It's happening. It can't be happening.

I hung up, disassociating from the moment, watching myself be fired. I noticed that everyone around me was still working at their desks, unaware I had just been culled from the herd. I moved quietly. Maintain your dignity, I told myself. Show no emotion. Make this a normal exit from your seat, a normal walk across the room, a normal walk down the stairs, a normal knock on the door of a glassed-in office that I'd never noticed before, a normal nod of the head to the woman who sat across the almost-bare desk who greeted me in a polite matter-of-fact voice and offered me a seat. I didn't argue, didn't fuss, didn't snarl. I just took the seat.

Philip was in the seat next to mine. He offered his hand. I shook it. His eyes were tearing.

Mine were clear. I listened numbly as the human resources representative explained the particulars of the layoff. She wanted me to go home and not think about anything for the rest of the day and perhaps tomorrow. Then I should look through the packet she was handing me. It would explain that I was to get paid for another 11 weeks, one week for each of my 10 years of service to the company plus one more as a bonus. I would find phone numbers for getting onto Cobra health insurance when the Tribune Company health plan ran out after the 11 weeks, and for obtaining unemployment benefits from the state when my severance from the company was complete. The packet would tell me how to enroll for a month's worth of job-seeking help from the consulting firm that the company had contracted to help me deal creatively with this important and hopefully positive transition in my life.

She handed me the packet, thanked me for my service and wished me luck. I shook hands again, stood, and walked out of the building with no goodbyes to any of my colleagues upstairs. Just that fast, I was no longer a member of the labor force. I had gone to work that morning as I had for 30-some years. A scant year and a half before, I had been somewhat famous in our county, a columnist, my words and picture published three times a week. Now I was an unemployment statistic.

It was 2:30 in the afternoon, the sun high and shining. It was hours before rush hour and my day was over. I watched myself driving home, obeying the traffic signals, pulling into my driveway, coming into the house, finding my wife in the living room and registering the surprise in her face to see me home at mid-day.

"I've been fired," I said. "They got me."

I watched her blanch. "Oh God," she said. "Are you all right?"

"I think so," I said. "I don't know." But of course I wasn't all right.

I went on Facebook and shared my news with a few hundred people. Then I spent a couple of adrenaline-filled days accepting people's commiseration. It was easier to write about my emotions than to actually feel them. I figured it was best to get the word out that I was without a job and looking; maybe someone would have a lead. Better that, than to hide out and look ashamed. Or to let anger eat at me. I was angry, of course. But it was an abstract anger. There was no one to be angry at. My industry's economy had gone under. And the technology I had grown up with and had always assumed would be there had been surpassed. I was a horse and buggy maker overtaken by the horseless carriage. So anger never became my ruling emotion. More often I was scared. Scared of not having an income – or of not having as much income. Scared of being unable to practice my profession any longer. Or scared that I would try to adapt my writing and editing skills to new settings – public relations, advertising, teaching – and wouldn't succeed. Scared that I was about to turn 60 years old.

It was now my unsought task to start seeing myself as a marketable commodity on the job market. For weeks I went to the seminars on resume writing, interviewing, networking. But networking was a joke. All the networking I'd ever done was for an industry now in triage. Some 31,000 people lost their jobs at American newspapers in 2008 and 2009. I was tossed in a wave of evacuees, including a lot of the men and women I'd networked with. And they were flooding the job market for the few

15

available scraps in journalism or its most predictable life rafts: PR, advertising, teaching. All those Plan B jobs were taken – those that weren't themselves eliminated because the recession was cutting into the ranks of corporations and schools as well. At one job opening, I was one applicant out of 600. At another, one of 800. At one university, I was told, sorry, sir, we can't accept your application. We've lost our funding for that job since we posted the opening. We can't hire anybody.

I did some freelance. I took some courses in commercial copywriting – how to write those pitches you get in the mail cajoling you to subscribe to a newsletter brimming with vital investment tips or urging you to contribute to a political candidate or begging you to sponsor an orphan's cleft palate operation. I watched my *Sun Sentinel* severance run out and applied for unemployment compensation. This was the point when my lawyer friend Michael told me that, given the realities of the U.S. economy, my job search could last a while. In all sympathy, he recommended I find work as a process server. Process servers are always in demand. I think he wasn't joking.

I was oddly serene. Or was I dumbly confident? I had, in any case, decided to trust in the prophesies of a friend who possessed no little store of psychic power. Her name was Bobbey. She called herself a "sensitive." She said that, without any effort on her part, she received frequent visits from angels who gave her information about people whose path she crossed. Strangely, the angels never gave her much information about herself – she couldn't predict winners in the stock market or horses at the track or know whether a house she wanted to buy was a good investment; she said her gift would never allow her to enrich herself. But those angels could be uncanny about others. When Bobbey met our daughter Rachel, for example, she looked at her a bit strangely just minutes after saying hello, and said that she sensed some problem with water. Then she got more specific. She saw a problem with Rachel's swimming pool. There was a leak, but no one would know about it for several months.

This was astonishing – no one had even told Bobbey that Rachel had a swimming pool – but it was also preposterous. Rachel's husband, Tal, a man with a general-contractor's license, had just had their swimming pool redone. Everything was new and perfect about their swimming pool.

But a few months later, damned if a gardener who was cutting Rachel and Tal's lawn didn't knock on their door to say he had discovered a puzzling wet depression in their back yard — as if water were gurgling underground. Sure enough, a little digging discovered a leak in the recently redone swimming pool.

I don't believe in the supernatural, but that prediction was way too specific and too peculiar to be dismissed as luck or coincidence. Who looks at a stranger and senses a swimming pool leak? When Bobbey said things, I took note.

We saw her infrequently. She and her husband John had retired to St. Augustine, a few hundred miles north of our town, Delray Beach. But we did see her at a party around Thanksgiving in 2008. She took one look at me and said, "Oh, dear, you're worried about your job aren't you? Really worried." Well, it didn't take a psychic to discern that much. The *Sun Sentinel* had started to lay off skilled veterans. The stress had deepened a few lines in my forehead and made me stiff in the neck and shoulders.

"Look, relax, nothing's going to happen for a while," Bobbey went on. "You're going to be fine all through the Christmas holidays." This was good to hear. I'd been worried I'd get lopped off around the first of the year, at the end of the company's financial quarter.

"You're fine until about April."

"Oh, yeah? Really?"

"Yes, and even after that you're going to be OK."

I chose to believe her. Decided not to worry through the Christmas holidays, through the New Year, through the first couple of months of 2009. Maybe the reason I had been so surprised when the ax did fall was that it wasn't yet April. It was March 25. I thought Bobbey had given me another week.

Now it was the beginning of May, and Ellen and I were coming up on our sixtieth birthdays that month, and decided we'd drive to New Orleans to celebrate at the great Jazz and Heritage Festival. On our way we stopped in St. Augustine to spend a night with John and Bobbey.

John, a transplanted Brit from the old school of hard-drinking Fleet Streeters, poured stiff scotches from the antique pub bar he'd set up in his den. Bobbey looked at me as if she were reading something that was as plain as day.

"You're going to be fine," she said, all confidence. "You're going to hear from someone from your past, someone who you have no idea is in any position to help you. But she is going to help you. She is going to offer you a fantastic opportunity and you should step right into it. And this is going to happen around July 15."

She paused a few moments, and then she spoke excitedly. "I see you working – you're in a place that's all gray. And you have these kind of schematics or drawings of newspaper pages all around – what do you call them, John?"

"Layouts."

"Yes, layouts. You're going to be working with layouts."

My face was now screwed into an expression of pure negation. "No, that can't be right. I don't do that kind of work. I haven't done that kind of work since maybe my first months in a newsroom, back in 1976."

"Well, maybe not," Bobbey said. "All I know is what the angels are telling me."

Angels, shmangels. And yet I started taking a mental inventory. What women were in my past who might be in a position to help me land my next job? I thought of old girlfriends, long-lost collaborators on news stories, old editors, past sources, spokeswomen I'd been friendly with. Even contacted a few of them over the next few weeks. Nothing struck.

One night in June, Ellen and I went out for Chinese food. My fortune read: "Be prepared to accept a wondrous opportunity in the days ahead!"

I put that slip of paper in my wallet.

An email happened to arrive a couple of days later. It was from the first editor I'd ever had, a brilliant and extremely kind man who ran the copy desk named Don Scarborough. Now retired, Scarborough had spent his whole career in Salem, Oregon, and still lived in the house he and his family had when I was there in the 1970s. He wrote to say hello, and was stunned when I wrote back that I'd been laid off. He replied right away: "That's the most shocking news I've heard in a long while. You are the best reporter and writer the industry has turned out in many years.... I feel sorry for you and the news business."

And then he wrote again, a day or two later, to ask if I'd be interested in doing what he had done for a short time after he retired — work at the English-language *Shanghai Daily*. "It's not exactly what you like to do. It's mostly copy editing," he said, "but I had an incredibly good time over there."

The instigator of this idea, I later learned, was Sue Hill. She'd been an ace reporter at the Salem paper, the Statesman-Journal. We hadn't communicated in many years. She was entirely off my radar. But, like me, she had stayed in touch with Scarborough. After I'd left Oregon to pursue my career eastward, heading for Ann Arbor, Kansas City and Philadelphia,

Sue headed in the other direction to Asia. She worked for the AP, Bloomberg and *Wall Street Journal* in Beijing and Hong Kong. She worked for the state-controlled English language *China Daily* in Beijing, and when a faction of the staff split off to start a Shanghai-based newspaper of the same sort in 2000, she went with them. She was a founding editor, in effect, of the *Shanghai Daily*. Now she was retired and living on the distant Australian island of Tasmania.

I was about to get my first lesson about China. Sue remained highly respected by the editors at the *Shanghai Daily*, who were still there, still running the paper. That respect was called *guanxi*, and it was like money. It had value that could be traded. And it was transferrable. Based on Sue's *guanxi*, she told me in a follow-up email, the *Shanghai Daily* would hire me in an instant; important decisions in modern China hinged on personal connections, just as they had in ancient China. The editors always hired a certain number of foreigners on one-year contracts. Was I interested?

"Listen, Howard, I know you. I know them. I wouldn't recommend everybody to them, but I think you'd really get on over there."

Someone from my past, whom I had no idea was in a position to help me, was going to offer me a fantastic opportunity …

I fully expected Ellen to reject the idea out of hand. Despite the terrible economy, she was prospering in real estate; she'd worked her way into a niche of the market that was bringing her a steady stream of business. We were just a 40-minute drive from the two cutest grandkids any grandmother could fawn over.

But I had forgotten about her yearning for adventure. "Hon, you know I've always wanted to live overseas," she said — but foreign postings during my newspaper career had eluded us. "I thought our chances to be expatriates were over a long time ago."

She gave it about two minutes' more thought.

"Let's do it."

Things moved incredibly fast. I quickly got off an email, as Sue recommended, to Jiang Jianjun, universally known as JJ, the *Shanghai Daily*'s key editor, expressing my interest and attaching my resume, and 24 hours later came a reply that thrilled:

"Dear Howard, I think *Shanghai Daily* should thank the economic crisis for giving the newspaper the chance to have you work with us. We are looking forward to seeing you in Shanghai soon...."

The paper would pay me 20,000 yuan a month — $3,000 in U.S.

money, tax free — with another $914 monthly paid by the Chinese government as a housing allowance. The money is "not great," JJ said, "but it is enough for you to live a comfortable life in China." The year-long contract would offer four weeks of vacation. It sounded wonderful.

It was June 27, 2009. Just that fast, my days went from a dispiriting tedium of searching online classifieds for job openings, writing cover letters, revising resumes to fit the would-be employer's requirements, sending letters and resumes out, and usually hearing nothing in return ... to letting go of all that. Just like that, I could walk away from the miserable economy and all the pessimism that went along with it. I could begin fresh. Put the house up for rent and get ready to live and work in a country that I had never dreamed of even visiting. Switch to a life in an alternate universe that, unlike the one I knew, was actually prospering.

After being laid off, after turning 60, after watching the opportunities vanish in my field of work, I had been all but sure that my world was shutting down and getting smaller, that money would be scarcer, work less fulfilling, and travel out of the question. Something similar had happened to my father when he prematurely lost his job as an executive around age 60. He tried hard to follow up with a great Act II for his career, but it never came. He had to settle for projects, hobbies and part-time jobs to fill the days of an enforced retirement. He carried it off gamely and with dignity, but it was always a drag on my heart that the avenues for his vitality had been shut off, and not by his choice.

So here was a strong rebuttal to that nightmare vision of life as an hourglass with the sands dripping away. Here was the adventure of China.

We were turning being let go into "Let's go!"

Had this opportunity offered itself a couple of years earlier, we probably couldn't have managed it. But our youngest, Ben, 19, had just finished his first year of college. For the first time in 21 years of marriage, Ellen and I didn't have children at home to take care of — the older two, El's daughter and son from her first marriage, were grown and long out of the house. We were, more or less, free agents. And improbably enough, Ben was studying Mandarin at school. Our leaving for China, rather than an abandonment, could actually be a benefit for him. He could come to Shanghai and take deeper language courses and we could share the foreign experience together.

It could be a family adventure. As a friend of Ben's put it, "Dude, it's like a weird, bizarro spinoff show, 'The Goodmans in China'."

We had one complication that precluded our leaving right away. Our 30-year-old, Mike, was to be married in Philadelphia in the approaching October. The *Shanghai Daily* agreed it wouldn't make much sense to rush out there, half the world away, then turn around after a few weeks to take part in the wedding. Better to finish all our family obligations first and go to China with an uncluttered mind. So we didn't hurry our departure. We made plans to take about two months to pack away our house and rent it out. We plotted a leisurely trip from Florida up to the Northeast, saying farewell to friends and family along the way.

Then, a couple of days after the wedding, we'd fly from Philadelphia to the most exotic destination either of us had ever seen on a plane ticket, Shanghai, China.

2
Back Story

Ellen writes:

DROP EVERYTHING in my life, leave my friends, family, put my career on hold and run off to China — knowing exactly one person in all of Asia? Scary. But if that one person was Howard Goodman, the answer was a no-brainer. He is my best friend, confidante, business partner, bullshit detector, therapist and booster. How could I not go?

We met way back in high school. I was 16 years old and my family had recently been transferred from St. Louis to Skokie, Illinois, just north of Chicago. We dated and even went to prom together. But I was more serious about an "older man," a guy one year older whom I dated on Saturday nights, letting Howie see me on Fridays. After we graduated in 1967, Howie went east to Cornell and I stayed in the Midwest. So did Mr. Saturday Night, which gave him the home court advantage. When I saw Howie next, over Christmas break, he had turned into a long-haired hippie, complete with navy pea coat. Attractive. But the other guy offered more of what I wanted then: security. My reasoning was simple — I wanted someone who could take care of me and he was going to be a lawyer. Attractive Hippie or Successful Lawyer? I told Howie we couldn't see each other anymore.

At the ripe old age of 22 I married Mr. Saturday. I helped him through law school in Ann Arbor, Michigan, and followed him to his first firm in Atlanta. On the surface, it looked like I had it made. I was married to a professional, had earned a Master's degree, had a house in the suburbs and two wonderful children. So why was I so unhappy? The marriage felt strained but I kept hoping it would improve. I had heard that you had to work at making a successful marriage, but it seemed no matter how hard I tried, I just couldn't get it right. Something was missing but I didn't know what it was.

I plodded along, doing my best to be a good wife and a great mom. I got my affection from my children and my intellectual stimulation from my girlfriends. Many of them had similar complaints about their marriages — their husbands were preoccupied with work, they felt overwhelmed with the demands of taking care of young children, there was no affection. I figured this was just the way it was. The kind of marriage I'd hoped for, the soul-mate kind, was just a fantasy you would see in a movie or read about in a book. I learned to lower my expectations for happiness. Once or twice we tried marriage counseling. The counselors couldn't believe how different we were. I was getting more and more liberal, he more conservative. Their advice was simple. If we wanted to stay married we would have to live more or less separate lives: go shopping separately, make social plans with friends separately, vacation separately. And so I'd go camping with a girlfriend whose husband also hated the idea of sleeping outdoors. I was quietly miserable but determined to tough it out until my kids finished school and I'd be free to leave.

One phone call changed all that.

It was my closest friend from high school, calling to tell me that our 20-year reunion was coming up. "Guess who's the only other person from our class, besides you, who's living in Philadelphia?" Rhonda said. "Howie Goodman. You should get in touch with him and see how he turned out."

So I called Howie and we met for a lunch, a lunch that lasted hours. I was so completely drawn to him. "You're losing your mind," I told myself. "You're a married woman." But I couldn't stop thinking about him. In less than a year — a tumultuous, crazy, painful, passionate year — I divorced my husband and I married Howie. I told him I felt terrible for the way I had treated him in high school and that, as penance, I promised to be a wonderful wife for the next 20 years. I have kept my word.

It sounds cheesy, but I feel like I'm still on my honeymoon. It's easy to feel that way when you're married to your soul mate. My single friends jokingly call me the poster child for successful second marriages. They tell me our marriage gives them hope. When people used to tell me how lucky I was, I'd smile and say that I would follow Howie anywhere. I didn't realize I'd have to prove it.

23

Howard:

I LIKED her the moment I saw her. That was on a yellow school bus, on our way to Niles Township High School North in Skokie, Ill., a postwar suburb just north of Chicago, a flat land of ranch-style houses and Jewish families proud to be in them instead of the walk-up apartments they'd left behind in the North Side or South Side of Chicago, happy to have lawns to mow, a spanking shopping center nearby and fresh new schools for their kids.

She had flaming red hair, a pretty face and an openness of expression that suggested she wasn't wrapped up in a clique. This was a result of her being new. She'd recently moved into town from St. Louis and hadn't been around long enough to realize how uncool it might be to befriend me, the high school newspaper editor. So she returned my smile and my hello and let me chat her up, and she grabbed my teenage heart then and there.

She was the first girl I really dated. But she wouldn't let me get too close. She was more serious about a guy who was a year older and a lot more focused on his adult financial future than I was.

I went off to college and got radicalized by the rising movement against the Vietnam War. When I saw her next, over Christmas break back in Chicago, our conversation went like this:

Me, channeling Eldridge Cleaver: "If you're not part of the solution, you're part of the problem."

Her, channeling June Cleaver: "All I want is a two-car garage and to go to Florida in the winter."

She dumped me. I felt terrible… and then somehow 20 years went by and I forgot about Ellen Rubin. Lots of other things happened. I ran from Mayor Daley's cops at the 1968 Chicago Democratic Convention protests, went to Woodstock, lived on communes, hitchhiked coast to coast, worked for McGovern, attended grad school at Berkeley, started a newspaper career in Oregon, worked in Kansas City and found professional fulfillment in Philadelphia, joining the Inquirer, then probably the best newspaper in America. I loved a few wonderful girlfriends. I got married, then divorced. More girlfriends. One of the girlfriends moved with me to Philadelphia.

And that's where Ellen found me again, calling me on the phone and asking me out to lunch. We met at at TGI Fridays, and as we were talking, the most peculiar feeling came over me. An experience I never had before or since. I felt myself pulled to her, a physical tug — as if my ghost or soul were moving across the table to connect with her, merge with her. Every other allegiance or attachment in my life melted away.

Just that fast, just that inescapably, I was aligned with Ellen Dara Rubin.

It made no sense. It made all the sense in the world.

She had a husband, two children, a dog and a suburban house on a cul de sac. I didn't sneer. On the contrary, I found myself jealous of her stability and her family life — found myself yearning for something just like it. I was in my late 30s and had been wishing, at last, after a long period of feeling unready, to be a father. My girlfriend was 10 years younger than I, enjoying the freedom of being a professional woman and in no hurry for parenthood. I had been wondering with increasing frustration when this part of my life might start.

In strangely parallel fashion, Ellen was telling me that she had settled for stability too young, that she envied my history of rambling, that increasingly she had been wishing for a less-structured, more intellectually challenging, more interesting life.

When we were college-age, I had veered left and Ellen had veered right. In recent years we had each altered course toward the middle. And now we met.

Everyone who met Ellen could see we were a great match. Some long-time couples finish each other's sentences. We did them one better. We found ourselves saying the same thing at the same time. And we did it weirdly, when there was no audible cue. A remark would come out of the blue — in stereo.

It wasn't our only similarity. We were born just two weeks apart in the same year, 1949. We were each the oldest of three kids. We were both Jewish, but wore the identification lightly. We each had master's degrees and were recognized as talents in our fields, journalism and teaching. We'd each had first marriages in which we had felt like the responsible ones. And now each of us wanted to be with someone who was as fully formed as the other. We wanted an equal.

I knew for sure she was the mate for me when we arrived in Venice for our honeymoon — and her suitcase didn't. Almost any other woman would have been frantic. No wardrobe! But she was calm. Her smile never wavered.

"Don't worry, I'll be all right," she said. "It's just part of the adventure."

For three days, until the luggage finally arrived at the Venice airport, she wore my shorts tied tight with a belt, and my t-shirts, knotted at the waist. In our photos she looks adorable.

With Rachel, Mike and Ben, we stayed in Philadelphia a dozen years, until it came time to leave the *Inquirer*, where circulation was collapsing, management was fumbling and reporters and editors were either seething or fleeing. I took an editing job at the Sun Sentinel, largely out of consideration for Ellen. I had always pretty much detested the Sunshine State, but South Florida had become the locus of Ellen's family. Her parents had moved there and so had the now-married Rachel. Ellen had always wanted the place in Florida and the two-car garage. The twist was she had them with me.

Our compatibility was off the charts. Our home decor was a blend of her folk art and my framed photographs and shelves of books. We liked the same movies, the same TV shows — though she never picked up the slightest patience for sports. I'm on my own there. When the ability to record TV shows came in, it was the death of us. We loved nothing more than to sit side by side on the long, white leather living room sofa, soaking in "The Sopranos," "Weeds," "The Wire." Hours of Turner Classic Movies.

We were each other's cheerleaders and support. I suffer from severe hearing loss, a congenital condition; Ellen's my translator. I'm much more widely read in history, biography, politics, music, movies, theater, literature; on those subjects, I'm her Google. She's got a great way with children, an eye for colors, an air-tight memory of movie plots and a mind for medicine, a legacy of surviving polio as a child. She's my Physician's Desk Reference on what pill to take for a sinus headache, which one for sore throat. I'm dreamy where she's practical; she handles most of the household money matters. I'm prone to self-doubt. She's developed a fine self-confidence. I'm inward-looking and analyzing. She's outgoing and straightforward. She laughs at my jokes, doesn't groan too loudly at my dumber puns and has a way of turning any story into something hilarious. When we get irked at each other, we'll almost never yell. If she's mad at me, she'll go silent. I hate that silence.

When I lost my job in 2009, I worried over the loss of income. Worried whether I'd be able to provide enough for Ben's future. Worried if I'd ever again find work commensurate with my talents. Worried about retirement and old age. But I never doubted the strength of my relationship with Ellen. I was jobless, uncertain, adrift — but with the best of mates.

In my enforced spare time, when I wasn't sending out resumes or writing the occasional freelance piece, I helped her with her real estate, taking the pictures and writing the copy for her house listings. Without a job to go to the next day, we spent evenings letting time and the world dissolve away. Our closeness tightened; sex grew sweeter, dreamier. You couldn't call it a honeymoon. But the fact was, we hadn't spent as much uninterrupted time together — just the two of us — since that romantic week of a lifetime in 1988.

Whatever we would experience on the other side of the world, we'd experience together.

3
Goodbye

A letter from Ellen:
TO MY friends and family,

I know many of you think that our planned move to China is crazy and that we're just shell-shocked and we'll soon come to our senses. I think that if I share some things with you, you'll have a better understanding of how we made our decision.

When Howie came home in the middle of the day and told me he had been laid off I didn't realize what that would mean to us and our family.

You hear about this kind of thing all the time, but until it happens to you it's just theory. My first response was to disassociate — I went right back to working on a real estate contract I was writing. Later that evening it began to sink in — my husband had lost his job. How was I supposed to bolster up his shattered ego? Could I keep us financially solvent? For the next few days my moods fluctuated between anger, shame and fear. How could this have happened to us?

I didn't blame Howie — it certainly wasn't his fault that the newspaper industry was spiraling downward. We knew it was coming, but even being somewhat prepared didn't make the reality less painful. We had Ben in college, a healthy mortgage payment to meet, and we were both turning 60 in a month. What the hell were we supposed to do?

I started to think about all the friends and family that we had and that gave me some comfort. I knew that we wouldn't have to live in our car like you hear happens to some people, but still, it was incredibly discouraging to have this happen to us at this stage of our life.

I always figured that if we played by the rules — get a good education, save your money, live within your means — that everything would work out fine. Not the case! OK, so now what?

After a few days the pity party I was throwing didn't feel right. I remembered the old saying, "When life gives you lemons, make lemonade" and that was exactly what I planned to do.

First thing on the agenda: Have fun.

You know that we took advantage of our newly freed-up schedule to take a road trip to New Orleans to celebrate our birthdays during the Jazz and Heritage Festival. By driving there and staying with Cousin Matt, the trip was affordable and we had an unforgettable time. This emboldened me.

"We're gonna make something good out of this. I don't know what yet, but something good," I told Howie.

Now here's the part you didn't know:

From the time I was little and first heard the word, I had always wanted to be an expat.

How cool, I thought, to see your country from the outside looking in. I came close once, when I was in high school and my dad's job at RCA Corporation almost transferred the family to Paris. When it didn't happen, I remember being really disappointed, but figured that I'd have lots of chances in the future. I thought about joining the Peace Corps, but got married too young instead. My honeymoon in Europe with my first husband re-kindled my love of travel, but instead of traveling, we saved our money and bought a house. I was hell-bent on being a grown-up and that meant home ownership and children. My Master Plan was to have my kids while I was young and then I would be free to travel later. As I've said to you many times, "Man plans, God laughs!"

When my marriage soured, I considered teaching abroad. I'd get away from my old life and see the world. I spoke to several agencies that place teachers in foreign countries but was quickly told that I wouldn't be invited to teach anywhere with two children in tow. So I struck out again. Looking back now, I realize how completely impractical that would have been, but I felt desperate and, at the time it seemed like the perfect solution.

My dreams of living outside of the USA lay dormant until I married Howie. His newspaper had some foreign postings and I hoped that we

29

might get a chance to be expats that way, but it never happened. My dream seemed to have ended.

So there I was, sitting at the kitchen table with my laptop, in Delray Beach having just turned 60, when Howie innocently asks me, "El, what do you think about moving to Shanghai, China?"

"Hold on a minute," I said.

The only thing I knew about Shanghai was that it was on water and that sailors in old San Francisco had to be careful not to get too drunk or they could get "Shanghaied," clobbered over the head and kidnapped into service on some shady freighter. I quickly Googled "Shanghai" and checked the latitude. I had heard how bone-chilling parts of China were and I wanted no part of frigid weather. On the map, Shanghai looked even with northern Florida and New Orleans. Nice. I could be comfortable there.

I barely looked up from the computer.

"OK," I said.

Howie couldn't believe it. He didn't think I'd give up my real estate career or our proximity to the grandkids.

"I have always wanted to see what it's like to live abroad," I told him. "I thought that boat had set sail without me. Let's do it."

So now you know that this isn't a half-baked idea that suddenly came up. As Benjamin Braddock says in "The Graduate," "Oh no, this is fully baked!"

I know this won't be easy. I will miss you like crazy and I'm sure there will be times when I want to run back home to the safety of your love and support. But I feel like this is all part of some master plan and I have to see it through.

I will always love you, no matter where I am.

Love,
Mom / El

Howard:

EMPTYING THE house was a chore that took weeks. It meant going through all the things we owned and deciding what to do with them. Every item — every chair and table, every pot and pan, every electronic gizmo, every book, every newspaper clipping (and there were hundreds) — required a decision: Store it? Lend it to someone for safekeeping? Throw it away? Take it along?

Our house was not extraordinarily large for American suburbia: Two bedrooms and a den, two baths, two-car garage. But it was, we'd soon learn, mammoth by Chinese standards. And in our combined 120 years on this Earth, Ellen and I had managed to fill it with an incredible amount of stuff. Kids' science projects. Dead computer parts. Airless basketballs. Thousands of photographs and hundreds of LPs and CDs, which I painstakingly digitized and transferred to an iPod to ensure I'd have an ample enough collection of listenable music in the Far East.

Many trips to the curb and treks to the Salvation Army later — after giving our living room sofa to young newlyweds, our dining-room hutch to a former *Sun Sentinel* colleague, our green chaise longue and Indian artwork to friends Michael and Angela, treasured framed photos to daughter Rachel — we stuffed the bulk of our things into a U-store-it the size of a one-car garage. We rolled down the metal door, secured it with a combination lock, and left our worldly goods in air-conditioned darkness in Lake Worth, Florida.

We turned our emptied house over to tenants, a hard-working young couple, with good credit, who promised to take good care of the place despite their large dog, and to pay on time. We would be getting the market rental rate of $1,650 a month from them, only about half of the $3,000 we owed each month in mortgage, taxes and other house expenses. House payments, storage payments, insurance payments: not only was the cost of living high in America, so was the cost of not living in America.

"We love your house. We want to buy it," the new tenants told us. We laughed. The thought was absurd. We knew we'd be back. In a year, the economy would look better. It had to. We'd have our year of adventure in China and then get back to where we were.

I said farewell to my mother in Chicago, who bravely wished us a good trip. If she felt pain at our leaving, she hid it. And later, I learned that she defended me fiercely when telling one of her friends about our going. "He's taking a job in Shanghai?" the friend said with horror. "What's the matter, he can't find a job here?"

Mom answered with steel: "He's going because he wants to."

We held a farewell party in Delray Beach, two farewell parties in New York for different groups of relatives, a farewell party in Philadelphia. At my old paper there, the Inquirer, we met with Jennifer Lin, a former Beijing correspondent. She plied us with tips about etiquette ("Don't hug people when you say hello and goodbye. The Chinese aren't huggers."), gave us books to read, showered us with enthusiasm.

"It will be exasperating, frustrating," Jennifer told us, "and the best year of your life."

A few days later, after Mike and Kate's wedding and a final flood of farewells, we flew off to the Far East, fully expecting the exasperation and frustration. And fiercely hoping she was right about the last part.

I had given myself a crash course on the Middle Kingdom. Histories. Novels. Analytical journalism. I studied Mandarin on Rosetta Stone, the language-learning software. And I got pretty good at it — as long as I was plugged into the program. For a while I was quite fluent in: "The girl is drinking juice." But the moment I stepped into the real world and tried to go much beyond "Ni hao," the Chinese hello, I was dumb as nails.

Years before, I had made two trips to Japan, one with journalists, one with wife and son, but the rest of Asia was a haze. What I knew about China had to be wrong, a mental welter of countless movies and stories and jokes and trips to Chinese restaurants. When I thought of China, I thought of the stereotypes in Charlie Chan and The Good Earth and the epic sweep of The Last Emperor and Crouching Tiger, Hidden Dragon; the child's idea of digging a hole to the other side of the world and emerging to find a boy similar to me, but wearing a coolie's rice-paddy hat; the black-and-white TV images of a billion fanatical people in baggy gray uniforms waving Chairman Mao's Little Red Book. As a high school freshman, I'd run through the dynasties of Chinese history in my Non-Western Civilizations course, and at Cornell I'd studied Chinese Communism as part of my Government major. I was very well educated and probably deeply misinformed.

The present-day China I learned about from the *New York Times* and CNN was a long-secretive place now panting for development, polluting its countryside, stealing American and European intellectual property, jailing dissidents when not shooting them at Tiananmen Square, censoring newspapers and TV, keeping its people chained to low-paying factory jobs and in lock-step fealty to the government. Along with everyone else, I was stunned by the TV coverage of the over-the-top Opening Ceremonies of the 2008 Olympics in Beijing, with their thousands of people mobilized in sync. Perfectly, scarily in sync.

I heard nothing much good about the place, other than the Great Wall. And Zen. There must be a third thing, give me a minute.

But now the door was opening. A fifth of the world's population was behind that door, the fastest rising fraction of the globe, coming onto the global stage after centuries of self-removal, subjugation and, for most of my lifetime, Red hostility to Westerners.

We were getting the chance to know the country that was giving Americans a new unease: a deeply uneasy feeling that our time at the top was coming to an end, that a rival was racing up behind us, coming out of nowhere, incredibly fast.

We left the United States when national unemployment was at a miserable 10.2 percent. Twenty hours later, we landed in a China where the economy was ablaze. Double digits didn't describe the unemployment rate. They described the growth rate. During our year in Shanghai, China would become the world's leading automobile market (the first time the U.S. failed to lead the world in car sales), the world's leading exporter (over Germany), the world's second-leading economy (overtaking Japan, but way behind the U.S.). In our year there, this land that still revered Mao Zedong would produce more millionaires than any other country in the world. The Disney Company would announce plans to build Shanghai Disneyland. And Shanghai, its sights on developing the next great financial center, would unveil its own copy of the statue of the Wall Street bull. Chinese officials couldn't help boasting that theirs was "redder, younger and stronger" than its New York counterpart. And whereas the Wall Street bull's head points downward, the Shanghai bull looked up.

As we arrived, Shanghai, a one-time cosmopolitan city that then spent 40 years closed off from the world in the gray stasis of Communism, was getting itself dolled-up on the grand scale. Expecting a record 70 million visitors for the 2010 World Expo — its coming-out party to the world — it was spending billions in public money to revamp its famed old-Europe riverfront called the Bund. It was widening roads, planting countless flowers and trees, building or lengthening a half-dozen subway lines. Shanghai opened its first subway line in 1995. We would see the opening of the eleventh line and the 260th mile of track. A city that barely registered in Americans' minds would have the longest subway system in the world.

We would see a China that started to push its newly acquired weight around. It was brash enough to brush off U.S. demands to readjust its artificially inflated currency. It was smug enough to give President Barack Obama a cool reception when he came to call. It grew stern with its neighbors, inflaming disputes with Japan and Southeast Asia countries over obscure borders and sea rights. It showed off a face to the world that seemed to take pride in being obnoxious.

But we would also see that, inside the country's borders, that same central government was doing a lot of things that were smart. China's leaders were becoming frank about the country's choking pollution, and were ordering steps to cut down on man-made greenhouse gases, with measurable targets. When the global recession hit, they forged ahead with billions of yuan worth of public projects — highways, railroads, airport terminals — and recovered far faster than did the U.S. or Europe. Whenever the rapidly growing Internet population (it became the world's largest, at 330 million, while we were there) railed against corrupt officials or dangerous food products, those complaints made it into Chinese newspapers — and the responsible officials or business people were usually promptly, and harshly, punished.

The biggest surprise was to see how broad, open and self-critical the Chinese media were about these topics and others — almost any topic, in fact, except the not inconsiderable matter of the Communist Party's grip on power. Any hint of a challenge to that, even a perceived hint — Tibetan or Uighar independence, Taiwan nationalism, references to the 1989 Tiananmen Square massacre, dissidents' sporadic calls for the formation of opposition parties — and the censors would spring into action. At the same time, you'd never know when they would pull out their scissors on some much smaller matter, like using a "too-violent" word in a headline. In fact, it was the unpredictability of the state's censorship that probably made it so effective; you could never stop asking yourself — will it be OK to put this item in the newspaper? To put it in an email? To ask a Chinese friend about it?

I would witness it all from an unusual perch, the newsroom of an English-language daily where the important news of China was pressed through the coarse filter of state control; readers of the *Shanghai Daily* got more "sort-of true" about China than rock-hard fact. But there was great fellowship and a wonderful lightness in that newsroom — just as there was a baseline of cheerfulness, friendliness and warmth among the Chinese people we encountered day in and day out. People who were living much harder lives, in general, than we live in the West.

WE DIDN'T know this on the first day we explored the city. We walked around agape at a jumble of old and new. East and West. Gaudy, neon-lit office towers and mysterious, inhabited alleyways.

We rode outdoor escalators that took us to footbridges over busy streets and marveled at the sight of flower pots on the upper walkways instead of graffiti. We weaved our way through a constant busy-ness, the relentless comings and goings and near-collisions and horn-honks of a city of nearly 20 million people.

After we ate our breakfast, we walked downtown streets awhile, struck by surprises. At one busy corner stood a large Buddhist temple, a collection of towers and buildings with pagoda roofs of gold leaf. It must have been hundreds of years old. Somehow it had survived the Communist takeover of 1949 and the Cultural Revolution madness of the '60s and '70s. Now it was surviving capitalism. Behind it were tall office buildings, a

35

looming wall of windows resembling Midtown Manhattan. To its right, an enormous shopping mall with the curvy heft of a Miami Beach hotel.

The temple itself was multi-use. There were jewelry and clothing stores on the perimeter; the moneychangers had literally taken over the temple, or part of it. If people went inside the courtyard, did they worship, we wondered? Was there religion in atheistic China? We would come back and check it out, we decided. We didn't have to satisfy all our curiosity in a rush. We weren't tourists. We were going to be here a year.

A year. How in the world were we going to cope with so much strangeness for a year

Then we spotted The Donut King. The sign may as well have said "Oasis." If ever we could use a couple of chocolate-covered raised donuts and cups of cappuccino, this was it. We sat at a little round glass table behind the restaurant as an excessively polite Chinese young man with painfully little English brought us our refreshment. We looked out at a park. A lush green park in the middle of traffic-choked city. Built, we later learned, over a subway stop and dozens of underground shops.

We looked out at children clambering over playground equipment, their mothers or nannies keeping a close eye on the family's precious one child. We watched a group of college-age guys and girls playing a netless game of badminton, awkwardly. We saw old people shuffling along, getting their dose of exercise.

"OK, I can make it here," Ellen said, her face relaxing a little. "If I know there's a park somewhere where I can look at trees every now and then, I'll be all right."

We sipped our coffee, savoring the taste of home, hoping that was true.

4
Change of Address

THE DENSITY of smog took us aback. Even at night we could see a miasma rising in front of car headlights and street lamps. And this in a city where people still smoked. If any single thing will drive me crazy about Shanghai, I told myself on our first night of exploring the city, it could be the assault of second-hand smoke.

It felt as if we landed someplace very far away from the freer air of America — and not just because our plane had crossed Siberia, that loneliest expanse of the map, all dark forests and forlorn political prisoners, to get here. Our Internet was bowdlerized. No Facebook, no YouTube, no Twitter. I couldn't access my own blog site. I'd have to think of some other way of communicating with friends and family and hope that the authorities didn't read my emails. I went to sleep after that first full day, worrying faintly about totalitarian pre-dawn knocks on the door.

But now it was Day Two and sunny, the air practically clear, the sky actually blue. We headed out for the French Concession, a part of the city that resisted the Shanghai frenzy to erase the past and that retained its colonial character—leafy streets with little traffic, oversize villas behind stately walls. When the British established colonies, they set up banking and trade; the French built boulevards.

There was a distinct international flavor in the French Concession. Foreign consulates were clustered here, as they are in Washington, D.C. Many expats, posted by corporations in Europe and America, settled here.

We ate breakfast at an outdoor French-style bistro in a quiet, gentrified alley, the menu boasting of its "Japanese funk." Whatever that was, we couldn't taste it. But we felt much hipper for having read the sign.

We had only walked a few blocks from our serviced hotel, but by taking a left on the sidewalk instead of a right, had found an entirely different Shanghai. If Day 1 in the teeming city reminded me of the dystopia of "Blade Runner," this next day felt like a trip back to the stately pre-war Vietnam of the movie "Indochine" — trees shading quiet streets, bicyclists gliding by, street cleaners brushing the curbs with straw brooms, women carrying their small sacks of produce down the sidewalk. Any minute, I expected to see Catherine Deneuve.

We liked this neighborhood. A lot. And it was only a mile from the newspaper office. Out of curiosity, we stopped to read the postings taped to the window of a realty office, and an agent popped out, a young woman of about 25, her broad face stretched in a big smile. Her name was Jenny, she told us in pretty good English as she handed us her business card — with two hands, as required in China.

Ellen introduced herself as a fellow Realtor, told her we were brand-new to Shanghai and wondering what my Shanghai salary could buy us in terms of an apartment rental. We talked for a few minutes about our budget and things we'd like in an apartment. Jenny snapped to it. Told us to give her half an hour and she'd have something for us to look at.

We explored a bit. The street was interesting. Hole-in-the-wall shops where Chinese men sold soda, beer and cigarettes. Gated lanes where old people exercised and huddled around card tables. But also Euro-style coffee shops and a pizza restaurant, wine stores and modern furniture showrooms.

Jenny lined up three places for us to see. To get to the first one, she led us through an intricate warren — a crooked alley of small attached houses and dangling laundry. We passed old women sweeping their thresholds and men puttering with their motorbikes. She unlocked a door and we stepped into a dark room with rusting basins, a beat-up table and a gloomy set of stairs. We stopped her before she led us up. It was like something from The Good Earth. If this hovel is all we can afford in Shanghai, we thought, we better buy our airplane ticket home now.

She took us to a second place even more dismal; her key failed to work the very ancient lock on the outside gate. "Don't worry about it," we told her. "We're not interested in this one."

And then she led us to a 20-story high-rise. With a lobby and doorman.

We walked into something amazing. We were 15 floors above the trees in one of the only two high-rises that had been allowed in the French Concession, which the city fathers were intent to preserve in close to its original state. In exchange for putting up the two buildings, the developer had had to put up an arts center in the sister building. Thus the apartment was next door to a theater. A French Concession concession, you might say.

The apartment had windows facing all directions ... meaning that Shanghai's forest of office high-rises and residential towers surrounded us but at a distance. Just below us, when we stepped onto the substantial balcony, were acres of tree tops and the peaked roofs of old Tudor and Victorian buildings that had been spared demolition by city statute.

The apartment had a full kitchen with the rarity of a stove (Chinese don't bake), a bathtub (another rarity — and a godsend for Ellen and her premature arthritis), and some of the most laughable, grandiose faux French furniture we'd ever seen: Versailles for the taste-impaired. Also a couple of features that seemed extremely Oriental: In the hallway near the front door, hidden compartments in the wall stored your shoes. In the main bedroom, a closet door opened not to a closet, but to another door. This door opened to the bathroom. You went through a Chinese puzzle to get to the john.

Two bedrooms, two baths — plenty of room for Ben when he'd come to study and work in January.

We never expected to pick the first one or two places we saw, but when something's irresistible, what can you do? The landlord was a bubbly guy named Frank, from Hong Kong, who did business around the world and who took extreme pride in showing each kitschy furnishing in the place and telling us how he'd got it special, from one world capital or another, just for this apartment, the very best in this part of Shanghai. For some reason he took to us, and we to him and his Yoko Ono-lookalike wife, Eva.

We made a quick call to Liu Hong, an editor at the paper who had offered to help us get settled. Could she speak with the realty agent and make sure we weren't getting ourselves into trouble? We handed the cell phone over to Jenny and after a very short conversation in rapid Mandarin, Jenny handed the phone back to us. Liu Hong said it all sounded OK. Just that fast, we had a deal. We practically had a *shidduch*. Frank and Eva had a daughter at Penn State; they swooned to hear we had a son the same age. And they promised to show us a hell of a time whenever we got to Hong Kong.

Who would have guessed? We'd made friends on our first full day of wakefulness. And found an apartment. A week after landing in Shanghai, we would move into a home for the next year.

DAY THREE in Shanghai. It was 10:20 in the morning and we were at the real estate office, where our eager-beaver agent Jenny Tang was offering us tea and presenting us with rental documents she'd worked into the night to prepare. They were written in both Chinese and English and they opened with the lovely phrase: "Party A and Party B, having had friendly discussion, hereby agree to enter into the following contract to be abided by both parties."

"Friendly discussion." This was different. In any other contract I'd ever seen, I couldn't recall friendship taking a part in it.

I was Party B. Party A was Frank, the apartment owner, who was indeed acting as if he'd rather be our pal than our landlord. I signed my name throughout the pages in the block English lettering you make as a child. Frank wrote in a precise calligraphy, Asian pictograms that despite being written in ballpoint pen probably could have been read by a medieval Chinese monk.

We agreed to pay 11,000 yuan a month ($1,611.34 in U.S. dollars at the day's exchange rate) for the two bedroom-two bath furnished flat, with two months payment upfront, plus an 11,000-yuan security deposit. Frank agreed to install satellite TV and Internet service. It was all clearly stated on the pages.

41

El and I struggled to keep the two currencies straight in our heads, hoping we'd brought enough dollars in American Express Traveler's Cheques to cover the half of the money we agreed to pay on the spot, and wondering how hard it would be to get access to our bank accounts and transfer the rest of the money to Frank in the next couple of days. It was late Saturday night in America and the chances of our reaching a banker for the next day and a half were about nil.

It was Sunday morning in Shanghai. And the crazy thing was, all these people were working. Jenny's realty office was filled with young agents poring over computer screens and scanning the sidewalk for customers. Restaurants were open. Laborers were scrambling up scaffolding to rehab buildings. Street sweepers were out sweeping.

Had no one here ever heard of the day of rest? It was tiring just watching these people. No wonder we were worried the Chinese were going to eat our lunch. Most of us Americans didn't want to work nearly so hard to eat it ourselves.

After we signed all the real estate docs, we got into two cabs and drove over to a branch of the Bank of China. It was a branch known for its comfort with the English language. El and I stepped up to a sober-looking female teller, and with Jenny easing us over the tough parts, told her that we wanted to open an account, deposit a bunch of dollars into it and then pay out most of those dollars to Frank, who was sitting with his wife Eva a few steps behind us.

What followed was a blur of paper and signatures and taps of the keyboard of our pocket calculator, as we converted a short stack of traveler's checks into a thick wad of yuan, about a brick's worth. I picked it up just long enough to hand it over to Eva.

When it was over, I was a customer of the Bank of China (Not Ellen. Bank of China didn't allow joint accounts). I got a passbook, just like the one I got as a kid in the 1960s from the Old Orchard Bank and Trust, in Skokie, Ill. And an ATM card. Unlike the Chinese currency, which bore the face of Chairman Mao, the card boasted a mascot: a cartoon of a pig. The card looked like a pass to Disney World.

With the bank account, I now had a place to deposit my Shanghai paycheck. And with the routing numbers that Frank gave us, I would be able to wire money into his Hong Kong bank account each month to pay the rent.

That was the theory, anyway.

Now all we had to do was round up $1,900 more for Frank.

My God. We were almost residents of China.

NOW WE were standing in the dim glow of an automatic teller machine, allowing an exhale of relief. This particular ATM with its merciful English writing was proving to be the savior of our sanity in the crazy scramble to scarf up the down payment we needed for our brand-new landlord.

We were in the hushed lobby of the Hilton hotel, a downtown landmark that was not quite luxurious, just very full of itself. Businessmen came and went, chatting over drinks at a corner bar tricked up to look like a library, or eating an off-hour meal at the Asian-Western buffet in the lobby restaurant that was soothed by the trickle of an indoor waterfall.

We had run into one dead end after another, just to get hold of about $1,900 — 3,000 yuan — of our own money.

Said money, of course, being held in bank accounts back in the States. Where we were used to accessing it without effort on a website. Our bank was Chase. Before we left for China, Ellen and I had thought we were being very smart by meeting with a Chase banker. He turned out to be a warm Palestinian-American gentleman named Majed who treated us like family. He set us up with a new business-banking account, complete with debit card and new passwords to remember. These would allow us to wire our money wherever we wanted.

So he said, and so Chase believed.

But no one had told these things to the Bank of China. The tellers there were unimpressed with our debit card and routing numbers. We kept asking them to take our money from overseas and put it in our new bank account. And they kept shaking their heads from side to side. Our Mandarin was poor, but we had no trouble understanding that.

The tellers would, however, give us cash from our credit card. Visa, they respected. But they'd transact no more than $1,000 at a time. And only after charging us 3 percent. (And Lord knew what Visa would charge us on top of that.)

OK, OK, we said — the response of the defeated foreigner.

Chinese banks didn't wire money around in matters of personal banking, we found. And people didn't use checks. Checks were too easily forged. People didn't trust them.

Which meant that paying the rent was not going to be the easy matter it seemed on the first day of our China banking tutorial. My employer was going to deposit most of my pay into the Industrial and Commerce Bank of

China, or ICBC, which had a branch in the lobby of the newspaper's building.   Unfortunately, our landlord Frank used the Bank of China. The banks here did not like it when you took your money out of one bank and put it in the other, even if these particular banks happened to have the same overall owner: the government of China. No automatic transfers here.

Each month, I would have to use an ATM machine outside the ICBC branch in the lobby to extract a mound of 100-yuan notes, and carry those notes — 110 of them — to a branch of the Bank of China for placement in the landlord's account for the monthly rent.

Carry wads of cash to the bank! In the USA we'd get reported as drug-dealer suspects. Here we would be doing ordinary business.

Our brand-new Bank of China account, opened with so many sheaves of paper and signatures just the day before, would be practically useless. Here, absolutely everybody who made a withdrawal left the bank counter carrying a bundle. Bill-counting machines were placed around the lobby to help people deal with the wads. And because that wasn't enough of an inconvenience, the highest denomination note was 100 yuan. Or $14.64 American at the then-current rate.

The same would go for paying utility bills. Forget sending a check to ConEd every month. Forget paying online. We would carry our electric bill or water bill over to a convenience store and pay in cash.

I tried to wrap my mind around this. China had become one of the richest countries in the world. It held a shitload of U.S. Treasury debt. And it did all this with banking methods only a step or two beyond the abacus. Come to think of it, every teller did have an abacus on the counter, a few inches from the computer keyboard.

We were not the only people confounded by Chinese banking. Our landlord had originally asked us to wire the remainder of our deposit into his account at his Hong Kong bank, HSBC — the Hong Kong and Shanghai Banking Corporation. Silly man! If Chinese banks disliked giving money away in general, they really and truly disliked giving it to a foreign bank. And as far as mainland China was concerned, Hong Kong — though under Chinese control since 1997 — was a foreign country in matters of money. Luckily for us, Frank agreed to accept a small satchel of cash.

Luckily, again, we found that ATM machine in the Hilton lobby. Unlike almost every other ATM we tried around the city, it was bilingual. And it accepted our new Chase debit card. And it gave us our money: a maximum 2,500 yuan per day. A whopping $366.

A couple of days of doing this, and we managed to gather the 130 100-yuan notes we needed to give to Frank to complete our securing of the apartment.

So this was how China, up and coming financial powerhouse, did its retail banking. We could not understand how this was even remotely possible.

HAND-OVER DAY. We met Frank and Eva at the apartment. They were accompanied by their friends Mr. and Mrs. Yao and their 35-year-old son, who mostly sat by himself and watched TV. Mr and Mrs Yao seemed embarrassed to introduce him to us. Their one child, the only chance at progeny that the government had given them, and he was, by all appearances, mentally disabled.

Frank and Eva and the elder Yaos had worked like crazy on the place. Cleaned everything, from the too-fancy chandelier in the front bedroom to the scroty filter over the stove. They went to big trouble to buy color-coordinated bed sheets and duvets – pretty expensive, we were guessing. They installed a satellite dish, allowing us to get an Internet connection and a "bouquet" of channels that includes HBO, Cinemax and – tee hee! — about a half-dozen adult channels.

"Young man channels," Eva called them, her hand covering her mouth, the embarrassed-giggle gesture.

The fuss they made over us, the handshakes and hugs and affectionate strokes on the arm! Mr. Yao was an old pal of Frank's, an older man with calm eyes, silver hair and a sense of humor. He used to be some kind of teacher. He was a native Shanghainese who had lived most of his life there and who insisted on our swapping phone numbers and email addresses because he wanted to be our guide to the French Concession and tell us the stories ingrained in the streets and lanes. He said that when Frank mentioned I was with *Shanghai Daily*, he had to drop everything and meet us. My guess was, he thought my job would afford me some pull with important people in the government and media. I had status, and if we connected, so might he. Of course he wanted to be my pal.

Yao wanted us to see he was no mere provincial. He understood our different nations. He told about a friend of his who'd traveled to the USA for a few weeks and came home complaining that all he'd had to eat was rice and noodles. Why was that? Well, the friend said, every time he met an American for a meal, the American would ask what he wanted to eat, and he'd say, all self-effacing, "Oh, just some rice and noodles." Yao told him: "There's your mistake. Americans are very direct. If you say you want rice and noodles, that's what they'll get for you. The rice and noodles. Exactly what you asked for."

Yao thought this was hilarious. His point was that, in China, conversation was indirect. It was built on intricate minuets of politeness, and, in this case, ritualized self-deprecation.

El and I felt a nice little buzz in our brains, the buzz you get when you feel an idea for the first time: Yao had put us inside the head of a man who couldn't imagine something that we Americans take for granted — the idea that a question was followed simply by its answer. For his friend, a question was always an opening gambit. The first answer or two was to be disregarded, and the questioner was supposed to follow up with increasing insistence — until he finally determined that the guest really would like to eat some pork or chicken or a hamburger.

Ellen, whose directness can verge on the blunt, looked a little alarmed. How were we possibly going to avoid offending people while we're in this country?

Suddenly, in the middle of all the housework, Frank hustled us out of the apartment, rounded up two taxis and sped us to a restaurant for lunch. It was a banquet, with the round table and the waiters delivering dish upon dish on a lazy-susan tray: A little bowl of spiced cucumbers. Small ham slices wrapped in a delicious fatty jelly. A whole chicken roasted in hoisin sauce. A steaming pot of barbecue-flavored beef and scallions. Steamed seasoned broccoli. A whole fish with a lightly crisped skin and moist white flakes inside. Fried pork dumplings. A barbecue platter of three kinds of beef and pork. A platter of sweet and sour shrimp with pineapple and another of fried rice — these were the only things we were used to. For dessert, a flat cake filled with banana and a black-bean paste. And soft white balls of gelatinous rice with a hot, sweet sesame paste inside.

Everything delicious. We all held glasses of Tsingtao beer and watermelon juice, and raised happy toasts.

"Frank has had many renters," Yao told us, "but he's never taken any of the others out to a banquet before."

Our new Chinese pals made a big deal out of my name, "Goodman," as in, "Oh, you must be a good man! Ha ha ha!" And for that moment, greatly enjoying connecting with these people, I felt like one.

The Mandarin word how means "good." That made "Howard

Goodman" a hell of a joke, my name combining in Mandarin and English into Good Good Man.

"That is good advertising for you," grinned Yao, like we were sitting at the Algonquin Round Table and he'd one-upped Dorothy Parker.

Back at the apartment, we made an inventory of all the furniture in the place and signed three copies of a checklist: one for me, one for Frank, one for the real estate agent. Ellen handed Eva the stack of yuan we'd been hauling around, more than twice the thickness of a deck of cards. Frank handed us the keys.

And lo and behold, one day shy of a week of our landing in Shanghai and setting sight on China for the first time in our lives, we took possession of Flat 18 C, No. 298 Anfu Road, Xuhui District, Shanghai, China 200031.

We had peace and quiet, a respite from the street. We had stunning views of the city. We had a maintenance man, Chou, who spoke not a word of English. We met him during the walk-through, when he came upstairs to inspect a balcony door that wasn't closing just right. He shuffled in, his clothes smeared, his mouth missing some teeth, and looked at us with rheumy eyes while trying to make out what we were saying.

Giving up, he yammered something in Chinese to Frank, who reported, "He says it's like ducks trying to talk to geese."

I barked out a laugh, and when Chou heard that, he started laughing too.

I felt we'd be friends, Chou and we. I was sure he'd try and keep the apartment running well for us. Because he liked us. And because Frank smeared him with a 100-yuan note.

SEVEN MONTHS to the day after I got the boot at the *South Florida Sun Sentinel*, my unemployment ended.

Granted, I had to travel half the globe for the privilege.

The first night's chores— some simple copy editing of four stories and a photo caption and making them fit properly on a world-news page — weren't the stuff journalistic dreams are made of. But I was working. Working in a city where people still read the newspaper.

I hadn't expected to be working that night. Ellen and I were on a sightseeing boat on the Huangpo River, getting ready to take a tourist cruise along Shanghai's scenic waterfront, when my cell phone rang.

It was almost 5 o'clock. The call was from an anxious Liu Hong, the assistant editor who has been helping us with the move. Did I know I was supposed to start work today?

Well, no, actually, no one had told me. Some days before, when I'd checked in with the editors upon our arrival in town, they had told us to take our time, get some rest, look around for an apartment, get used to Shanghai.

Oh! Liu Hong said quickly. No problem! Take your cruise, come in when you're done.

And so our 45-minute ride — up the eastern shore of the river, the modern Pudong side; down the historic European-built Bund — was bittersweet.

The sun was setting, casting a hazy orange glow over the gliding landscape of buildings and boats. Lights twinkled on as the sky turned to black. El and I watched it, and held each other, and felt a sundown kind of sadness.

We'd been through a lot since I got laid off. Disappointment and uncertainty and worries about income.

But it wasn't all bad. Being home so much, we spent more time together, just the two of us, than we'd ever had. We travelled to New Orleans for JazzFest because we damn sure weren't going to let a loss of a job keep us from enjoying our life. We did everything as a pair. We talked over all the job applications I was filling out, the freelance pieces I was writing. I accompanied her on real-estate listings. We rediscovered all sorts of ways of enjoying each other's company, and refamiliarized ourselves with lost pleasures and lovemaking that had become dulled or forgotten over the years.

Our closeness only grew as we plotted this adventure of leaving the States and we worked like mad to make it happen. We became closer still in our first days in Shanghai, because at most times we were, literally, the only other person the other could talk to. We shared every new perception, every thought, every new discovery.

And now I had to go to work. Had to take time from exploring Shanghai to go sit at a desk. Had to leave El to occupy herself in the foreign city alone.

We felt something special ending for us.

The sun went down, the boat docked, El and I found a taxi and took a chance on a tiny restaurant near the newspaper office. We were the only foreigners. It wasn't a welcoming room. The patrons seemed planted there for the evening. They smoked as they paused between courses and stared at us. The wait staff, irritated with our lack of Mandarin, called over a bilingual customer to take our order, then served us hurriedly. The food was good — a garlicky chicken and some soft moist beef in onions — but when we left, no one told us to come back soon.

Ellen and I made our goodbyes and I watched her walk away on Shaanxi Road, my heart filling a little as she was swallowed up by the city.

I took the elevator to the 38th floor of a downtown office building on Weihai Road and sat down at a dusty desk to begin my time at the *Shanghai Daily*.

IT WAS a light first day. Some instruction in how the Mac-based system worked. Where to find the computer queue for stories that needed their English "polished." What queue in the computer system to put them in when done, so the next editor in the production chain could find them.

Then some actual work: Edit the stories and write the headlines for everything that was going to appear on the next morning's Page A11: World News. The stories were already selected, the page already laid out. My job

49

was to make sure all the words fit correctly in the allotted spaces and conformed to *Shanghai Daily* style.

One by one, I trimmed the stories to match the space and wrote the heds:

Korean stem-cell scientist Hwang convicted of fraud
'Net's next trick: Non-English addresses
Castro sister: 'I spied for CIA'
3 in 10 UK teachers falsely accused

I muddled through, hitting unfamiliar keys and squinting at an unfamiliar style:

"11am" (No spaces or periods).

"Dr Liu" (No period for doctor).

"US$5,000" (Always specify the currency's nationality).

My new bosses didn't expect much on the first day. They wanted me to ease into things. It'll get more interesting, they assured me, when I start working with the reporters.

I left at 11, while most everyone else on the night shift remained, still with work to do.

I was employed again. I had an office to go to, a commute, a lunch hour, coffee breaks, colleagues, gossip.

When I'd been first hit with the shock of unemployment, my only thought was: can't wait to get another job.

Now I'd started that next job. And my first thought was: hope it doesn't take too much time away from exploring Shanghai and China.

5
Twenty Million Strangers — And Me

Ellen's blog:
I SAID goodbye to Howie at the paper last night and walked out of the building into the street.

For the first time, I was all alone in China.

"Okay, don't panic," I counseled myself for the first of many times. "Just take it one step at a time. First, figure out how to get home from here."

I walked to what I thought would be a good place to hail a cab. The lighting was very bright in some parts of the sidewalk but shadowy in others. After a few minutes without any available cabs appearing, I took the stairs up to an overhead walkway.

It dawned on me that without Howie as my navigator, I really didn't know where I was going. "Just keep walking," I told myself. Up ahead I saw a middle-aged Asian man in a trench coat. He was smoking a cigarette and staring hard at me. "Should I be scared?" I asked myself — for the first of many times, I'm sure.

I had a nervous moment as I passed the guy, until he averted his eyes and continued to smoke his cigarette. He was probably staring because he wasn't used to seeing people who look like me. I forgot how unusual my long red hair is in this part of the world.

"Whew! I definitely have a lot of new experiences ahead of me," I thought as I hurried away and tried even harder to find a cab. From the vantage point of the elevated sidewalk I was able to get a better sense of where I was and where I should be standing for a taxi. I walked back down the steep stairs — and I hate stairs — and started flapping my lowered hand as I've seen other people do.

Like so many other things, even hailing a cab is different here. People look at you like you're nuts if you wave your raised arm high in the air, Manhattan-style. In China, it's a low gesture, a wave that's about waist high, what the writer Peter Hessler calls "petting the dog."

It seemed like a very long time — in reality, probably no more than five minutes — but a cab finally stopped for me. I got in, and in very slow and halting Mandarin, gave him my address. He nodded, sped off, and in a short time delivered me to our apartment building.

Yes! One small success!

I gave the Mandarin-only guard at the front desk a *ni hao* and took the elevator up. Inside the apartment, I took off my shoes, put down my purse, and sat down on the couch.

"Now what?" I wondered.

The apartment was different without Howie in it. We had been inseparable since we left the States. Now I was acutely aware of being alone.

"Sound. That's what's missing!" I though. "If Howie were here, the stereo would be on, a bit too loud, and we'd be rocking to The Grateful Dead, Bob Dylan, Van Morrison, or a thousand other artists in his collection. Or we'd be slow dancing to Gershwin or show tunes."

One of the first things Howie did when we set up the apartment was to buy a nice little pair of speakers (300 yuan: $45) to play the 12,000 songs on his iPod. I tried to figure out how to turn it on and was quickly reminded that Howie is the audio-visual point person in our house. I believe in division of labor, but at times like these I realize I need to step up my knowledge of the home electronics.

"OK, El, just turn on the TV. God knows you grew up in a household where the TV was on constantly. You used to refer to it as 'The Eternal Light'."

But even that turned out to be complicated. There were three remotes — one for the TV, one for the cable, and a third for the speakers. Which one did what? What button do I push first? Why did I suddenly feel like a moron?

Promise to self: "Pay attention next time."

I finally got the TV working, only to be rewarded by a dial-spanning spectrum of absolute crap. I had made a very strong point to my landlord that I absolutely had to have cable with HBO, figuring if I had to be alone in the apartment all night, at least I'd have something good to watch. What I did not know is that all the world's HBO is not equal. The network sends its worst TV series and movies to Asia, I suppose so that the rest of the channels don't feel outclassed.

The first English-language channel offered a movie with a little girl, crouching in a closet, hiding from a man with a knife —
CLICK.

Another movie. Three guys walking around a jungle with creepy-crawlies coming out at them —
CLICK.

Oh great. This next channel had vampires attacking a town, and people shooting at them and waving torches Why does every other channel have to remind me of Michael Jackson's "Thriller" video? For someone who has to close her eyes during movie previews with any kind of scary stuff, this was not good.

That was it for the satellite channels. I'd sample the local TV.

How bad could that be?

The first thing I got was a samurai movie. People in historical costumes getting ready to chop off people's heads.

CLICK.

A war movie with Asian soldiers in World War II-era costumes fighting…who? Japanese? Chinese Nationalists?

CLICK.

A talent show. A woman dressed like a little girl singing a chirpy pop melody in Mandarin.

CLICK.

A talk show. The host in a brightly colored suit and a big bow tie, mugging to the audience and saying … what?

CLICK.

Finally, the news. Something I could watch and enjoy. Except it was in Chinese without English subtitles.

CLICK and OFF.

The apartment went quiet and it would be hours before Howie came home.

This could be the first night of a very long year.

6
Crazy Town

Howard:

WHAT WAS it like, this new city of ours?

Start by imagining a cluster of very tall office buildings, high-rise apartment towers and neon-lit store fronts. Now fill the scene with foot traffic and floods of vehicles. In an ordinary place, this would be the downtown. In Shanghai, it was just one of a dozen. We found "downtowns" in every direction, spread over a very wide landscape. We'd ride to an unfamiliar part of the city to discover yet another cluster of skyscrapers. And in the distance, we'd see another.

It was a runaway metropolis — with architecture drawn directly from the id. The skyline was a canvas of weird shapes and unexpected angles, like a comic-book backdrop for superheroes. Important buildings looked like Transformer toys or Buck Rogers set designs. One was the world's biggest can opener. Another, a towering jeweled phallus. No building worth a damn greeted the night without flashing a Miami's worth of Day-Glo colors. Some office buildings turned into nightly advertising screens, their animations visible from miles away.

It was striver architecture, a city begging for attention, proud of its newly prosperous self. New York once expressed this kind of exuberance in its skyline — at the beginning of the 20th century. Fifty years later, after World War II left America as the most powerful country still standing, New York's building style turned quiet and confident; the clean Bauhaus boxes of Sixth Avenue in Midtown are serenely certain of their own importance. Maybe in another 50 years, Shanghai will tone it down the same way.

But in 2009, Shanghai crackled with adolescent energy. Bursting out of its own clothes, betraying its insecurities despite its shows of bravado, the city and its people seemed mature in certain ways, childish in others — wearing a bra and losing a baby tooth all at once. You could be craning your neck, looking at one of the world's tallest skyscrapers, but you'd better watch your step because you'd be walking past a food-seller hacking apart a chicken on the sidewalk or cutting off frog's heads with garden shears and dropping the heads in a mucked-up bucket.

Everybody wanted to buy a car, and everyone was a brand-new driver. This was a country with more than four times the population of the United States that in 1990 had fewer than 6 million vehicles. By 2009 the number had exploded to 62 million; and though it was still officially a communist country, 26 million of those vehicles were privately owned. (The U.S. had almost 255 million passenger vehicles in 2007). It was the greatest surge in car ownership in world history. It often felt as though all the cars in China were on the streets of Shanghai at the same time — dashing headlong into the same intersection.

The streets were crammed as well with bikes, motorcycles, pushcarts. And jaywalkers who must have had a death wish. Drivers had no respect for the painted crosswalk. None at all. Ellen and I nearly got hit one night by a motorbike while we were standing on a nearly empty sidewalk. Hey, the driver wanted to be on that sidewalk too.

A taxi ride — any taxi ride — was a thrill ride. Your driver felt it his duty a) to swerve into whatever lane he was not currently occupying and b) to spurt ahead to close any gaps between himself and the car in front. Like nature, Chinese drivers abhorred a vacuum. The mainland Chinese drove, as Peter Hessler said in *Country Driving*, his unbeatable account of China's roads, the way the mainland Chinese walk — like schools of fish, dashing and darting among each other in a mysterious harmony. They should have crashed, but didn't, not usually. Still, there were plenty of road accidents. According to the government's figures, which independent researchers believe to be seriously understated, more than 73,000 people died on China's roadways in 2008 — 200 people a day. Given the close shaves we had almost every time we hopped in a cab, we couldn't believe the number wasn't way, way higher.

The driver would invariably drive in the wrong gear, grinding it out in second when he was trying to go at full speed. Jesus, doesn't this guy know how to drive? I'd ask myself, feeling the transmission's pain. Ellen heard the cabbies did it to save money. They believed they'd have to buy less gas if he drove in a lower gear. If the car were damaged as a result, their boss would be stuck with the repairs.

Almost none of Shanghai — or any other large city we'd see — looked like the Asia we imagined. You could find more traditional Chinese design in the interior of a suburban Kansas City chow mein house. Most of the city looked like Lefrak City in the Bronx. But Shanghai did have an Old City. And here we saw the pagoda roofs and dragon-sculpted curlicues we had in our heads. To be honest, most of Old City's pagoda-style buildings weren't so old. They were reconstructions. But the site was real. It's where Shanghai started as a small, walled fishing town, minding its own business for centuries before the Europeans came crashing in, in the 1840s. Now it was a busy bazaar where tour buses dropped off tourists looking for deals on pearls or delicious steamed dumplings. You'd walk through mazes of stalls stuffed with cheap sunglasses, Chinese fans, toys, paintings, t-shirts, silk scarves and decks of cards in kitsch: pictures of Kobe Bryant, old-time Asian erotica, Chairman Mao.

Yet right in the middle of all the ersatz and the hubbub of relentless shopping was an actual ancient garden with an actual ancient teahouse. There was a lagoon, crossed by a bridge that zig-zagged nine times. It was called — wait for it! — the Nine Zig Zag Bridge. It was built more than 400 years ago in the Ming Dynasty, its sharp 90-degree turns designed to keep away evil spirits. Because, as everyone in the Ming Dynasty knew, an evil spirit could only travel in straight lines.

Now the Bridge of Nine Turnings (as it was more loftily called) was a mecca for tour groups led by resolute guides who carried colored pennants so as to be visible to every member of the group. Chinese tourists poured into Shanghai from the hinterlands to see the amazing modern city for themselves. They were always in groups, and the groups always wore group t-shirts or baseball caps. It was like being surrounded by teams of the world's retirees.

Nine Zig-Zag Bridge during Chinese New Year

It was crowded: the bridge teemed with people, railing-to-railing, for all nine zig zags. When you got to the end, you found a high wall and an admission gate and a kiosk selling disposable cameras and spare flash-memory cards for taking digital photos. And for 40 yuan ($6) you could buy entry to the garden beyond the wall.

The Yu Garden was serene. Stepping behind the walls shut out the jostling city. Inside was a five-acre park with 30 genuinely old pagoda-roof buildings along winding pathways that offered clever views of luscious ponds, rock formations and greenery. Along the top of the surrounding wall were seven sculptured dragons.

During our first week in town, we got to the garden on a late afternoon, a half hour before closing, and had the place — and the quiet — almost wholly to ourselves. We soaked in the peacefulness.

Serenity itself: Inside the Yu Garden

Outside the walls, Shanghai was an enormous construction site. Chinese work crews were working ever harder and faster to make the city shine for the World Expo that was set to open in about six months. They were tearing up streets for new subways and river promenades. Or tearing them up just to make nicer streets. They were putting up new buildings and putting new fronts on buildings already standing. They were building a new terminal and runway for Shanghai Hongqiao Airport, the airport for domestic flights.

And they were building the ridiculously huge Expo itself, turning a riverfront area of rundown warehouses into a horizon of futuristic pavilions. Shanghai's leaders fervently hoped for a knockout attraction that would put rival Beijing's 2008 Olympics to shame. At the time of our arrival, the propaganda effort was already intense. Likenesses of the Expo mascot — a blue Gumby-looking doofus called Haibao — were everywhere: on billboards, as statues, as toys and magnets and toothbrushes.

The most famous symbol of Shanghai is the Bund, a row of European buildings facing the Huangpu River dating from the 1800s, when British opium traders and bankers claimed a big chunk of Shanghai for themselves. The ersatz Europe is on half of Shanghai's postcards. Yet for months we couldn't see the Bund. The Victorian piles were dark at night because the street and riverbank had been turned into worksites. They were being torn apart and rebuilt. The result would be beautiful. Through-traffic would be redirected underground, while up above would stretch a couple of lanes for local auto traffic as well as a wide, tiered walkway enabling people to stroll directly along the river.

But now the site was a mess. We tried to walk on the Bund, but wooden walls blocked the view of the river and the dazzling new financial center on the other side, Pudong. It was all dust, concrete, rocks, noise. Pretty soon, the sidewalk ended, consumed by the construction project. Now we were on the street, clinging to a wooden wall as cars, scooters and humongous buses barreled toward us in the dark. There was nowhere to go but forward, toward the recklessly oncoming traffic that grazed our elbows.

Oh God, I kept thinking, is this the end of Ellen and Howie? Killed on a street in China, a week after their arrival?

SHANGHAI WAS an important port town for the Chinese until 1842. Then it became important to the West.

The British, seeking ports and rest stops for their trading companies' trips around the world to India, contrived a war with the Chinese emperor, breezed to victory and exacted a very stiff price. In the name of Queen Victoria, the Brits claimed the island of Hong Kong and hefty pieces of five port cities on the mainland. Their slice of Shanghai became, in effect, British territory. It operated under British law and British courts and British trade officials. This was most agreeable for the traders and merchant shippers who set about making fortunes importing opium from India and selling it in their newly seized market. Not so great for the Chinese who got hooked on the opium and became second-class citizens in their own county. The French and Americans, not to be outdone, soon grabbed other sections of Shanghai for their own.

It didn't take long for the the city to bear the markings of foreign masters. The Bund became a mini-London. The British built Tudor mansions with wide lawns suitable for a pleasant spot of afternoon tea. They put up Anglican churches, cricket fields and an enormous racetrack that became the center of social life for decades. The French turned their "concession" into a beautiful ville of leafy, curving streets shaded by plane trees — a sultry Paris. The Americans left few footprints; they soon merged their concession with the British and left the chores and glories of empire to the cousins more enchanted with its trappings.

The Chinese were consigned to the old walled city and to stretches of Shanghai that lay outside the foreign concessions. While it is not true that a French Concession park once bore the warning, "No dogs or Chinese allowed," the story was close enough to the spirit of things to endure for decades. Each of the European powers governed its concession with an obsessive regard for its own sovereignty. The British streetcar could not connect with the French streetcar because each was made to fit the track width particular to the home country. When autos came in, a driver needed three licenses to get across the whole city.

Those affectations aside, Shanghai became a commercial powerhouse. By the 1920s and '30s, the city was the romantic and notorious Pearl of the Orient, a sophisticated, wide-open town alive with mobsters, jazz and brothels, a place of international business and intrigue, a hub for artists and revolutionaries. Art deco dance halls and music theaters from the era are still standing.

Then came the Japanese, their soldiers ominously joining the city's mix in the late 1930s. In December 1941, on the same day that other Japanese forces were bombing Pearl Harbor, Japanese troops stormed the city and took unquestioned control, rounding up Shanghai's foreign residents and throwing them in detention camps.

The defeat of the Japanese in 1945 brought another kind of war, between Mao Zedong's Communists and Chiang Kai Shek's Nationalists.

When the Communists won, in 1949, a darkness fell on Shanghai. A literal darkness — the bright lights of the old hedonistic city were turned off, scorned as excesses of the bourgeois past. The fine mansions were carved into communal housing for groups of families. Not a single tall building was erected for 40 years. A visitor in 1985 said it looked as if no building had been cleaned since the 1940s. And like the rest of the vast

China landmass, the city was closed off to the Western world.

Mike Revzin, an experienced Asia buff from Atlanta who runs an educational site called ChinaSeminars.com, remembered Shanghai in the 1980s, when it was so dark at night you could hardly find your way and the habituation of communist doctrine had drained people of any enterprising spirit.

"You'd go to a newsstand and you'd see four or five people standing around, and you'd ask for a newspaper, and a guy would say, '*Mei yo*, the newspaper clerk is out to lunch,' " Mike told me. "The guy talking, his job would be merely to sell the candy. He couldn't touch a newspaper. There was so little actual business going on in the city, and so little incentive to actually work, that the government would assign a bunch of people to a place like that newsstand — because the country was forbidden to have unemployment — and the workers would divide up the small number of tasks to give everybody something to do.

"To me," Mike continued, "the greatest achievement of the Chinese Communists was in succeeding in turning the Chinese population into a lazy people. Everywhere else that Chinese people migrated – Malaysia, Vietnam – they were the most industrious people around."

How industrious? In Malaysia, that government had to institute affirmative action programs to help out the native, majority Malay people — because the Chinese who had immigrated there so dominated the country's business and industry.

It all changed in 1990. Deng Xiaopeng, the leader who recognized that Maoism had failed spectacularly and had decided in 1979 to open up the country to the rest of the world and to business, declared that, after having loosed Shenzhen and a few other controlled experiments in capitalism, it was time for Shanghai to wake up.

Whammo.

The place exploded like Champagne with the cork popped. At a downtown museum called the Shanghai Urban Planning Exhibition Center, El and I looked at dozens of pictures of Shanghai street scenes — the same locations, then and now. A two-lane road was now a street with a second tier of traffic overhead. A two-story building had given way to a 40-story high-rise. A field of farms now looked like the Bronx. On and on.

They were just like the side-by-side photos you've seen of street scenes in New York, Chicago and Los Angeles, the same dramatic changes in architecture, transport, pedestrians' dress. But those would show you a

New York street in 1900, compared with the same New York street in 1950 or 2000.

Shanghai's "then" shots were from 1990. "Now" was less than 20 years later.

The pace of change was most staggering in Pudong — the area of Shanghai east of the Huangpu River. When Deng called for economic reorganization, Pudong was a nearly empty landscape of small farms and low-slung warehouse buildings. Now it was a sci-fi vision of futuristic multi-colored towers, an electric metropolis, a fast-arriving financial center. A symbol for the whole newly awakening Chinese nation.

Months into our stay, our son Ben, then 20, stood on the Bund with a family friend from America named Molly, who was also 20. They were taking in the skyscrapers, the space-age shapes and Day-Glo advertising facing them from Pudong.

"Can you believe," Ben said, motioning across the river at the alien skyline. "We're older than all that?"

7
Poked and Prodded

WE WERE in a government building, wearing Japanese-style robes over our topless torsos, being guided from examination room to examination room by women in nurses' uniforms, getting inspected, detected …

It was all very "Alice's Restaurant." To get my work visa and for Ellen to get her trailing-spouse visa, China required us to pass a medical inspection. Hence this trip to the Shanghai International Travel Healthcare Center, a knuckle-whitening half-hour cab ride from downtown.

We were in the care of Miss Yan, the perky young secretary from the *Shanghai Daily* who was in charge of handling the details of our visa application, a task that took weeks. She was all nervous energy at the healthcare center, clutching our passports and the dozen passport-size photos we had to distribute to various bureaucrats in a string of offices. Chinese bureaucrats apparently couldn't get enough of our looks.

We had expected a short visit to a doctor's office. Instead we are on an assembly line of health assessment.

One by one, Ellen and I were taken to a closed-door room to measure our height and weight. Another room for blood tests. Then a sonogram; EKG; eye tests (color blindness and vision acuity); chest x-ray. In the seventh room we saw a mild-mannered doctor whose job was to take our blood pressure and give us a general OK. He checked us out the old-fashioned doctor way, with a stethoscope to our chests and probing fingers on our necks and bellies.

It wasn't so bad. No peeing in a cup. No coughing while a guy with latex-covered fingers poked your groin.

After reading and hearing so much about human-rights abuses in China, we'd been apprehensive about coming to a government medical clinic, but the place proved cleaner and the staff more attentive than any American public health center I ever saw. We asked Miss Yan if this was typical of Chinese healthcare. She laughed. This pristine facility for incoming foreigners was nicer than most Chinese clinics by many degrees.

Jarringly, the Chinese government now knew more about our health than the U.S. government ever did. We wondered why they were so goddamn interested. Why should any government care to know whether my asthma was allergy-induced or exactly how many surgical scars Ellen had from her childhood polio of 50-some years ago? But rest assured: the Chinese government knows. They asked me detailed questions about my asthma. They took careful count of Ellen's scars.

On the other hand, we now had the peace of mind of knowing that we were starting our time in a foreign country in good condition. No hint of SARS or swine flu — words that, in Asia, had the power to frighten. And the exam was free. I'd recently had a few of these same checkups at Delray Beach Medical Center and been slapped with a bill for $800.

This wasn't the first time we were objects of official curiosity. The day after we moved into our apartment, we walked a few blocks to the nearest police station to report, as required, our change of residence. One-party China is not a totalitarian state; you don't worry that you're constantly being watched and that spies are trying to overhear your every word. It's not 1984. But the authorities always do want to know where you are living.

The police station was run-down and grimy, a small building down a short lane from the street. Unlike your typical American cop shop, there was not a gun to be seen. In one scuzzy corner of the place — near an ashtray piled high with cigarette butts under a "No Smoking" sign that clearly was not doing its job — a young guy in t-shirt and jeans with an aversion to conversation looked at our lease agreement, jotted down our new address and scanned our passports into a Windows Explorer program. The People's Republic database of Goodman mug shots was getting larger by the minute.

One more thing about that health center. I'd expected to see a lot of Westerners being processed there. That's who "foreigners" are in China, right? People from places like America and Europe.

Not so. Almost everyone else arriving in China for an extended stay was an Asian: Japanese or Korean or Singaporean or Malaysian. I couldn't guess the many places they'd come from.

It's a big world, I thought. Much bigger than we realize back at home, living our day to day in our familiar neighborhoods and social circles. It was dawning on me that as a Caucasian having forever lived inside the USA, I'd never thought deeply about the distinctions among Asian countries and peoples — their characteristic facial traits, their rivalries, their not-insignificant prejudices toward one another. Unable to tell a Manchurian from a Filipino from a Vietnamese, I must have sounded, to an Asian, as ignorant as if I didn't know a Frenchman from a Pole from an Irishman; a Catholic from a Baptist from a Jew.

I'd never had occasion to think much about Asia. Never placed the continent in the center of my mind before. For most Americans my age, the national pageant is something that started in Europe, a saga that began with the explorers and the immigrants, with sub-stories involving slave ships from Africa and doomed cultures of Native Americans. Asians? Purely peripheral, their home countries a blur of stereotypes and muddled geography. Sorry, Charlie Chan. We just don't know that much about you folks — or care. Randy Newman nailed it back in 1970 with a vicious sendup of the average American's view of the Asian character: "Eating rice all day / while the children play. / You see, he believes / in the family. / He holds his money tight in his hand / With his yellow woman, he's the yellow man."

I came to learn a lot: That Hongkongers look down their noses at mainlanders as rubes or nouveau-riche big spenders. That mainland Chinese disdain the Hongkongers as money-grubbers. That Singaporeans condescend to Chinese as bumpkins, and Chinese resent the Singaporeans as snobs. That Chinese in Shanghai denigrate Chinese from the countryside. That the Japanese are to Asia as the French are to Europe: they place great store on style in food, clothing, art, manners. And they have an air of superiority about it.

I'd learn that mainland Chinese are nicer to white Americans than they are to their own brethren who live outside the mainland. And that if any one thing unites all Chinese, it's a deep-seated fear and hatred of the Japanese. In this part of the world, the horrors of World War II don't mean Auschwitz or the Bulge. They mean the Rape of Nanjing, the 1937 slaughter of tens of thousands of Chinese by the invading Imperial Japanese Army. Those memories were still raw.

8
Clueless in the Cleaning Aisle

THE BIG store made us stupid.

We stood before row upon row of plastic bottles of cleaning products. The market was immense, spotless, fluorescent-lit. Modern in every respect. We couldn't read a word.

It was unfair. Hadn't we come to a country intertwined with the world economy, if not practically running it altogether?

Well, then, how dare they not use English? How could they cling to a writing system that looks nothing like English or any relative of English?

We were helpless in the Carrefour, the French-owned hypermarket that you must pronounce "Cally-foo" if you want the Shanghai cab driver to drop you there. One after another, I picked up plastic bottles that differed in appearance, and turned them around slowly, squinting closely. I could gain no clue as to their contents. All the writing was in Chinese characters. Chicken scratches, for all we could tell.

We were after essentials. Our apartment had been advertised as furnished, but "furnished" in China was not the same as "furnished" as in a Tahoe vacation house, door key to salad forks. The apartment came with furniture, yes, but no dishes, cookware, silverware or towels. We would have to buy the gamut and try not to dwell on the fact we already owned perfectly good versions of all these things and had just stashed them in a storage locker in Lake Worth, Florida.

At least, we would pick up great bargains in China. That's what we told ourselves. We had arrived at the world's factory. We were in the country that makes everything that we in Americans buy at Walmart and Target and stuff into our split-level houses. All the sneakers, blue jeans, board games, iPhones and wine glasses. The throw pillows, tools and tires. All the stuff we love and lust after and can't live without.

And here we were at the source. This whole country, we figured, had to be the ultimate factory outlet. Everything had to be cheaper, if only because it didn't have to be shipped across the ocean to get to us.

Imagine our surprise, then, at the proliferation of lousy goods in the Shanghai Jing'an Carrefour. Bath towels too thin to qualify as dish rags. Shirts just two wearings away from their first ripped sleeves. Zippers that pulled apart in your hands. The textiles all colored in powder blue, pink and strawberry and decorated with cutesy drawings of kittens, so saccharine they should have come with a warning for diabetics.

It was an early lesson in Chinese economics. Those cool things that say Made In China didn't stay in China. They were from factories that got special tax breaks for making goods for export. They were immediately boxed and stacked onto container ships for the USA, Europe and South America. The government got a big cut of the proceeds on the sales made to the foreign purchasers, the factory owners became millionaires, and the workers got a pittance. The Chinese worker who was making clothes for The Gap could not afford to shop at The Gap. She had to settle for domestic versions of the cool jeans and tops. Much cheaper versions. It was as though all of China were a giant dollar store.

I often wondered, the longer we spent time in the country, how long would the Chinese rank and file put up with this? Working at factories to make goods they couldn't afford? Able to buy only the low-end toys that broke the first time you gave them to your grandson? (Something I learned from personal experience.)

As a national economic policy, China's highly engineered strategy to become the West's manufacturer had been brilliant — so far. Those low-pay factory jobs lifted tens of millions from severe poverty, the fastest, largest such rise in human history. But sooner or later it would dawn on many Chinese they were being cheated. It would hit them that, better off though they were, the quality goods they slaved to make were still much beyond their reach. And when that happened, look out. Several hundred million Chinese getting discontented all at once would not leave the world unshaken.

In the meantime, Ellen and I had to outfit our apartment with the second- and third-rate stuff that filled the Carrefour. Just now we were looking for dishwashing soap. We were in the cleaning-goods aisle. We could tell that much.

But what was this bottle I was holding? Floor cleaner? Window wash? Shampoo? Laundry detergent? There was no English lettering anywhere in sight. No Western script of any sort.

The small army of six or seven sales people were no help. They'd hustled over to us as soon as we'd paused to study the shelves. They traveled in a flock, like birds, and like service workers we'd find all over China, wore matching plumage — in this case, uniforms of beige pants, blue shirts. Our English didn't work on them. But one young man did light up when he recognized some sound we uttered. He trotted off and came back a minute later with a young woman who smiled at us and spoke in English.

"Can I help you?"

"Yes, thank you," we tried. "We're looking for dishwashing soap."

She didn't get it. She studied us closely. She wanted to get it.

"We want to wash dishes."

She kept studying.

"Dishes."

By now we were pantomiming the scrubbing of a dinner plate.

Got it!

"Ah, ah, ah, ah, ah. OK. OK!"

Nodding and smiling, she turned to her colleagues for a conference. She spoke Mandarin or Shanghainese, we couldn't tell which.

Now they were all in motion. Three reached toward the shelves. Each pulled down a different bottle and pushed a competing brand at us, arguing loudly among themselves over the one we should take. We didn't understand this at all. They couldn't have been working for commission; Carrefour was a self-service store. You put your stuff in a shopping cart and checked out at a cash register. Yet they seemed deeply invested in whether we picked the green bottle, the yellow bottle or the pale red bottle.

We went with the yellow. But was it really dishwashing soap? Granted, it worked fine when we got home and tried it on the breakfast dishes. But for all we knew, it might have been just as effective on the bathroom floor, the kitchen counter, a load of laundry or in giving us that fresh-as-springtime smell in the shower.

What a relief, then, to discover the Shanghai Ikea. Blue and gold and big-windowed, it was exactly the same as every other Ikea we'd ever been to, except for the Chinese characters added to the otherwise familiar labels for Billy bookcases and Ivar chairs. We didn't need a translator to make sense of the store, and we knew the goods would be good enough.

In the store's cafeteria overlooking a busy elevated train line, we joined the Chinese customers snacking on Swedish meatballs. It felt like comfort food. These were the same Ikea meatballs we'd known in

Philadelphia and Florida. Strange to say, the globalization of this simple and endlessly replicated little treat from Scandinavia made us feel at home.

We piled into a taxi with bags full of cookware, flatware, dishes, towels and toothbrush holders — grateful to have escaped the Great China Dollar Store.

Matters grew more serious when it came to our coffee.

9
Coffee Crazy

Ellen's blog:
HOWIE AND I are addicted to coffee. We admit it. Early in our marriage we tried to end our caffeine dependence by stopping cold turkey. We got headaches, grew irritable. The whole world sucked, and everything in it. Inside a week, we came close to killing each other.

We keep that painful chapter in mind. Ever since, we have been very respectful of the importance of coffee to our personal well being and to the healthy maintenance of our marriage.

The Chinese are a tea-drinking people. This was the country that invented tea. Caffeine here is overwhelmingly delivered by the leaf, not the bean. Coffee, we found, was mainly for foreigners and for the young aspiring professional class of Chinese. Starbucks had dozens of stores around Shanghai, and so did the British chain Costa Coffee, but the locals went mostly for the status.

Coffee seemed to be expensive almost everywhere we went in Shanghai. Our first couple of weeks in town, we had breakfast out every day. The coffee portion of the bill usually surpassed the food. Considering that a great motivation for our move to Shanghai was financial, it quickly became obvious that two cups of coffee for each of us every morning was not a great idea.

"This is nuts," we told ourselves. "We've got to start making coffee at home."

Sounded easy. But the grocery stores rarely stocked decent joe. They almost always sold instant. If you ever wonder where all the world's Nescafe has disappeared to, check out Shanghai's 24-7 convenience stores. The local grocery on Anfu Lu that catered to expats had actual coffee beans. But the several brands ranged greatly in price and even more greatly in obscurity. Was this bag from Cuba? Brazil? The Philippines? We couldn't tell. We decided on Yuban, a mid-priced name that we at least had heard of.

For a coffeemaker, we picked up a cheap French press from Ikea. We toted home bottled water.

(We had been warned repeatedly against drinking the tap water of Shanghai. Not that the water itself was unsafe — it was the city's pipes. The municipal water system was so old that bits of metal were apt to mingle with the water you poured into your glass.)

Next step: Buy some milk. This should have been easy. But every carton was written in Chinese. We studied box after box, and finally chose a small one that looked kind of friendly. It had a picture of a cute teenage boy on it, a kind-of Asian version of Disney's Aladdin.

Next morning we heated water in our one saucepan, another Ikea purchase. We filled the bottom of the press with the ground coffee and plunged.

We were excited. Our first cup of home-brewed coffee in our own kitchen. Aromas of home!

Something made me try the milk before pouring it into the coffee.

It tasted like lemon.

"You have got to be kidding!" I shouted at the carton.

"Lemon-flavored coffee? How on earth am I supposed to know this? Where does it say lemon?"

The carton didn't answer.

Chocolate milk, strawberry milk we could understand. But lemon? The flavor of milk gone sour? How crazy was this? What kind of strange creature is the Chinese consumer?

We did not stay this helpless for long. Little by little, we got to know the dairy section. We turned coffee shopping into a hobby, trying different brands from different countries. We eventually found a very good ground bean from Yunnan province at a good price.

It became our staple.

A lot cheaper than marriage counseling.

10
Hooking Up

Howard:

THE APARTMENT, much as we loved it, had its peculiarities. Strange smells wafted through the kitchen window: fishy oils, cabbage-y vegetables, odors we couldn't identify.

The water pressure would fail without warning. There'd be no showers those days. The management offered explanations to the residents – we could tell by the commotion in the lobby – but no one spoke anything but Chinese, so we were in the dark.

Then came the day when I realized that when I woke up the next morning, I'd be unable to watch Game 6 of the World Series on my TV or over the Internet. My beloved Phillies against the hated Yankees in what looked to be the decisive game. The apartment's TV and Internet connections were down.

Everything was intertwined: the TV, the satellite dish, the router to which we attached thick blue LAN lines to get the Internet on our laptops. And the whiz kid who installed them — a friend of realtor Jenny's — had used a wire that wasn't quite the right fit for the satellite box it was supposed to attach to. The line kept falling out of the connector hole. I'd stick it back in and get things working, but if I happened to jostle any of the wires plugged into the box — which happened all the time, because when you use a laptop you constantly shift from position to position — the damn thing fell out again.

We had wanted the satellite TV because it boasted HBO and CNN International. In English, miraculously enough. The CNN was nice to have, as was the BBC World Service, although both were known to go blank with no notice because the censors took issue with what was being reported at the moment.

HBO, however, was a major disappointment, a lame, scrubbed version of the programming we got in America. Terrible movies from the

1980s and '90s that make up the backwash of the HBO schedule back home — these were leading fare on HBO Asia. Series like "Hung" or "The Wire" would show up months after they aired in the States, the sex scenes blurred out or excised altogether.

On the other hand, only foreigners were allowed to get any satellite TV in China at all, we were told. So no matter how thin the offerings, our TV was still a window to the outside world that was closed and curtained to most people on the mainland.

Eventually a repair guy arrived. Jenny showed up too, to translate. The wrong-size wire? That wasn't this guy's department. He was from China Telecom. The wire had come from Jenny's satellite-pirate friend. Regardless, China Telecom Man got down on his knees and studied our phone wires for a minute, made a quick change and — voila! — the Internet was working again. And so was the satellite TV.

Then he showed me the problem. In moving some of the furniture around, I had mistakenly plugged a phone line into a connector hole for the Internet. And I'd stuck the Internet line into the slot for the phone.

He showed me, like he was explaining to a very slow child, just where on the connector the directions were written.

Written in plain Chinese.

How dumb of me! The problem wasn't the gray wire that always fell out of the satellite box that the first guy had so sloppily put together. It was my inability to read the directions.

The same sort of directions that sat there, quietly essential and mockingly mute, on every appliance in the apartment.

Take, for example, the heater/cooler unit in each room. El and I expected these to work pretty well. They carried the Mitsubishi name, not some Chinese brand we'd never heard of. They worked by remotes. Very convenient. We would never have to get out of bed to adjust the temperature.

But the only writing on the remotes was in Chinese.

During an early cold snap, I furiously pressed every button. And succeeded in making the machine blow colder air into the bedroom.

This was where the language barrier really hurt. When talking to someone face-to-face in Shanghai, you could usually pantomime enough to get your point across, especially if the message was simple. When you needed something complicated — like asking the doorman to keep his eye out for an upholstery-fabric delivery — you could get hold of a Mandarin-speaking friend on the cell phone and have them explain it.

But our illiteracy in Mandarin turned us into helpless morons when we were at home and trying to get the heat to work or the Internet connected or the gas stove to light or the bottled-water man to bring a new delivery.

My solution was to bring the remotes into work with me one day, show them to Liu Hong and ask her to translate. As she did — with an amused little smile on her face — I drew diagrams of the devices and labeled the buttons "On," "Off," "Warmer," "Cooler," "Fan Only," "Automatic."

Yes, my knowledge of Chinese characters really was that weak.

When I got home, I taped the guides to the gizmos and felt immediately empowered, as only a man can feel with a remote in his hand. And let me tell you, we really needed those translations. Because when the temperature dropped (dropping in Celsius, another puzzle to our American brains), the house got cold. And stayed cold.

Our perfect apartment had not an ounce of insulation.

11
Wet Head

WE'D EXPECTED the difficulties with Internet and TV connections. After everything we'd heard about censorship in China, we were glad to have any outside communications at all.

But we hadn't anticipated trouble in drying our hair.

This was a personal priority of mine. In packing for China, I had actually used some of my precious suitcase space for a hair dryer. That's how important this was. I figured I would pick up an electricity adapter when we arrived. This was not to be. No adapter seemed to work.

So I quickly moved on to Plan B: Buy a new hair dryer.

We found several models to choose from in Tesco. Tesco is a major discount store, very big in Britain and a big deal in Shanghai, too. Think Kmart with a giant grocery and a piped-in children's chorus endlessly singing a dirge, in Mandarin, to the tune of "Happy Birthday."

The saleslady spoke nothing close to English but understood my pantomime. She picked out a small travel-model hair dryer and patiently took it out of the box and plugged it in to show me how well it worked. A good deal at 89 yuan. About $13.

I brought it home. The next day, rushing to go out, I hurriedly washed my hair, plugged in my new purchase …. and got blasted with smoke and the smell of burning plastic.

I ran to the balcony, cursing the incredible fact that the stupid thing had worked perfectly fine in the store and had no business exploding when I got it home, and hoping that sun, breeze and some stiff brushing would dry my hair at least a little. A tequila shot later, I was ready to face the world.

We had a date to check out a new sofa. We were determined to rid ourselves of the Bad Versailles sofa and arm chair that had come with the flat. These furnishings were worse than ugly. Full of lumps and with cushions that slid forward every time you sat on them, they actually made you less comfortable the more you tried to sit in them.

On Craigslist Shanghai, we found a promising lead on a replacement. The woman on the phone spoke with an Australian accent and said she was in a hurry to sell. "You want to pop on over now? That would be great," she said.

We took a taxi to a spacious, funky apartment in a towering complex of copycat buildings. The Australian was a sparkling 20-something named Jacinta. She and her Chinese girlfriend, Chris, were unloading their stuff because they were moving to Beijing.

Their couch was flat and L-shaped, minimalist modern, but its blue cloth covering had been shredded by their cats. The women were very knowledgeable about life in China, and they seemed kind of fascinated to meet people as new and raw as we were.

As we sat on the couch talking about our adjustments here, I mentioned unexpected problems — like the hair-drying fiasco I'd just had. In describing the frustration, I almost broke into tears. The jolts and exertions of uprooting ourselves to China were leaking out, just a little.

We talked for about 45 minutes. Eventually the conversation swung back to the sofa. They were asking 2,000 yuan (about $300) for the sofa, but it was too torn up for us to be interested. Would we consider 1,000 yuan? Jacinta had connections in the furniture business and knew an upholsterer who could probably re-cover the couch for another 1,000. Well maybe.

We'd think about it.

We made our goodbyes, feeling like old friends already, and agreed to talk more about the couch the next day.

Howie and I went into the hallway to wait for the elevator. All of a sudden, Jacinta came running out of the apartment. Holding a hair dryer.

"Please, take this."

It was such a surprise. And so touching.

"I don't need the hair dryer," Jacinta said. "I have short hair. And we really have to get rid of our stuff."

That wasn't all.

"We want you to have the couch," she said, "for free."

There was still more. Jacinta would set us up with her upholsterer friend and take us to the fabric mart to help us buy new material. Even though she was so busy with her own move. Just out of friendship.

This time, I think I really did produce a tear.

A couple of people had told us we'd have moments — or days — when we'd be completely frustrated by Shanghai. And then moments when it would all turn around and everything suddenly would feel exactly right.

This was what they meant.

Choosing upholstery with Jacinta at the fabric mart

12
Getting the Chinese Price

Ellen's blog:
ANOTHER DAY, another problem with our cable TV. So I stopped by the real estate office to see if Jenny, our real estate agent, could help us with it.

She eagerly agreed to come over later in the day to see what she could do. And she gave it a good try. She unplugged wires and plugged them in again, turned switches on and off, pressed lots of keys on the remote. Then she stopped. She announced we needed to get the installer back for "professional assistance."

She asked if there were anything else I needed help with and I admitted that the washing machine labels, all in Chinese, were a puzzle. So she studied the machine and translated the instructions for me.

After the laundry tutorial, I invited her to sit on the new couch for a chat. Soon, we agreed to help each other in our language studies.

First I showed her pictures of Mike and Kate's wedding and explained the Jewish custom of the bride and groom being lifted up on chairs during the hora. That led to questions about who pays for the wedding and how much these grand events cost.

We compared Chinese weddings (groom's family pays) to ours (bride's family, or split). She followed my English very well, and when we came to an unfamiliar word, we'd stop and I'd explain it and she'd repeat her pronunciation until she was satisfied that she had mastered it.

She told me she was one of six children from a poor family outside the large industrial city of Wuhan, a six-hour train ride west of Shanghai. She said that hers was one of parts of China that had known great poverty and that many babies starved because their parents couldn't feed them.

I asked about the large number of children in her family — wasn't there a government policy restricting family size? Yes, she said, but her grandparents strongly believed in having a male heir and so her parents paid huge fees to the government for the privilege of having more than one child.

I told her of the large number of Chinese girls adopted into our country and how I had just had dinner in New York with such a girl, the adopted daughter of one of our best friends.

"She is very lucky," Jenny said. "Many, many children are not so lucky."

I asked her if she had known hunger growing up.

"Yes," she said. "But even though we didn't have anything, my parents made sure we were a family. My mother made sure I had a good education."

Jenny, who is all of 24, already had a masters degree and was helping two siblings with their college expenses. And she sent money back home to her widowed mom.

Her goal, she told me, was to be able to afford to buy her mother a home in two years.

She said that in China every generation strives to be more successful than the previous one. I taught her the English phrase for that: upward mobility. I said it used to be that way in the USA, but not so much anymore. The economy had grown more difficult for most people. Now, children just wanted to live as well as their parents, and many parents seemed fine with that.

She said it seemed Americans wanted to play a lot — goof off.

I agreed, and explained there was a term for that: "Free time."

Then Jenny asked me a question that I really couldn't answer, not then:

"Why is it that Americans are so rich when they don't work very hard?"

IN MY first days in this new land, Jenny was my guardian angel. It felt completely natural for me to drop by her office with a bill in hand.

"What is this and how do I pay it?"

"Oh, this is the telephone bill. Would you like me to walk with you to pay it?"

"Sure — If you can spare the time," I said, never turning down her offers of assistance.

It turned out to be a very short walk. We had only to go to the convenience store on the corner, similar to a 7-Eleven, where I had previously paid my water and electric bills.

A quick 68 yuan ($10) later, we were out of there.

"OK," she said. "What else do you have?" as she gestured to my filled IKEA shopping bag.

I pulled out a shoe with a wobbly heel and a purse with a button-clasp that needed to be reattached.

"Do you know where a shoe repair shop might be?" I asked her.

"Sure," she said and starting walking me down busy Wulumuqi Road. Two minutes later we stood in front of a tiny open-air shop.

The lights were on, but no one was inside. Jenny asked the laundry owner next door if he knew where the shoe guy was. The laundryman was ironing a shirt. He told us the shoe repair man was away for dinner. Just then the shoe repair man pulled up on his bicycle.

Jenny showed him my shoe. They talked and talked for what seemed five minutes. "OK," she said, "he'll do it for six yuan." That's 88 cents.

I was curious. "What were you talking about for so long?"

She said he'd first asked for eight yuan. Jenny had countered with five. He told her five was impossible. They settled on six.

I agreed on six. Then I showed him the purse with the fallen-off clasp. He studied it for quite a while. He said he would do it for five. We agreed and stepped away to let him get on with the work.

Ten minutes later, Jenny and I returned to see how the work was progressing. The shoe was done. The repair looked good to me. I asked about my purse.

He walked to the back of the shop and started shouting up a flight of stairs. After a minute, a woman came down, holding my purse. She was wearing pajamas. This was a Shanghai custom, pajamas as street-wear. And at the moment, it was a custom under fire. With the World Expo approaching, local moralists feared that the wearing of pajamas in public would convey a hick image of the city. Defenders of the tradition said the reformers were trying to root out a crucial article of local color. The *Shanghai Daily* ran columns on the controversy, pro and con.

And us? We delighted in every pajama-sighting. We thought the people wearing their striped flannels and slippers looked like escaped mental patients. We loved it.

Down the stairs she came, gesturing at my purse, complaining loudly to Jenny. We both looked at the purse. It looked fine. The clasp had been reattached. So why the commotion?

Jenny understood. The woman was a neighbor of the shoe repair man. It turned out, he could not see very well. He had asked her to do the repair and she felt he had quoted too low a price. She wanted 10 yuan. Jenny told her the price had been agreed upon beforehand. She couldn't go around changing it after the fact. Pajama woman backed down.

My admiration for Jenny rose all the higher. I paid my 11 yuan, collected my repaired items and walked away. Out of curiosity, I asked Jenny to find out from the laundry owner what he would charge to clean six shirts. He looked at me, then told her 48 yuan. With a smile, I told Jenny that my cleaner across the street had just done six shirts for 36 yuan.

"That's good," she smiled. "You paid Chinese price." Not, in other words, the foreigners' price.

Walking back up Wulumuqi Road, I paused at a small shop that sold pajamas and robes. I hadn't brought a robe from America and I knew it would soon be getting cold. I would want one.

"I'll help you buy one," sweet Jenny offered.

There were many to choose from, but I quickly spotted one I liked. It was bright orange and lined in orange fleece.

"I'll take it," I announced.

"Really?" asked Jenny.

"Yes. I like it, it fits, and it's a good price. Is there something I'm not considering?"

Jenny gave a huge grin. "No, it's just unusual. Most women would want to think about it and come back in a few days. But it's OK," she added, remembering how we'd picked the apartment 10 minutes after seeing it. "It's your style."

I gave the saleslady a 100-yuan note ($14.65). She studied it for a second and nodded her head: all right.

"Was she checking to see if it was counterfeit?" I asked Jenny.

Jenny nodded.

"How can you tell if it's real or not?"

Jenny and the lady were happy to give me a demonstration. Each bill, they showed me, had several places that changed color when you moved the bill in different directions. The coolest test: The lady placed a piece of paper over a blank part of the bill, then rubbed a coin on the blank paper. As in a parlor trick, a picture of Chairman Mao appeared, proving it was a genuine 100-yuan note.

Turns out, you had to use a specific type of coin — a 0.10 yuan (kind of a dime) that is much lighter than other coins. Aluminum, I believe. Other coins didn't work. I checked.

So, thanks to my guardian angel, I paid my phone bill, got my shoe and purse repaired, bought a robe — for Chinese price — and got a lesson in sussing out counterfeits.

Just a little walk in the neighborhood.

Ellen and Jenny

83

13
The Dirt on Shanghai

Howard:
PEOPLE KEPT asking us if we'd gotten an *ayi*.

An *ayi* (literally, "auntie") is a domestic who comes to your house or lives with you and cleans, does your laundry, makes your breakfast, watches your kids — whatever you'd want her to do. *Ayis* were cheap. All labor in China seemed cheap. Hence their attraction and one of the reasons that many expats lived much better in Shanghai than they could ever hope to back home in America or Australia or wherever else the bank or corporate headquarters had sent them from.

Any self-respecting expat was expected to have an *ayi*. And not just expats. Chinese people hired *ayis* too, as soon as they made it to middle class or anywhere near. People who hired *ayis* made it sound like an act of generosity. These young women had come to the city from their poor towns in a desperate search for money, we were told, and whatever small wages we could pay them would be a lifeline.

But El and I held off, because a) we were cheap, b) our social conscience balked at the inherently unequal relationship we'd be entering into, and c) we didn't have enough household chores to worry about.

We soon started to reconsider c.

Nothing in our apartment stayed clean for long. Before we moved in, our landlord had hired a crew to scrub the place. But we still found plenty of grime. On the gas stove, black crusts of grease adhered to every burner. The plastic wrapping that covered the bedroom lampshades was gray with dust.

We grumbled about the lousy job that cleaning crew had done, We bought some Mr. Muscle — China's answer to Mr. Clean. We scrubbed. And made the place look a lot better.

Not for long. We began to notice that, no matter how often we swept the floor, it was soon covered again in dust. By the time we went to bed, the bottoms of our bare feet were gray.

We knew we weren't tracking the dirt in with us; trying to do as the Asians do, we generally left our shoes at the front door. Dirt got in anyway. It got in through open windows, and it got in when the windows were closed.

The fact was, Shanghai was dirty. We just had to get used to it. It must have been like London 100 or 150 years ago, when England was rapidly industrializing and asserting great global power and the city was growing like gangbusters. That romantic London fog of Sherlock Holmes's times — it wasn't actually fog at all. It was coal dust.

That gauzy London was today's Shanghai. The air was often hazy with something you could taste. One October day, the *Shanghai Daily* reported on an especially bad fog that rolled in with "a peculiar dark quality that reminded some residents of the disaster film 2010." A spokesman from the city weather bureau called it a combination of fog, dust and "airborne particles from the north." It read like a weather report from the Red Planet.

On brighter days we'd see automobiles with conspicuous dust on their roofs, as if they had been sitting on some unswept shelf in the attic instead of outdoors in the supposedly fresh air.

The sidewalks were constantly dirty, despite armies of street sweepers who were out all day with blue uniforms, bamboo brooms and push carts – attacking industrialization's grunge with Tevye's primitive tools. There was almost no such thing as a clear window. Buildings that were only eight or 10 years old looked like America's beat-up 30-year-old public housing.

Part of it was the stirred-up dust from the construction that went on, almost round the clock, to prepare for the World Expo.

Part of it was that many Chinese people just seemed a lot more tolerant of shmutz. We saw plenty of people who were freed of all inhibition against spitting on the sidewalk, a habit that public-health reformers had ended in America at the turn of the 20th century. You had to be very careful of ever sitting on a curb or a stoop in Shanghai. You never wanted to put your purse or briefcase down there.

We saw men take a seat in a large crowd and unselfconsciously blow hockers clean out of their noses. They actually had a rationale for it: it was believed unhealthy to hold in the phlegm.

To be fair, Chinese people generally thought it perverse of us Westerners to blow into a handkerchief. They must have thought we were barbarians for carrying our snot around with us. I did see some Chinese men use tissues to empty their noses, especially after eating food with chiles, and I always wondered if these guys thought of themselves as a cultural avant-garde.

In a restaurant, we didn't always get napkins at dinner, and sometimes when we asked for them the waitress acted like she doesn't know what we were talking about. Often, instead of a napkin they'd give us a tissue. Not the easiest way to dry your fingers. But that provided a use for all the tissues that weren't being used for the blowing of noses.

There was one more reason the city was dirty. China, the would-be world leader in so many ways, was rife with inadequate cleaning products. The stuff called Mr. Muscle came out of a slickly packaged plastic bottle, just like the ones in American supermarkets – but it didn't work magic on household dirt the way we expect from Comet or Ajax.

In our kitchen in our Shanghai apartment, there was one spot on the counter that El tried to remove with our watery Chinese cleaning spray. Day after day, she tried. But it ignored her, no matter how hard she attacked it. She finally voiced her frustration.

"I'd give my kingdom," she said, "for some Soft-Scrub."

Which cracked me up.

We went on a quest for an American-like cleaner. We looked and looked, and finally, inside a grocery specializing in imported foods, we found a close equivalent: Cif, a "powerful cream cleaner" from Unilever

Hong Kong & Malaysia. We didn't care that it cost over $7 a bottle. We saw that it contained a mild abrasive and, our hearts leaping a little, we had to have it.

We took it home. And, yes, we took out that spot.

I don't know if China will supercede the U.S. as the globe's leading economic power, but I do know this: Mr. Clean will kick Mr. Muscle's ass every time.

14
Scaredy Cat

Ellen:

SHANGHAI WAS scary. From the moment I walked out of my apartment I saw nothing but hazards.

The uneven, broken pavement — what if I tripped and broke a leg? Not an unreasonable fear when polio leaves you a little unsteady on your left foot.

The man standing on a bicycle, using it for a ladder while his soldering gun sent down sparks on the unbarricaded sidewalk — what if one of those sparks went into my eye?

That dangling electric wire I had to walk past — would it zap me?

Crossing an intersection, I could be fodder for any taxi, truck, bus, or motorcycle that wouldn't care that I have the right of way.

Everyone and everything on the street was playing a colossal game of Chicken.

What if I got hit? What hospital would they take me to? What if the ambulance driver didn't speak English? That was a good bet. How would they know how to contact Howie? How would he ever learn what had happened to me?

When my children were little, they used to ask me "what if" questions. "Mom, what if I can't fall asleep? What if I fall asleep and have a nightmare? What if you don't hear me when I call you for help?"

My standard answer was, "What if the sky falls?" It was my way of telling them that there was always going to be something to worry about if you were looking for a worry — there'd be no end to it.

That usually ended the conversation.

But here, it felt as if the sky might actually fall.

It exhausted me, just thinking about all the ways I could be in danger. One day I spoke to my American friend Amanda about my concerns. She was anything but comforting.

"Oh, it's bad out there," she agreed, and proceeded to tell me about a horrifying incident she had witnessed.

While walking home on a dark road she watched as a man driving a motorcycle hit a large, uncovered pot hole in the middle of the street. The guy went sailing over the handlebars and landed in a heap. Before Amanda could do anything, another motorcycle hit him. Now he was unconscious.

She rushed over to him, hoping to attract a police car, as she stood in the road diverting other vehicles from the fallen driver. Finally, the police came and soon a truck arrived. To Amanda's complete shock, the truck driver and his assistant lifted the unconscious man by his arms and legs and placed him in the back of the truck. No stretcher, no board to support his neck and back. Nothing. They drove off. Then the police departed, never thinking to put up any type of barrier to block the pot hole from ensnaring another victim.

Later, we found out something maybe worse. Many Chinese who are injured in an accident will sue whoever comes to their aid, alleging blame for exacerbating their injuries or even for causing the accident itself. With the actual perpetrator nowhere in sight, this was the only way some poor man or woman might see any redress from the accident — or get an easy payday. The situation was so bad that most passersby refused to get involved when they witnessed something awful happening to someone. Now we realized that, God forbid, if Howie or I got hurt in the street, we might lie there for a very long time until some brave gambler decided to help us out.

So this was what I was dealing with. I tried to remain rational under the circumstances.

"OK, El," I asked myself, "what if you did get hurt and went to a doctor or a hospital? What would you do?"

Back in the States, I'd know exactly. I'd slap down my United Health Care insurance card and let the professionals take care of me.

Could I do that here?

Using Skype one night, I called the 800 number for United Health Care. I reached a service representative and explained I was living overseas. "What do I do if I have a health problem?"

"Well," she told me, "you can't use your United Health Care card overseas. If you do get sick or injured you'll need to pay out of pocket and keep your receipts and maybe we'll reimburse you for some of it."

I thought about what "maybe" might mean. I was pretty sure it meant "never."

Here we were, paying tons of money each month to Cobra to be maybe reimbursed if we needed medical assistance. I was badly missing the insurance coverage, or rather the double insurance coverage, that for years Howie and I had when I was teaching and he was working for the Philadelphia Inquirer, each of us belonging to strong unions. Medical visits were routine. Now they would be luxuries. I'd really have to weigh things before deciding to see a doctor.

At 60, I was starting to feel that I was slipping from my rung on the middle-class ladder. How much farther were we going to fall?

I wouldn't allow myself to dwell on the subject. Not with this exciting city and country to explore. I'd take the advice I gave to my children when they worried so long ago —"What if the sky falls?"

15
'The Government Won't Like That'

Howard:

THE SHANGHAI DAILY jumped out at you from a Shanghai newsstand. Often it was the only publication in English. It was tabloid size, 40 pages every day, a decent roundup of city, world and business news; sports, with a lot more stories about soccer and volleyball than the NFL and major league baseball; and features, ranging from cosmetics tips and movie-star gossip to advice on Chinese traditional medicine.

The weather map could have been lifted from any U.S. newspaper, except for the temperatures being in Celsius and the cities being Chongqing and Harbin. And for the weather predictions being predictably wrong. Fair, foul, foggy — whatever the Shanghai Meteorological Bureau confidently forecast for the next day, you'd be smart to bet against it.

The paper was quite a convincing copy of a Western newspaper — so long as you didn't depend on it for news of China.

The editors were a very smart group of people who knew quite a bit about the American and British media — Western journalists' standards, their frankness, the unflattering truths they often aired about China. The editors also clearly loved their jobs and knew the system they lived under, just as any long-surviving species knows its environment. They weren't going to publish very much information that Xinhua, the state-run news agency, had not released first.

Everyone in the *Shanghai Daily* newsroom had constant online access to the *New York Times* and the British *Guardian*, meaning that everyone knew that, when the subject was China, there was far more to the story than they were going to be able to tell in their own newspaper. The newsroom's TV screens were always showing CNN International — except for those moments when the screens would go blank, sometimes in mid-sentence. Some good bureaucrat in the Propaganda Bureau would have decided that the news report of the moment was too offensive for the citizenry's eyes and ears, and CNN would suddenly disappear. This reliably occurred when the subject was the Dalai Lama, the quasi-religious Falun Gong, or the Tiananmen Square massacre of 1989. But other subjects, far less obvious a threat to any regime's sense of security, would be censored, too.

I found that out on my second day of work.

The *Shanghai Daily* had hired me to perform the strangest job I had ever had in journalism: Polisher. The job was needed because the reporters were Chinese and were attempting to write news stories in English, their second language. Only a few had strong educations in journalism. Fewer had the bulldog inquisitiveness that good journalism requires or knew how to write a news story well. Many, it seemed, were there only for the security of a job in a semi-state-run enterprise. About a dozen reporters covered city news. Another eight or nine wrote business stories. Four or five translated stories from Chinese newspapers and press releases into English; that's where *Shanghai Daily* got a lot of its news about China beyond Shanghai — the paper had no reporters of its own in other cities (except for nearby Hangzhou, whose city government paid to have a page of news to promote their city). Another eight or nine Chinese reporters, and the occasional Westerner, wrote features, but features weren't my concern. I was part of the news-side polishing crew. We came in around 5 in the afternoon and worked till midnight or beyond.

It was quite an amazing ambition, to put out a daily newspaper not in your natural language. And to realize it, the *Shanghai Daily* needed us, the dozen or so Australians, Canadians, Scots, Singaporeans, Indians — and the rare American — to turn the reporters' tortured Chinglish (their word) into publishable English. The job was part-editing, part-code breaking.

We would read sentences like: "He reminded Zhang that Wei had complicated social intercourse." We had to figure out that the writer really meant: "Wei had disreputable friends."

We would read that "a girl's right lung was punctuated" and that "the price will be rescannable." We corrected those to "the lung was punctured" and "the price will be reasonable."

We would read police stories that required a Major Case Squad to crack. The police, of course, spoke in Mandarin or Shanghainese, and it was up to our reporters to translate their statements into English. One day I read this supposed quote from a police official: "We will not notice them beforehand. No more face-work and no more hide-out." I called the reporter over for an interrogation. It took some questioning, but I determined that the official had said, "We will not notify them beforehand. And we will do no more surveillance."

Then there was the criminal defendant who was judged "inguilty."

The job would routinely turn my brain into a knot.

My first night had been easy. I did the world-news page, and all the stories were written by wire services.

But on my second night I started working with pieces written by the staff.

My very first story regarded the fallout from a recent city scandal. Investigators had gone overboard in a crackdown on illegal cabbies. That Monday, in two separate cases in different parts of town, authorities had been forced to apologize to innocent people who had been fined and brought to court for allegedly operating "black cabs" — using their private cars as taxis without having gone to the bother of getting a license. These guys had been stopped by plainclothes police decoys who demanded rides to, say, the hospital because they were supposedly having an emergency, and the drivers obliged. Shanghai officials admitted that these poor shmucks had been entrapped by overzealous "watchdogs," who probably received bonuses based on the number of scalps they brought in and didn't care how they got them.

The story I was to polish started out by mentioning the "peak of criticism" over these pit-bull cops. The reporter's copy then rambled along to touch on a number of related topics, in roughly this order: A) New city bus routes were being added in suburban areas to limit the demand for illegal cabs in far-flung neighborhoods. B) The main Shanghai transport bureau had warned the investigative teams they had better play fair from now on, or expect punishment. C) A member of the city's political advisory board had urged the city government to promote car-pooling by setting up a website where riders can get matched with people offering rides. D) Something-something about efforts to get gypsy cabbies working for legit companies.

Now, of all the elements in this story, what was the most newsworthy? Well, B), of course: the warning to the watchdog teams to shape up. So I flipped the paragraphs around to lead off with that. The Number 1 polisher, Dave, the only other American on news-side, approved, and told me to make sure to take the basic step — which the reporter hadn't done — of filling in the context. The writer had failed to tell readers why we were following the story in the first place; that, earlier in the week, two government bodies had been forced to apologize for entrapping innocent people.

It took me a while, being new at it — about an hour and a half to figure out what the writer's sentences meant, discard excess language and rearrange all the paragraphs into a sensible order. Then I spent another half-hour trimming it all to fit on the page just-so, and writing a headline:

Bureau warns taxi watchdogs: Play fair

Great, all done.

Except behind me I started hearing JJ, the main news editor, jabbering in Mandarin to the night metro guy called Skye. That was the English name he'd picked for himself. And leaping out of the unfamiliar strings of Chinese, I heard an English word every now and then, "taxi ... taxi ...." Something was up with my taxi story.

Sure enough, Skye came over after a while and showed me that page A4 had been remade. Taxi was no longer the lead story. It was at the bottom of the page. It was a third of its original length. All reference to entrapment cases was gone.

What the hell happened?

Skye quietly explained: "It's been cut by the government. They said we can't discuss the entrapment."

Me: "You're kidding. It's all over the TV today. It was all over our paper this morning."

Skye: "They said the government has had its say in the matter. And that's enough talking about it. No more."

So there I was, mind-blown and drop-jawed. Of course I'd expected to find censorship in China. But that was theory. I hadn't expected to run into it on a subject as innocuous as taxi-law enforcement. I hadn't expected the censor to be thinking ahead to our next day's reporting on a municipal news story and telling us, before the story was finished, that one part had to be cut but another part could be published. I hadn't expected it on my first fucking story!

I had never seen pre-censorship before: In all my years on American newspapers I'd written many stories that angered officials. They let me know it after the stories ran. To have authorities telling me — while I worked — what the story may include, and what it must leave out? I couldn't believe it. Who were we working for here?

JJ took it as par for the course. It was no big deal, remaking the page around 11 p.m. because of an objection like this. "Happens all the time," she said.

Dave the American, who had a history of serially quitting the paper and coming back, murmured, "This is a big reason I'm leaving." Which he did for the last time, as he planned, five weeks later.

I dutifully reworked the story. The much-shortened, much duller story. My new headline:

More buses set for suburbs

I didn't get mad. Not even annoyed. I just laughed to myself and thought: This is absurd. And felt a little sorry for the hundreds of millions of people living here, whose information was so meagerly meted out to them. Whose government treated its people like they're children: God forbid the kids should be told the facts of life.

It's not my newspaper, I told myself. Not my country. It's the editors' paper. I'm just here to help them produce it.

I found this to be a very useful denial of responsibility. I doubted I would make it through a year if I approached it any other way.

I WAS hired on a year's contract, the *Shanghai Daily's* standard pact for foreign experts. It was much like any other employment contract I've ever seen, except for the clause that I agree to "respect China's religious policies, and shall not conduct any religious activities incompatible with his/her status as a foreign expert." (Did this mean no Chanukkah candles? No, no, I was told, don't worry. The government would only take an interest in my belief system if I joined the Falun Gong.)

The contract also wanted me to "respect Chinese people's ethics standards and customs." Did this mean I should abandon my moral qualms against buying bootleg DVDs? Respect the standard and custom of censoring stories and hassling journalists who stepped over the line? It seemed odd, even ridiculous, to see these things in an employment contract — but also intimidating. The authorities were letting the little people like me know that they had a big country to run and were serious about how they went about it. It worked. I felt myself receding into a lower profile, shuffling into a meeker version of myself. I vowed to rock no boats.

The newsroom was in a 45-story building topped by squiggly

antennae from the Godzilla Tokyo Skyline school of architecture. The lobby doors were manned by three or four guards in blue-gray military caps and jackets. They looked like stern doorkeepers of the state, until I noticed that by evening they would be napping, their thin white socks showing beneath hiked-up blue-gray pant legs, their heads cradled on criss-crossed arms, a thermos of tea at the elbow. Even during the day, when they stood attentively and looked the part, there was no real security. No one ever asked to see an ID. There were no gates to cross in the high-ceilinged lobby, which had a faux-Grecian-style interior, a bank branch office, a Chinese-language bookstore, a never-busy coffee shop, and a convenience store that never closed. I bought many an ice cream bar and Coke Zero in that store, using a company auto-pay card that was one of the great perks of the job (about $25 worth of snacks a month), without ever exchanging a single intelligible sentence with the ladies in the green polyester uniforms who worked the cash register at all hours.

We occupied the 38th floor. Outside the floor-to-ceiling windows were the astounding night lights of Shanghai's high rises: Flash Gordon shapes in bright, ever-changing neon. Some of the city's most iconic sights — the gaudily phallic Pearl Tower, the Shanghai World Financial Center (then the third-tallest building in the world) — seemed close at hand though they stood across the Huangpu River, which was two and a half miles away. And nearer than these, just below us, we could look down on hundreds of three-story rowhouse-like buildings of a much older Shanghai, holdouts of the disappearing city. They were called shikumen, old-style houses whose alley-like streets once served as communal living rooms, four families sharing the outhouse.

The smog, however, had to lift to give us this clear view. Most days the wall-size windows were curtains of gray, the skyline peeking through wavily, the night lights blurry and smeared. I had been in the office for a couple of weeks when I looked away from my computer screen one day and noticed the gray outside the windows — and saw that it matched the gray of the newsroom's walls, the gray of its file cabinets, the gray of the top of our desks.

I see you working – you're in a place that's all gray.

Goddamn Bobbey and her predictions.

Shanghai Daily news meeting

MY DAYS started with the 5 p.m. news meeting, the first time in the daily process when the senior editors would see what stories were coming down the pike for the next day's paper. Or as I came to think of it, the time when the top editors would see how dumb the day's reporting assignments had been, how poorly they had been carried out and how it was too late to do anything about it. It was a terribly inefficient way to do business, and the top editors knew it was inefficient. But they kept it doing it the same way because … well, just because.

I'd usually be one of two Westerners sitting at the conference table with about 20 Chinese staffers: day editors who had made assignments or sifted the news wires since morning, and night editors who were going to take the resulting stories and edit them into shape and put them on pages for the next day's paper. The meetings were conducted in English, and when side conversations broke out in Mandarin or Shanghainese, people would be very thoughtful about pausing to translate for us Westerners. There were jokes, and light chatter, and snacks passed around. These were the best-humored news meetings of any newspaper I had ever seen.

The news budget — the list of stories, in summary form — would be projected on a screen. Almost any day, you could count on a story about a corruption trial in some part of the country. Corruption was a big subject in the *Shanghai Daily*, despite the paper's being under state control: Officials taking bribes, then going to prison or the executioner. Companies padding powdered milk with melamine, a compound used in making plastics, with sometimes deadly consequences. Dialysis machines making kidney patients sick because of lousy sanitation. A zoo where all the animals, including rare tigers, were dying because the managers didn't spend any money on their upkeep. Mine accidents. A lot of mine accidents.

And almost every day, a story about natural disaster. Heavy snow in Xinjiang Autonomous Region. Earthquake in Qinghai Province. Drought in Yunnan. Place names that became as familiar to me as the names of states.

At the meeting, someone would read each item in a tentative drone, although the words were perfectly visible to us all. The only things that kept the meetings from coming to a standstill from the drag of their mounting boredom were the piercing questions or blunt criticisms from JJ.   " W e don't need that story. We had it yesterday," she would say, four or five times a week. "Let's not look stupid." This was a favorite phrase, which she often shortened to: "That's stupid." Or the even more succinct, "Stupid!"

Most of the other Chinese in the room never said a word. I didn't know if this was because they hated to risk incurring a "stupid" from JJ or whether it was a manifestation of a cultural trait I'd heard about, expressed in the aphorism, "The raised nail gets the hammer." It meant you'd be a fool to stand out — in school, at work — because chances were that someone would criticize you or resent you, and you'd have to deal with a loss of face. This was not an attitude conducive toward generating initiative.

Sometimes, one of us Westerners did the talking. We'd stop the proceedings and ask a question because the stories were so hard to understand in their raw translation.

"What is an illegal horning?" I once asked, secretly hoping it was some exotic sex act known to the Orient, only to be told it referred to truck drivers who banged their horns too loudly.

"What does he mean, 'The Metro operator said no massive passenger strand were reported at the four stations along the glitched area.'?" I inquired when I was new on the job. After a few months I wouldn't have had to ask. I would have understood at a glance: The subway authorities had declared that the system delays which affected four stations did not make too passengers late. You can get used to anything, I learned at the *Shanghai Daily*, even the most mangled of English sentences.

The meetings gave me the chance to see what the stories were supposed to say — a great advantage, because the reporters' copy I'd be receiving in the next couple of hours wouldn't be decipherable without some form of decoder. And because it gave me the chance to roam around and ask the reporters for details or to see if they could use some help in figuring out how to write up the information they had.

Most of the metro staff were young men and women looking barely out of college, now working hard in their cubicles, their desks cluttered with takeout noodles, pots of tea and iPods. They answered my questions with smiles and thank you's, but most of them were passive and unambitious — jarringly so.

I'd ask: Did we get a comment from the acquitted man? No, the government didn't want us to talk to him. Do we have statistics to back up such-and-such an assertion? No, the government didn't provide them. Can we compare that official's claim with our own verification? I'd get a blank stare, an apologetic smile, a short shake of the head.

I felt for the reporters. Even the aggressive among them knew the drill — you'd ask the officials your questions and get nothing off-script in reply. After a while you wised up and quit asking. And only a few of the reporters were aggressive. Only a few had journalism experience or aspirations. Some had merely gotten good school grades in English.

There were exceptions, like the young man Zha Minjie. Minjie was a sweetheart. He was only 23, but he had studied some journalism in college and he loved American writing and American styles. On his desktop he kept a book about Al Capone and the other legendary Chicago gangsters. In English. I gained big points with Minjie simply by telling him I was from Chicago.

Rachel Yan, the city editor, had studied at the University of Missouri Journalism School in Columbia, Mo, the granddaddy of American j-schools. She was about 30, very pretty, and dressed less like a career woman than a college student. She knew what good news stories were supposed to be made of — a questioning spirit, above all. When talking to me about certain reporters, she would sometimes make an eye gesture of retreat — a glance to the side and down — as if stepping away from someone else's shortcoming.

She'd say the reporters were young and badly trained. They didn't know how to organize their information and spent too much time staring at the screen, which made them late in handing in their stories. These were complaints known to almost every city desk editor at every newspaper in America.

I felt for them all, fundamentally, because the job they were doing was extremely difficult. Imagine putting together a newspaper in a second language. Even in a first language, writing for newspapers is hard. You have to know how to describe things accurately, you have to condense, you have to weigh the various facts you've picked up with judgment and proportion, you have to have an understanding of your readers. Not many people have the ability to write well in any language.

And long before you sit down to write, you have to know how to seek out information, get to the newsmakers, ask good questions. Where would young Chinese have learned this?

AROUND 6, I'd be eating. At my desk, usually — beef or chicken, rice or noodles that I had grabbed from a hole-in-the-wall across the street. Or a sandwich delivered from the aspirationally named New York City Deli, or Urban Soup Kitchen, or some other Shanghai approximation of a Western restaurant.

No matter what I brought in, JJ would walk over to take a look. She'd lean in, take a sniff.

Invariably, she'd ask: "How much was it?"

I'd tell her. Almost always she'd say: "Too much."

Now and then she'd say nothing, but give a brief little nod. Made me feel I'd passed a test, and I would enjoy a moment of pride, like I was on my way to becoming a real Shanghaier.

One of the great dividing lines between the Chinese and foreign staffers was the canteen on the Wenxin Xinmin United Press Group Tower's 10th floor. The food was subsidized by the company and very cheap. To Westerners, it was also inedible: greasy concoctions of pork, little fried fishes and unrecognizable pools of vegetables ladled onto the tin food platters seen in James Cagney prison movies.

At 10:20 every night, the Chinese staffers would disappear en masse for a night-shift feeding, returning from the 10th floor with big, doughy steam buns for tomorrow's breakfast. I considered myself a great cross-culturalist because I began to make those nightly treks too. The cafeteria ladies quickly knew me: the one guy who didn't speak Chinese and pointed his fingers to order a plain bowl of noodles, half filled with hot water, sprinkled with scallions and vinegar, sometimes topped by a dollop of Chinese greens. I needed the late-night, 20-cent carbohydrate boost. I had at least another three hours of work to go.

None of the Chinese staffers ever seemed to bring in food just for themselves. If they had an orange or a bag of candy, they'd offer you a piece before eating one. Every time a staffer got married, you'd know it because they would leave a decorated piece of candy on your desk — whether you knew the person or not. The staff was young and primarily female. In my year at the paper, eight of the women had babies, an amazing number in a country with a one-child policy. Marriage was much on the staffers' minds. Either they were getting married or lamenting that housing prices were so high that they couldn't afford to get married. Lots of the staff — men and women in their late 20s and early 30s — were living with their parents. They had finished their educations and had their jobs, but in every other respect they were waiting for their lives to start.

There was a nice familial looseness to the *Shanghai Daily*. People were always bringing their infants around for inspection, and work would stop as beaming staffers played pass-the-baby. No one minded if Ellen hung around for an hour or two while I worked. She'd surf the Net on an idle computer or she'd visit friends she'd made among the editors and polishers. When JJ learned that Ellen had been an English major, she tried to hire her as a proofreader, but her working hours would have been even later than mine. Hearing that Ben was coming to join us in Shanghai, JJ immediately offered him a newspaper internship — which he gladly accepted.

"When Ben comes to Shanghai," JJ said one day, giving me a sly smile, "maybe he'll get a Shanghai girlfriend."

"Yeah, maybe."

"There are a lot of pretty girls in Shanghai," JJ said.

My boss, the yenta.

AT 7 the reporters' stories would start to appear. The nightly hit parade of bad news writing.

One of the veteran polishers had been collecting gems for years:

> The minute you look up for haircut prices, young ladies dressed virtually in underwear would ejaculate a hot smile from the corners of their eyes. —

2005 opinion piece about barbershops that provide "additional" services.

The Hercules heel lies in the mentality of the table tennis giant. — *2003 profile of a ping pong player.*

Touched by it, I had a long and sincere talk with my mother which helped a lot tightening the tires between us.

Balls began to visit my home as well as my neighbors. — Man sues golf course.

According to Yang, among the two women, a 24-year-old girl living there was in bad mood as her mother, who went to have a bath with her, was dead during the accident.

The administration released a draft policy after strong appeals from consumers and the media was ignited by the case of Mitsubishi Pajero, in which a woman went into a comma after a break failure. – *Story about automobile safety measures.*

"All I could do was lie in bed, becoming unconscious, even when going to piss," the 56-year-old recalled.

Two babies compete in a creeping match at Westgate Mall on Nanjing Road. – *Photo caption about an infant crawling competition.*

The finger-off man has been transferred to Huashan Hospital for better treatment. – *2006 article about a fight in which one man had two fingers chopped off.*

Chen later excreted 56 eggs of heroin bags that contained 376.41 grams of heroin in the total. – *Story on a drug trafficker busted by police.*

The giant cock, which weighs over 50 kg, needs 5-6 people to lift it, with its body and feathers in 10 colors. Equipped with a sound system, the lantern can even crow as a real cock. – *2005 story about Chinese New Year decorations for the Year of the Rooster.*

We polishers read this stuff with exasperation and hilarity. We worked mainly in silence, but every now and then you would hear a wild peal of laughter from someone like Sarah, an Australian, who had just read the words "ass glue." Turned out, the writer meant a product made from boiled donkey.

There were the criminals who had been "burst for stealing taxi meters." The capital of Haiti renamed as "Port-au-Prison." The folk-arts museum described as a "village with humanistic flatus."

My friend on the features desk loved this bit of wisdom from a travel story about bat caves. For once, the English was crystal clear, if not quite ready for family publication: "When bat watching, it would be better if you wear a hat or cap because the bats might dump shit on your head when they feel disturbed."

Editors' row: (from left) JJ, Joyce, Adam

THE CHINESE editors — the bosses, we called them — often complained that the polishers were a bunch of complainers. Which was true. The thing that polishers usually complained about was the refusal of the Chinese editors to become more efficient, to take any actual steps to improve the writing as they often promised to do, or to enforce in any way the many examples of plagiarism we found.

One writer was a particular culprit. A man in his 30s, he had worked as a lawyer but had chucked that to come to the *Shanghai Daily* and translate Chinese-language news stories into English, a job he performed with no appreciable ability. Yet he liked it. Very much. "It's so much easier than being a lawyer," he told me. "I work at the paper and I have no worries." Apparently he was unemployment-proof, for he would write sentences such as this one, which led off a story about — well, see if you can guess what it's about:

Six traffic officers in an Inner Mongolia city has been sacked for delivering local truck drivers package prices as fine in advance for their overloading violations.

(Time's up. The answer: Six traffic officers were fired after allowing truck drivers to pay bribes to guarantee that the cops would overlook future weight violations.)

His paragraphs would clunk along this way, each one at war with itself and with logic — until, shockingly, you'd come upon a passage that was perfectly cogent, clear and sensible. Invariably, it was directly lifted from Wikipedia. We Westerners would be badly perturbed. In every other news organization we had known, plagiarism was a firing offense. At the *Shanghai Daily*, the bosses seemed embarrassed that we would bring it up. No offenders ever faced consequences.

Some of the Chinese editors could not bear to admit to error. An Australian named Alex, proofreading a page, found a story where the math didn't add up. He took it to Liu Hong, a supervising editor who had already approved the page, and they argued for quite a while. She couldn't win the argument with logic, so she ended it by saying, "It's Chinese math." Alex was beaten. After that, he sometimes started arguments with her for their entertainment value, just to see what dumb excuse she'd come up with to defend herself.

The dozen polishers had knocked around the world of journalism at a variety of levels, from provincial sports rags to the AP. About half of them had been at the *Shanghai Daily* five years or longer. A guy from Singapore, named Calvin, kept himself in a constant state of rage about the primitivism of Shanghai. The people had no manners! The drivers didn't know how to drive! The cabbies spoke no English, none! They didn't even know the words "Hilton" or "Sheraton"! In any other city in the world, the cabbies know what the Hilton is! Yet every time his contract ended, Calvin renewed, and he would spend another year reading unexciting stories for the business pages and erupt in same old fury.

The sweet-tempered man in charge of sports, Bivash, had been at the *Shanghai Daily* since its founding, steadily putting in his shifts with quiet professionalism and faithfully sending money to his wife and two children who lived in Mumbai, where the kids could get an affordable education. Marc, from Canada, had married a Chinese woman, a real beauty. They had a year-old son, with another child on the way. They shared a crowded apartment with her mother, father, and — for one touchy period — an elderly, needy grandmother. All these family ties meant that Marc, who read Toronto's *Globe and Mail* every day and followed the baseball stats as faithfully as a diabetic checking his blood-sugar level, was bound to work at the *Shanghai Daily* for a very long time.

There was Dave, the American, who had joined the paper and quit and rejoined, then quit for good. He, too, had acquired a Chinese family, but had never picked up the equanimity it required to deal with the most basic reality of working in the Chinese media: the censorship. He let his anger spill out in caustic arguments with JJ; she would listen, not visibly annoyed, and then quietly go ahead and do it her way. She was the boss.

Dave was howling at the wind. There was no such thing as beating the censors. You had to go along. That was the condition of the job. To produce a newspaper that could actually get published in Shanghai, you often had to remove little facts or whole passages from stories that would have made them fairer, more informative, better rounded — but also would have made them less flattering to the Chinese. Dave loathed this.

"My job is sort of like the colon," he once told me. "I extract all the nutrients and pass the rest on to the anal aperture." The eventual droppings were for the readers to ingest.

Some foreigners just couldn't stand it. The aforementioned Alex had arrived a few months before I did, and figured out that the best way to get through a shift was to leave the building for a smoke or a coffee every 40 minutes. The story I got was that he'd made some glaring editing errors in his first few weeks, and JJ had reacted with something less than delicacy.

"Alex!" she'd yelled within everyone's earshot. "You're stupid! Stupid!"

Alex had stepped into a stock role. According to the long-timers, the bosses always singled out one foreigner to pick on. This year, it was Alex's turn to be berated — loudly, publicly, repeatedly. Next year it would be someone else.

By the time I arrived on the job, Alex had settled in a muttering sullenness, and JJ had arranged to give him the most harmless and boring pages to edit. The tension in this cold war broke only when Alex came into the office one night when he'd been scheduled to be off. I couldn't say for sure, but he just might have hoisted a few Australian beers before coming in.

JJ addressed him with a cutting tone. "Alex, what are you doing here?"

Alex spread his face into a smile. "It's because I'm madly in love with you, JJ!"

A moment's pause. Then JJ cackled with laughter.

16
'You're Learning About Journalism Now'

FROM MY desk, reading the computer screen for hours at a time, I'd hear a constant background noise of office talk in Mandarin — not understanding a word. It took a while to figure out that these people weren't mad at each other, weren't arguing, weren't barking orders, weren't scolding poor performances. Conversational Chinese just sounds harsh.

I also heard a constant background of CNN International: Larry King and his unchallenged guests. Obama and his critics — our divided government with all our partisan chatter on display, making our political figures and failings far more familiar to many Chinese than their own leaders or policy debates.

The other TV in the room belonged to the two sports editors. Lots of snooker, curling and soccer, and a ton of racquet sports. I'd never seen so much tennis on a TV set before. Every minor tournament got a lot of play on Chinese TV. Also ping-pong. Volleyball. And badminton — not the backyard game we know, but badminton played for keeps, at slashing speeds, with dance moves in victory and anguish in defeat.

Also a lot of NBA games. Pro basketball was the only American sport in which people on this side of the world had any interest, despite the presence of an Major League Baseball souvenir store in downtown Shanghai, more an MLB beachhead for future market penetration than a result of actual Chinese enthusiasm. But basketball — that was a phenomenon. Of course there was a lot of interest in Yao Ming, especially in his hometown of Shanghai, but even when he was sidelined with a knee injury, games of his Houston Rockets got full coverage on national Chinese television. LeBron James, then of Cleveland, and Kobe Bryant, of L.A., were close to folk heroes. You saw Chinese kids playing basketball everywhere, even though they weren't tall and not particularly smooth with

107

the ball-handling. They played defense by jumping up and down, twitchily, as if the goal were to stay in motion rather than block the guy with the ball.

Over the hours, I'd edit a stream of stories, write headlines and make sure the three or four pages I'd been assigned that night looked just as the editors wanted them to — no widows in the lines of type, no repeated words in any of single page's headlines, not too much white space showing around the heads.

It was a slog, as desk work always gets.

JJ, THE hands-on editor of the whole paper, was wicked smart. She would have been a star at any American newspaper I'd worked on. She was about 60. She wore her hair in a plain bob and round glasses much like Uncle Duke's assistant Honey in "Doonesbury," and almost always sounded cheerful no matter the circumstances — but she was no innocent. The story was, she had spent years pushing authorities to gain the release of her husband, who had been jailed in the Cultural Revolution years of the 1970s for the heinous crime of listening to Voice of America. She was one of the few editors in all of China who was not a member of the Communist Party. By normal practice, editors are vetted by the party to get their jobs, but JJ got a pass because of her unique skills: although thoroughly Chinese, she could swing the English language with ease and aim right to the heart of any news story.

I knew this because I'd seen her write, quickly and effortlessly, the copy for the front page — leaving almost nothing for any polisher to do. Her writing of that front-page news summary was, by a long sight, sharper, livelier and more interesting than the turgid thing that was the original story.

Ah, yes, turgid stories. For the most part, the *Shanghai Daily* was a great facsimile of a Western newspaper. We were surprisingly frank about a lot of the bad news of modern China. We covered the fires, the traffic accidents, the Metro subway lines' extensions and breakdowns. We ran stories on corrupt Party officials, earthquakes, floods, shoddy construction. Like other Chinese news media, we covered a frightening, bizarre rash of knife attacks on kindergartners; the numberless criminal ties between Chongqing's police and political leaders and mobsters; and protests — many protests. Over government land acquisitions and home demolitions. Massive fish kills caused by pollution. Horrific road deaths caused by dump trucks speeding from construction sites. Escalating tensions with Japan over obscure offshore islands.

We also ran a million stories about the World Expo, in keeping with the *Shanghai Daily*'s position as "official sponsor." We couldn't publish enough about the booming Chinese economy. Any paper in any boomtown would have done the same.

But the paper never forgot that it was also a political instrument. If the Chinese president made a speech on a matter of national policy or economic policy (basically the same thing), that became the lead story. If the president was quiet that day but the premier made a speech, that became the story. This meant we'd run essentially the same speech on back-to-back days. One day's top story: President Hu says China will continue its loose-money policy in the new year, looking for stable growth in 2010. The next day's top story: Premier Wen says China will continue its loose-money policy in the new year, looking for stable growth in 2010.

If Hu or Wen traveled to another country, it was odds-on that their speeches on that foreign soil would be the day's top story. In American media, most of the statements and press releases that roll out of the White House or a governor's mansion are seen as self-serving exercises in image building, and summarily condensed or discarded. When our chief executive does say something of actual importance, he will be quoted at length, but so will political opponents, analysts, other foreign leaders. The Chinese media don't work like this. The Chinese leader will be quoted in full, with no empty cliche omitted. A professor or a financial analyst might be quoted as well — or not — but almost always to affirm the wisdom of the leader's remarks.

Thus, readers of the *Shanghai Daily* would sometimes find, on the paper's front page, the earthshaking news that President Hu had gone to Turkmenistan and announced that China looks forward to continuing its cooperative relations with Turkmenistan and hopes to find more opportunities to worth with the Turkmen people for the mutual benefit of both countries.

(China's two top leaders were a colorless pair. The media wrote almost nothing about their personalities, habits, private lives, wives or children. However, ever since winning points for showing up at the scene of the horrendous 2008 Sichuan earthquake, Premier Wen got in the habit of having himself photographed greeting and consoling victims of floods and droughts. In China, this was major image-making. I wasn't even sure of the top leaders' names when I arrived in China, though all the Chinese we met knew who Obama and Bush were, and how they felt about them — Obama good, Bush bad. I was delighted when I learned the top men were called Hu and Wen. I could fit those names into any headline. Now, all we'd need were a few leaders named What, Where, and Why, and we'd have all the elements that your first journalism teacher said you needed for a lede.)

The nationalism that threaded through the paper meant that Taiwan was never portrayed as a separate country, but as an estranged province of the People's Republic. The nation was always "Chinese mainland," not "mainland China." We never referred to the "Sino-Japanese War," always the "War of Resistance Against Japanese Aggression" (1937-45). The "French Concession" became "former French Concession," until that name too was to be avoided whenever possible.

The Dalai Lama, the 1989 Tiananmen Square protests and massacre, the Falun Gong, world-famous dissidents like Liu Xiaobo and Ai Wei Wei — they rarely claimed a mention in the *Shanghai Daily*.

The censor also fretted about stranger things. Innocuous things.

Once I wrote a headline. A few minutes later, a smart editor named Meng Tiexia, who had Anglicized his name to Adam, came over to correct me.

"You can't say 'dispute' in a headline. The Chinese government doesn't like 'dispute'."

My face must have shown my amazement.

He grinned. "You're learning about journalism now," he said.

It turned out, the authorities didn't want the newspapers to publish anything that might suggest violence and discord. A mere word in 36-point type, it seemed, could subvert their endless efforts to create a "harmonious society." Thus, a headline couldn't say "Fireworks explode." You had to change it to "Fireworks light sky."

Peter Zhang, the paper's top editor, looked every inch the modern executive, always wearing a suit jacket (no tie) while peeking at his smartphone and keeping a constant eye on CNN International and the BBC on his office TV. A true intellectual, he loved to probe the etymological origins of Mandarin words. He had published a guide to Chinese idioms, wrote a column on Chinese slang, had translated or co-translated more than a dozen books, and used that smartphone to play high level games of Scrabble, in English. He had a wide, easy smile. He played what seemed a very odd set of roles. At the same time that he was editor in chief of the *Shanghai Daily*, which was officially under the private ownership of a big media group, he was the No. 2 man in Shanghai's propaganda department, the office charged with making the city look good.

I never figured out how he balanced these supposedly conflicting responsibilities. It was all the more puzzling because he seemed so genuinely excited and entertained by the latest scandal or screwup — whatever fresh outrage cropped up in the news. Maybe when he was on site at the Information Office of Shanghai Municipality, he wore the assenting aspect of an organization man, but in the *Shanghai Daily* newsroom he appeared as delighted in the world's gossip and as unsurprised by its failures as every good journalist anywhere.

Peter, JJ and a few other top editors were the same core of people who had founded the *Shanghai Daily* 10 years before I arrived, in a convoluted breakaway from the Beijing-based *China Daily*, their nationally distributed, more richly endowed and better-known rival. They were people who constantly read and watched the Western media and knew what was what. I often wondered how people as smart and able as they could stand to work under such restrictive conditions.

Then I got it: They reminded me of the good journalists I knew who, after 20 or 30 years with a newspaper, went to corporations or universities or non-profits and became spokesmen. Their hearts and minds still burned with a good journalist's well-practiced ability to seek out both sides of a controversy, to look unflinchingly at the bad news — but their jobs required them to tell the best-looking version of an event, to spin a story in the employer's best interest. Sometimes, when I'd interview ex-reporters who had turned flack, they would let me know, sotto voce, that they were well aware of the unflattering parts of a story they weren't supposed to talk about. It seemed a way of venting their reporters' souls.

At the *Shanghai Daily*, the venting would come in the news meetings. As the editors discussed the next issue's stories, there would be hoots and guffaws at every new revelation of another minister caught with illicit millions and angry mistresses. There'd be shakes of the head at a report that Chinese nouveau riche gulp their wine rather than sip it: what a hick country we are! It is a universal rule, transcending generations and geography, that finding entertainment in these embarrassments is what journalists do and what propagandists abhor. In their semi-private moments outside the act of publication, the *Shanghai Daily* staff showed the souls of journalists.

Or maybe they were showing a more general tendency toward self-deprecation. Here you had China rising spectacularly, starting to make a historic claim to superpower status — and the Chinese I met never seemed to mention it. Exclaim about the country's astounding advances, and they'd deflect the compliment. "We're still a developing country." Or, "We're a poor country, you know." Or, "Our people only earn one-seventh of what Americans do."

JJ made almost all the important judgments about what went into the next day's paper, assigning the stories for every page of local, national and international news. She decided which business, sports and features stories would get a teaser headline for Page 1 and those that would make it out of their ghettoized sections and run on Pages 2 and 3, the "Top News" pages. She was married, with a grown son, but appeared to have no life outside the paper. She'd arrive around 4 in the afternoon and then never seemed to leave. All her meals would be take-out delivered to the paper, and no matter how many times I worked until 2 a.m., she'd outlast me.

This was a problem, actually. Over the years, she had developed the habit of delaying the key decisions — choosing the stories for pages 1, 2 and 3 — until late in the process. And then later. And later. Frequently, it would be 12:30 at night, and I, as the polisher for Top News, would still be waiting for JJ to say what the front-page lead story was going to be. Only then could the page designer create a layout, and only after the page designer was done could I do the finishing copy-edit, write the page's headlines and photo captions — the most important page in the newspaper, mind you, composed when I was the most tired — and at last get my weary bedraggled ass back home. Once in a while there was a valid reason for waiting so long: midnight in Shanghai was daytime in the U.S. and early evening in Europe. Breaking news from the awake side of the world was always a possibility. But more often, JJ lingered over inconsequential things, like updating the death toll of a flood in Guangzhou Province. She would scour the wires right up to the last possible deadline — often, past deadline — to make sure our readers that next morning got the very highest fatality number. As if the flood would be any more tragic, or our readers better informed, if the story said "more than 250 dead" instead of "more than 240 dead." As if there were no such thing as TV news or the Internet to render obsolete any toll we printed by the time people opened their newspapers in the morning.

Maybe she did this out of competitive pride — she did like to boast that the *Shanghai Daily* ran later-breaking news than the *China Daily* or Shanghai's several Chinese-language papers.

Or maybe obsessing over the little details on these stories was a proud professional's way of compensating for all the news she could never run.

AFTER MY first few days, a polisher named Bernie, a very able newspaperman from Australia, sat me down for a coffee and gave me a few hints on how to wade through the muck of poor prose. When you get a new story, read it all the way through and don't touch it, he told me. Sit on your hands if you have to, but don't so much as correct a misspelled word. Just read the thing and try to make sense of it. Once that's done, go back and untangle the mess.

I'd do that for 10 or 12 stories. It would take about four hours, half the shift. Then came the second part of the job. A news-desk editor, a Chinese, would design a page for the stories. When he or she finished, I'd call up an image of the page on my computer screen. The stories I had edited would be there, a little too long or a little too short, and so would photographs in need of captions. I'd write headlines and have to nip and tuck the stories to make everything fit neatly on the page.

One evening early in my tenure, I realized I was doing the far-fetched thing that Bobbey had predicted. You're going to be working with layouts.

The combination of rewriting stories, fitting them to the page and writing headlines and photo captions is common in the British newspaper world. It's called sub-editing, and the editors are called subs. In American newsrooms we have copy editors, who write headlines and captions, but don't do significant rewriting. There was a British colonial flair to the whole polishing thing — the British-style work system, the hires from the Commonwealth countries — but, curiously, the *Shanghai Daily* used American English spellings and locutions. We used flavor, not flavour; defense, not defence; a party, not a knees-up. Most nights, I was the only person around who was born to this language. That made me the in-house expert. ("No," I'd say, "the court didn't jail someone for 10 years yesterday, it sentenced someone to 10 years in jail yesterday.") Measurements, however, were metric. We described distances in kilometers, not miles; temperatures in Celsius, not Fahrenheit. With these, I was an idiot.

My work would be done a little after midnight. But I couldn't leave until the pages were proofread.

The proofreader was never in any particular hurry. The minutes dragged.

When I finally got the all-clear to go home, it would be after 1 a.m. and I'd be feeling every over-extended minute of it.

The streets, so crowded during the day, would now be dark and quiet. My taxi would take me past food sellers who set up portable grills on the street for customers who ate their kebabs while sitting on crates or on their haunches. Past hookers showing their netted legs on Huashan Road near the Hilton Hotel. Past rag-pickers clustered on an empty side street for a nightly exchange of goods, dividing the spoils for efficiency's sake, so that one of them could redeem the day's haul of scavenged cardboard; another, the paper; a third, the plastic bottles — bringing a touching sense of order and camaraderie to the lonely, unremunerative business of riding your bicycle over very long distances and hours to collect and sell Shanghai's garbage, for a pittance.

And I'd be thinking, wow, this is what it's like to work in China. You work hard.

17
Praying for a Friend

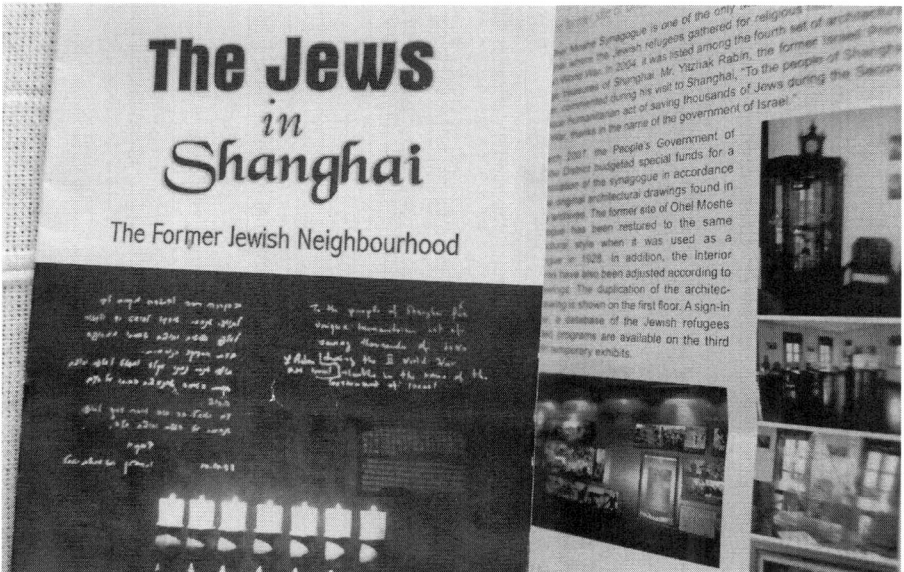

The Jews *in* Shanghai

The Former Jewish Neighbourhood

Ellen:
I DON'T consider myself a religious person. I'm Jewish, same as I'm a redhead — just born that way.

With the kids grown and out of the house, I didn't feel the need to attend synagogue or participate in Jewish activities.

Moving to Shanghai, I wondered if I would even feel like "being Jewish," whatever that meant. When we removed the mezuzah from our door as we departed Delray Beach, I asked Howie, "Do you think we should bring this? Can we put one up in an atheist country? Do I care?"

We did bring it, and I put it on top of the intercom box by the front door — sort of a compromise. Not attached to the doorpost, as the Hebrew Bible instructs, but close.

I knew Shanghai once had a large, vibrant Jewish community and was a haven for European Jews during World War II. During one of our day trips I picked up a pamphlet entitled "The Jews in Shanghai." My interest piqued, I googled "Jewish community, Shanghai."

Up popped a website about an active synagogue that catered to Jewish travelers as well as local residents. You could even make a reservation for Shabbat dinner using PayPal.

OK, What did I have to lose? Howie would be away at work and maybe I'd meet some interesting people.

I clicked in my order.

Late Friday afternoon, I dressed in my most modest clothing — long skirt, dressy sweater, high heels, and walked downstairs with Howie to catch a cab.

"You're making a mistake. You're going to hate it," he warned me. "This is a Chabad house. They're Orthodox. They're going to proselytize."

"It's not a mistake — it's a blog entry," I told him.

On the way, I chatted with the cab driver who happened to speak some English.

"Are you going shopping?" he asked.

"No," I told him, "I'm going to … pray."

The word sounded strange to me. It's not usually in my vocabulary. I could see that it thoroughly confused the driver.

"You know," I said, "Buddhist, Christian …"

He smiled and showed me a blue bracelet he was wearing.

It said: "Peace, Love, Life, Jesus Loves You."

About the last thing I expected to see from a random cabbie in Communist China.

A few minutes later, I arrived at a large brick villa inside a residential complex. I took a deep breath and pushed open the heavy wooden door. In front of me was a sweet-looking woman in her thirties holding an adorable little girl.

"Shabbat Shalom. I'm Deena, the rabbi's wife. Welcome."

I thanked her and asked how observant the congregants were. She explained it was a very mixed group — some very Orthodox, others not at all. The service, however, would be Orthodox.

"Have you been to an Orthodox service before?"

"Only once."

She assured me I'd be fine.

We walked downstairs to a large room divided into two sections by a wooden trellis draped with plastic ivy. The left side was filled with men praying. Some looked like figures from an 18th-century shtetl: Huge fur hats, long black coats, beards, and long curls at the sides of their faces. Others were more modern, in black slacks and white long sleeve shirts. A few were in t-shirts.

On the other side of the ivy were the women — about 10. They were as diverse a group as the men.

A few were really beautiful young women. They turned out to be the teachers. There were several middle-aged women quietly sitting, about three or four animated women who stood and prayed aloud, and Deena, holding a child in her lap and quietly talking to another child sitting next to her.

A few minutes after I arrived, an incredible-looking woman came in carrying a child. She had short cropped blond hair, a mini-dress with black tights and the most amazing stiletto-heeled short boots I have ever seen.

So much for stereotypes.

After the service, a group of Chinese workers quickly went to work. Down went the trellis, and out came the dining tables. It took all of about 10 minutes to have the room remade and ready for over 100 diners. There was a large buffet with pasta salad, salmon, and salads — the appetizer table. Another table was set with huge challahs and bottles of wine.

After a prayer over the bread and wine, we began our meal. After eating Chinese for two weeks it was great to eat familiar food. The main course consisted of two types of chicken (OK, one did seem vaguely Cantonese with a sweet sauce and pineapples), rice, roasted potatoes, and cooked vegetables. My grandmother would have been delighted.

The rabbi, a genial man from Israel, said it was the tradition to have all newcomers stand up and introduce themselves.

"Say your name, and where you're from. But not what you do," he instructed — a reminder that you shouldn't discuss business on the Sabbath.

I was knocked out by the diversity as the people stood and introduced themselves. People had come from Baltimore, Los Angeles, Miami, London, France, Brazil, Iran and Israel. Everyone clapped at the mention of Israel.

In his role of MC, the rabbi would lead the diners in a new song every few minutes and encourage us to clap our hands along with the music. The melodies were different from how I'd learned them — a lot of the people were Sephardic, and my family Ashkenazi — but I was tickled to realize I recognized them. It was like hearing cover versions.

The rabbi even walked around with a bottle of vodka, offering to fill anyone's empty shot glass. Now this was the kind of Shabbat dinner I could get behind.

I visited with some of the other participants after dinner. The young teachers were from France. A woman from Chicago had been born in Soviet Russia. There was an American photojournalist. An expat family from California with three young boys. Deena from Cleveland and her Israeli husband. They all blended into a Jewish community in Shanghai.

But the best friend I made from that night wasn't even there. Deena told me about an American woman from San Antonio, by way of Cleveland, who had been in the Far East for a few years and made it her business to serve as a one-woman welcome wagon to newcomers.

This was Jackie. We occupied different economic spheres in Shanghai. Her husband, David, had been sent by his American company to supervise its Chinese operations and their corporate package included the transport of all their furniture, including museum-worthy Asian artworks, a full-time maid and a huge apartment that was completely ruled by an enormous, rambunctious and saliva-dripping dog.

But she proved a kindred spirit: like me, a former teacher and the mother of a grown son — and an eager traveller and enthusiastic hostess. We would spend a lot of time together.

18
Hard To Swallow

Howard:
THE CHINESE restaurants were nothing like the ones we'd known back in the States. They were filled with groups of men who smoked cigarettes as much as they ate, and drank as much as they smoked, and sat at a table for hours, their restaurant-going being as much about socializing as eating.

We had expected something else from a Chinese restaurant. Rice, for instance. In Shanghai, rice was not — as we had always thought — the staple of the Chinese diet. Rice was not used as a bed for other dishes. Rice was not served at all unless we asked for it, and when we did, we were likely to get a funny look from the waitress. An explanation came from a guidebook, which said that rice was eaten by Chinese people only at the end of a meal if they wanted to get that filled-up feeling.

The varieties of Chinese food we knew from restaurants back home – Cantonese, Sichuan – were not the norm. Many restaurants in Shanghai featured other Chinese cuisines: Hunan, Uighar, who knew what else. Since we couldn't read the signs on the doors and windows, we almost never knew what fare we were in for when we stepped inside.

The menus only added to the mystery. Most had pictures, which should have helped. But the photos offered no way to tell how to create a coherent meal: What went with what? How big was a portion? Was that beef dish an entrée or an appetizer?

One night early on, we tried a promising restaurant on our nearby shopping street, Wulumuqi Lu. The food, served in heated pots on the tables, looked interesting and the smokers were clustered in just one corner of the place.

Luckily for us, the menu, a big glossy book with at least a dozen pages, contained English translations.

Thus, we were able to consider such choices as:

Explodes Fries The Sacrificed Beef
Chops The Pepper To Steam The Taro
Saliva Chicken
The Aricularia Auricula Fries The Meat
Hunan Superior Does Fragrant
Old Godmother Cattle Tendon
Fries Additional Ingredients The Boletus
The Homesickness Fish
Hunan Strong-Smelling Fermented Bean Curd
Miniature Is Drunk The Fish

We went with the "Sheet Iron Unwearied Effort However Beef."

Also the "Stir-Fries Before Stewing The Jack Bean Dry," the "Clam Egg-Custard," and the oddly decipherable "Seafood Soup."

We very much liked the soup, which was a hearty and flavorful broth; the beef, which came soaked in cumin, reminding us of Mexican food; and the green beans, which were garlicky and irresistible.

The custard tasted like a soft-boiled egg ruined by the essence of fish oil.

None of the familiar Chinese dishes ever seemed to be on the menu. No General Tso's chicken. No egg rolls. No orange beef. Instead, we'd find dishes made from parts of animals we never, ever wanted to think about eating: intestines, stomachs, balls.

We learned that there was at least one commodity that America successfully exported to China. These were chicken feet. U.S. poultry farmers had found that, instead of throwing these inedibles away, they could ship them to China, where chicken feet are considered delicacies.

All I can tell you is that, one day at work, I ordered a "special chicken soup" from the hole-in-the-wall restaurant next door to the newspaper building. I lifted the lid and there, poking out of the broth amid bits of vegetables and white meat, was a pair of black chicken feet. Gnarly, ugly, amputated, black chicken feet. With claws.

I put the lid back on. For some reason I wasn't that hungry anymore.

19
First Month In

Ellen's blog:
I CAN'T believe it's already been a month since we arrived in China.

The other day I got lost on my way to IKEA. I was on my own, and had taken the subway and when I got out at the street, I wasn't sure what direction to head for. Being a resourceful person, I waited until I found a foreigner carrying an IKEA shopping bag and asked for directions. My guide was a young American guy who had moved here four months ago. As we walked, he asked me how I liked it here and what were my impressions. It got me thinking ...

First, I have to sort out my feelings about moving to a city — any city. Up until a month ago I'd been living a very suburban life with a house and a yard and a two-car garage. I drove everywhere.

If you had told me I would be riding the subway, talking to strangers and walking home alone on dark streets late at night, I would have thought you were nuts — and yet that's exactly what I do and feel very comfortable doing it. This city is safe, and it feels it. Even for women walking alone at night.

There are times, however, when the street traffic can be scary.

I'm not just talking about cars and buses. Howie and I almost got run over by a motorcycle while standing on the sidewalk. The sidewalk! And riding in a taxi can be horrifying. It feels like everyone on the street — pedestrians, bicycles, motor bikes, cars, taxis, buses, is playing a colossal game of Chicken.

Sometimes it feels that I not only moved across the globe, but I also time-traveled. There's somewhat of a 1950's or 1930s feeling with odd machinery and appliances, laundry hanging out to dry and so many people smoking. Service workers frequently stand at attention in uniforms and white gloves. When's the last time you saw that in the States outside of a Shirley Temple movie?

Some things are hard — like always making sure we have good drinking water and trying to keep the house warm and clean. Many of the local products leave something to be desired. I bought some transparent tape that just doesn't stick, scissors that lasted for less than a week before breaking. Imagine a continent-size "dollar store." That's everyday shopping in China.

Communicating with people can be really frustrating. I have become quite skilled at pantomiming but some ideas just don't translate into a gesture. The language is baffling and I often wonder if I'll ever have anything more than a rudimentary understanding of Mandarin.

Yesterday I met a restaurant owner who was born in China, moved to Toronto at age 10, and came back to Shanghai to open up a restaurant. He described himself as "a banana — yellow on the outside, white on the inside." Although he speaks fluent Mandarin, even he can't read it. Now that's what I call one difficult language.

There are many things we are loving about Shanghai. The strangeness, when not frustrating, is really exciting. Our apartment is great and the neighborhood, which combines "China Old World" and "International Trendy" continues to intrigue.

The people are very friendly and curious about anything having to do with the USA. Our money will go a long way if we choose to eat like Chinese, from local markets, rather than foreigners. We're giving up wine — the imports being unaffordable and the domestics undrinkable — for Tsingtao beer.

This first month has been a really steep learning curve for us. When I think about all the things we've accomplished — navigating our way through the city, finding and setting up our household, learning the intricacies of currency and banking, getting our work visas (almost there), I think we've done pretty well.

I'm hoping this next month will be a little bit more relaxing because, frankly, I'm bushed!

20
Sitting There and Doing Nothing

Howard:

ALMOST EVERYONE who comes to China soon gets sick.

We foreigners are not used to the foods. Or the foods aren't sufficiently washed before they're served. And in a country where human fertilizer is still used in some places, we didn't want to go without washing that food.

Yet wash it in what? The tap water was untrustworthy. We drank bottled water: the delivery men on bicycles, laden with stacks of five-gallon bottles of purified water, hundreds of pounds in accumulated weight, were a common sight. But you couldn't entirely keep the tap water, and the hard minerals and chemicals it contained, mainly from Shanghai's antiquated water pipes, from getting into your system. We washed the dishes with tap water. We washed the fruits and vegetables in tap water. We just hoped to God, irrationally, that the impurities disappeared when we toweled off the apples and let the plates dry on the rack.

Hence the ubiquity of bad stomachs, which were quite openly discussed in China, there being far less social stigma attached to body-function conversations than we knew in America. Huashan Hospital, a huge medical complex in our neighborhood, opened an addition over the summer, and blared the name in electric lights: "Diarrhea Clinic." The bright red letters were in plain view of patrons of the Café Montmarte on the other side of the street. Which must have done wonders for their appetites. For once, we would have appreciated a sign purely in Chinese characters.

125

But after several weeks in Shanghai, I had the opposite problem.

I was stuck.

It was as if my intestines had forgotten their purpose. My system went numb from duodenum to rectum. My lower GI went AWOL.

Days went by like this. At first I was kind of happy that I'd lost the need to evacuate, because it freed me from having to contend with the terror of the foreign toilet. I realized that I was fine with living in a different country so long as I didn't touch anything too intimately. I was comfortable not touching. I was happy enough to observe.

But you had to be an active participant if you were going to answer the call to nature, and I harbored a deep mistrust of the cleanliness of the mainland's bathrooms. This was a culture where people were used to squatting over a hole in the floor, even in a modern office building such as the tower that housed the *Shanghai Daily* (in our men's room, we had four Western-style toilet stalls and one squatter). And when you did see a Western toilet (a favorite brand being the aptly named American Standard), you were often discouraged from flushing down toilet paper. In the old sections of Shanghai, we were told, the pipes were too fragile to accommodate paper. People were required to take their soiled squares of toilet tissue and toss them in the waste basket. My brain reverted to a 6-year-old's. Whenever I stepped into a bathroom in an old Shanghai neighborhood, such as the men's room at the Starbucks in the Westerners' shopping and dining haven of Xintiandi, all I could think was, "Gross." I made a conscious effort to avoid the waste baskets. Tried not even looking at them.

Whatever the cause of the problem, I needed a cure.

With Ellen as my loyal ally, we began looking for medicines. We rummaged around convenience stores, a false lead. These 7-11-like shops, where we'd buy ice cream and pay our electric bill, displayed colorful packages of condoms by the cash registers, but surprised us by stocking few medicines, and nothing that looked like a laxative. We went into a Watson's, a kind-of Walgreens without the pharmacy — lots of cosmetics and vitamins and hair products. But again, few medicines. We were scanning the aisles, looking for some promising box or bottle, and soon had company. A young woman in a smart blue blazer stepped up to us with a bright smile and a "Ni hao!" and flow of words we didn't understand, until we stopped her with a "Bu putongua," which we hoped she heard as "No Mandarin." Ellen pulled out an English-Chinese pocket dictionary and pointed to the word "constipation."

"Ah," she said. We'd caught her interest.

Ellen pointed to me. The girl looked me up and down, her eyes centering on my belly. Out of nowhere, two, then three other clerks appeared, all wearing matching blue blazers, all talking among themselves, all turning their eyes toward the same spot on my belly.

Suddenly the Watson's sale force sprang into action. A female clerk spun around to the shelf behind her and pulled down a package and held it toward me. One of the guys scurried away and came back with a bottle of something else. The two began arguing. It sounded heated. They were in passionate disagreement over my remedy. Another clerk joined in, and soon the three were arguing. Ellen and I asked to see the bottles for ourselves. The writing was all Chinese, but one green rectangular box had a drawing on it — a simple illustration straight from the days of 1950s American TV ads. An intestinal tract, no doubt about it, and a fat arrow running down and through and out. Sold!

When we got home, I found that the miracle product was nothing more than fiber in capsules. I was way past fiber. I needed something more like Drano.

So we walked over to Wulumuqi Road – Ellen worriedly, I painfully – and into one of Shanghai's pharmacies, shops with green crosses on the front of them and long glass counters displaying boxes of ointments and pills instead of, say, jewelry. Half the store was filled with Chinese traditional medicines: dried leaves, pastes, dark vials of sour liquids. The other half looked familiar — packages of Western capsules, creams, neck braces – but with nearly all the writing in Chinese. In the front window, in the biggest block letters in the place, was a sign beckoning walk-ins: "Viagra." Someone had learned enough English to entice the expats.

There were two women and a man behind the counter, all in white lab coats, none speaking English. Ellen approached one of the women, phrase book in hand. Discreetly, wordlessly, she pointed to the now dog-eared page for "constipation," and pointed to me. The woman looked at my belly as if deep in thought. Soon the other woman came over. Then, the man. The first woman spoke to the others. The man chimed in. The woman nodded. She went looking for something in the back of the store and came back with a look of triumph, as well as a green, rectangular box. The same ineffectual fiber pills.

"No, no, no!" I said, shaking my head.

"Bu, bu!" said Ellen, the linguist. Our purchase of Rosetta Stone had not gone to waste.

Our impromptu medical panel looked confused. Ellen thumbed frantically through her dictionary for "stronger."

"We. Need. Something. Stronger." I said, in the reflexive American belief that if you say something in English slowly enough, you are bound to be understood sooner or later. A reflexive belief, but a false one. My listeners stared at me with admirable politeness and complete incomprehension.

Trying charades to get the point across, I flexed my arms as if making a muscle.

"Ah!" said one of the lab-coat women in a flash of understanding. She trotted away, then trotted back with a bandage for a sore arm.

I left the charades to Ellen, and eventually she got our listeners to understand what part of the body we needed help with. The man in the lab coat brought us a package containing small bottles of a dark medicinal liquid. "Work very good," he said, nodding vigorously.

I took it home and tried it. But the the foul stuff did not work. It was time to go to the doctor. A real doctor.

This was Dr. Andrew, a Chinese gentleman of extremely good manners and a store of patience. He had a Western medical education and an Eastern propensity for unexpected holistic diagnoses. His practice was unusual. You had to catch him on a day when he wasn't making one of his frequent trips to Hong Kong to stock up on medicines unavailable on the mainland. Before you showed up for your appointment, a nurse would ask the general nature of your problem. When you arrived, a specialist in your particular problem would be there – one of the semi-retired professors or hospital department heads that Dr. Andrew kept on retainer. You'd find the wizened gentleman standing next to the doctor, along with three young women in identical navy-blue vests and skirts and pale-blue blouses. His nursing/receptionist team. One of the women would ask if you wanted coffee (not tea! Dr. Andrew knew his foreigners), and bring it to you in a cup and saucer of fine china. It was a most civilized way to begin a line of questioning about bowel movements, laxatives and enemas.

When the doctor and his team saw you, they gave you their exclusive attention. No other patients were seated in the waiting room after you. You wondered, if you hadn't gotten sick, what would the doctor and his staff have done with themselves all day?

Dr. Andrew asked many questions and the professor at his side listened to the answers as avidly as he did. How long had we been in Shanghai? What had we been eating? How long had it been since I'd had a productive turn at the toilet? My answer – about four weeks – caused both doctors' eyebrows to shoot up. I showed them the medicines that had done me no good. The old professor looked surprised and murmured something in Chinese. Dr. Andrew translated: "He says that's strong stuff." I felt a perverse rush of pride. My Western belly had repelled the best laxatives the East could throw at it.

Dr. Andrew was beyond thorough. He examined my eyes, poked at my belly, took a blood sample. He wanted to see if I perhaps had some kind of hemorrhoid. Inspecting me on an examination table, he found something so fascinating that he called the nurses over. Now three Chinese young women in matching navy-blue outfits were peering at my bare rear end, making comments in a foreign language and jotting notes in Chinese characters. My butt had become an object of intense curiosity.

"Oh, this is very interesting," Dr. Andrew said, referring to some barely perceptible patch of skin to which he ascribed some huge significance. "I would like for your wife to see this. Would that be all right with you if I called her in here?"

"Oh sure," I said. "Let's ask over the neighbors while we're at it."

So Ellen came in and joined the viewing party. The doctor suggested an ointment to be administered at home. He also wanted to give me some transfusions that very afternoon because he had determined that my potassium levels were too high. But first, of course, he wanted to get those stubborn bowels moving and wondered if I would consent to an enema.

"Yes," I gasped, "please."

Three applications later, I was cured. I never had a recurrence of the problem again. And I lost my self-consciousness about foreign bathrooms. Something changed.

Somehow I told myself: Wherever I am, here I am.

And from that time forward, I quit feeling so much as though I were in a foreign place. I learned that if there is the smallest part of you that is hesitant to touch your surroundings — that if some deep part of your brain associates "foreign" with "unclean" — you are never going to be more than a spectator. But if you relax those fears, you can feel at home when far away from home.

I never knew I had those fears. It embarrassed me to acknowledge them. I wanted to be a man of the world. Instead, I saw that I was just another uptight, insulated *laowai*.

21
Water Woes

Empty water jugs, waiting to be picked up at our front door. The key piece of forensics was the white cap on the bottle at right.

Ellen's blog:
THE NEXT time you pour yourself a glass of water from the sink, stop for a second and appreciate how easy it was to do.

It's a lot harder to get a glass of water here in China.

When we moved here, Howie and I made a conscious decision not to live in an expat "bubble" where everyone speaks English and things like house cleaning and cooking are all done for you. Almost all the people in our building are Chinese and our conversations with them are limited to polite smiles and nods of the head.

The doormen and women are very friendly and are always giving us big smiles and hellos — or ni hao's. Any speaking here is Chinese only. Most of the time we are able to communicate by pantomime, but that form of communication has its limits.

Which gets me to today's topic: ordering water.

The tap water in our part of Shanghai is not dangerous — no bacteria or parasites lurking like water in other parts of the world.

It does, however, contain some heavy metals (not like the rock bands) that make it wise to use bottled water for drinking and cooking. Our apartment came with a dispenser for 5-gallon jugs of water, right in the kitchen, so I understood that ordering water would be part of our routine.

Jenny, my first Chinese friend, was good enough to write me a script so I would know what to say when it was time to call and order another bottle of shui (pronounced shh-weh-aye with a wiggle in the aye). The process is a little complicated:

Step 1. Estimate when you are almost out of water.

Step 2. Call the phone number on the almost empty bottle and pray that someone who understands a little bit of English answers the call.

Step 3. Order two bottles of water (liang tong shui) to be delivered the next day.

Step 4. Empty the remainder of the water into reserve bottles.

Step 5. Place the empty bottles outside the front door.

Step 6. Go down to the lobby and give the water money to the doorman. This part was also simplified by Jenny who was nice enough to write an explanatory note in Chinese characters that I show the doorman if he doesn't understand why I'm handing him money and saying "shui."

Step 7. Receive two new bottles at the front door the next morning.

Did I mention this is all there is to do as long as nothing goes wrong?

While preparing to write this post, I got busy taking photos of the empty bottles in the hallway. I didn't pay attention to an important detail — making sure you don't leave a piece of the water dispenser in the top of the empty bottle.

The next morning, as Howie was installing the new bottle of water, he made a crucial discovery. The little white piece of plastic that sits inside the dispenser was missing. It's a small thing, but it makes all the difference. Without it, the water will hardly flow into the spigot.

"El, do you think that you might have left it in the top of the empty bottle?"

"Anything is possible. Let me check the photo."

When we enlarged the picture, the evidence was plain. It was just like the movie Blow Up.

There it was, the crucial piece, stuck in the top of the empty bottle.

But the empty bottle had been collected, along with the thousands of other empty water bottles collected that morning from front doors all over Shanghai.

Now what? we wondered.

"A picture," I thought, "is worth a thousand words."

I marched downstairs and began my pantomime with the doorman. I pointed to the photo, with an arrow pointing to the piece of plastic sticking out of the top of the bottle. Then I dialed the water-bottle company, and handed him the phone.

He tried, but the operator at the bottling company sounded less than encouraging.

OK, on to Plan B: Call Amanda.

Our lifeline.

It was a lucky day when I met her, an amazing American girl in her early 20's who is fluent in Chinese. We met in an American-style coffee shop late one afternoon, when the place was empty except for one other couple, a young blonde and an older man. It was a tiny restaurant, maybe 20 seats, and we could easily hear these two speaking in American English. We quickly struck up a conversation and found out that the young woman was Amanda Rose McCreight from Pittsburgh. The older man was her father, visiting from the States.

Amanda said she was working for a Shanghai law firm as a translator. She had learned to speak Mandarin in a total-immersion language program in Nanjing and she spoke it very well. With a twinkle in her eye, she said she enjoyed seeing how shocked

Chinese people were to meet her after having only spoken with her by phone. Her apple-pie American looks didn't match her flawless Mandarin.

We finished our snacks and started to say good-bye. I mentioned that I needed to go to the Carrefour for some household things.

"I'll come, too," Amanda said. She needed a few things, and her dad was heading home for a nap. "Is that OK? We can share a cab."

And just like that, I had a new friend.

Besides the language, she knew the customs of modern-day Shanghai and was always happy to help us if we got stuck.

I called her and explained our water crisis.

"I'll be right over," she said.

Things started to happen after Amanda called the company. Later that day, a representative from the bottling company called and said the piece would be delivered the next day.

And it was.

We attached the two inches of plastic, hoisted the 40-pound water jug, set it on the machine and pushed the tap. We filled a glass and drank.

Simple.

22
Thanksgiving

Howard:
NO ONE at the *Shanghai Daily* gave thanks for Thanksgiving.

The holiday didn't mean a thing to the Aussies I worked with, nor the Scot, the Canadian, the Singaporean, nor the two guys from India. Even the young generation of Chinese, who considered themselves very up on things American, knew almost nothing about it.

I was broadened by foreign travel simply by seeing that our warmest American holiday has no meaning outside our borders.

And yet, we did get together with a small group of Americans, thanks to El's friend Jackie. Jackie was originally from San Antonio and her husband David from Houston. So they reserved a table for nine people at Bubba's BBQ, an example of American enterprise with a down-home theme over on Hongqiao Road.

The company was nice. Most of the people had been in Shanghai a few years: David was an executive with American Greeting Cards, in charge of the Asian factories where the cards were manufactured for sale back in the States. Another guy was from General Electric. Another was in property management. He and his wife were Australians, and were tagging along to see what an American Thanksgiving was like. El and I hoped they had good imaginations, because we did not see a single reference to Pilgrims. No one sang, "Over the river and through the woods."

The dinner was a buffet, cooked by a Chinese staff, and the wine and beer, flowing freely for the two hours we'd paid for, were served by Chinese waitresses. The meal was a bit of a miracle, because, as a rule, no one eats turkey in China. This turkey, imported from God-knows-where, was barbecued rather than roasted. The cornbread stuffing and pumpkin pie were pretty good. But there was no cranberry sauce, nor whipped cream for the pie, because Bubba, the Texan owner of the place, disliked cranberries and lacked appreciation for the proper presentation of pumpkin pie. "I'm not good at desserts," he shrugged when we asked him.

Yet, somehow, we spoiled denizens of the First World overcame these setbacks and found reasons to reflect on our blessings.

We were healthy, Ellen and I told each other. We were living in a part of the world that was infinitely interesting. We had the love and support of friends and family from afar ... and we had a growing wealth of stories to tell when we got home.

23
Shivers in Shanghai

Indoors, it felt like outdoors

WE WERE freezing.

Our first two weeks in Shanghai, we had been in shorts and shirtsleeves. But on the night of Halloween, as if scripted by witches and ghouls, a cold front blew in and took root. It stayed chilly and rainy for weeks.

On November 16 we learned that we were in winter — and that we had been in winter for five days. It was Shanghai's earliest winter in 28 years.

Early winter? Say what?

A season in China is not a quarter of the calendar. It doesn't start on a set date. A season is declared by the official weatherman, just as a recession in the U.S. is declared by economists. If the indicators are low enough, long enough, people are told they have been in a recession. Or winter.

Winter's early arrival was just the latest example of extreme weather in Shanghai. Before we landed, Shanghai had had its shortest spring in years, then the hottest summer day on record, then an unusual string of storms. The head of the Shanghai Meteorological Bureau blamed it all on man-made climate change — and no one thought he was saying anything controversial.

Winter had been declared in Shanghai because we had five days in a row under 10 degrees Celsius. That's 50 degrees Fahrenheit.

That doesn't sound so bad. But in fact it was frigid. That was partly because of the damp. And partly because Shanghai did not believe in insulation.

Shanghai is in what's considered "southern" China. Forget that on the map the city is smack in the country's middle. We were south of the Yangtze River, and in the boundless wisdom of Mao Zedong, people south of the Yangtze didn't need insulation.

Since builders weren't required to insulate, they didn't. As a result, any cold that got into our apartment stayed there. It attached itself to the walls and moved in with us.

Touch the wallpaper, and we were inside a refrigerator. Step on the floor, and we felt a chill to the sole.

As Floridians, we had to adjust. We went to Wulumuqi Lu and bought fur-lined, house slippers. Ugly but warm. We trekked to a European sporting-goods superstore and I bought waterproof shoes and extra gloves. El got a few long-sleeved pullovers.

We learned to dart into a cold room, turn on the heat and wait for it to warm things up before we ventured inside ourselves. It was like growing up with Chicago winters and heating the car for 10 minutes before daring to get into it. Only here, we did it inside the house.

We bought an additional space heater. And we kept shivering until we took the advice of some friends who'd been through it, and bought ourselves long underwear made of silk. Which was the best advice we got about living in China. Silk underwear. It felt like a second skin. We wore it under our clothes when we hung around the apartment. We wore it to sleep, along with knit caps.

Night caps! We were the old couple who shamble off to bed in "The Night Before Christmas." We were back in the 19th century.

This, we realized, was how hundreds of millions of Chinese people lived for half the year. As quickly as China was lifting itself into a modern economy, the basic living conditions were basically threadbare.

At first I thought the Chinese were damn stoic about it: If it's cold, put on a jacket and carry on with whatever you were doing. But soon, I determined that Chinese people cultivated a relationship with the cold that was just perverse. They liked it cold. They thought it invigorating. Salubrious. They invited it in. They embraced it. When the temperature dropped, they opened their windows. They threw wide their doors.

They padded around the house with coats on, blowing into their fingers, thinking they were keeping healthy.

We bundled up, too, and dreamed about spring.

24
Duct Tape Duchess

Ellen's blog:
IF YOU'RE wondering how I'm keeping busy while Howie is at work, I can answer you in two words: duct tape.

When we were given two rolls of duct tape by Americans here who were leaving China I didn't realize what a wonderful product it was. Like magic, it holds things together without harming the surface it adheres to.

Now I am officially, clinically addicted to duct tape.

Like any addiction, it started out slowly — a little tape around a window ledge to keep out a draft. It was a rush to feel that I had some control over the cold seeping into my home. If that worked, I reasoned, I could apply duct tape to other places. So next I taped around the window — much better.

Our bedroom was awfully bright early in the morning, so I covered the window with aluminum foil attached with duct tape.

Then I attacked the very drafty front door in the foyer, using rolled newspaper and duct tape to make a weather strip at the bottom. That worked so well that I continued taping the rest of the door cracks.

Now I was empowered. I attacked our freezing bathroom using plastic wrap and, yes, duct tape to make an air pocket between the window pane and the wrap. The bathroom is now significantly more comfortable.

I am now the Duchess of Duct Tape. I dream about duct tape. I wonder where to strike next with duct tape.

I still have several windows as yet unadorned. Ah, the choices!

The duchess attacks: Among the kitchen cabinets

25
The New American President

Howard:

WE WERE joined by a few more Americans in Shanghai in mid-November. President Obama and his entourage checked into the Portman Ritz-Carlton Hotel about a mile and half from our apartment. It was the new president's first trip abroad since gaining the White House. China was said to be much honored to be his first destination.

In any American city where I'd worked, the arrival of a president was generally met with all-out assaults from the local news channels. Unless the prez was in town for strictly private fund-raising events, you got wall to wall coverage of his every move.

But Obama landed in China to a curious quiet. The time and place of his arrival, even his scheduled appearance before a college-age audience — none of it was published in advance. So he was met at the airport merely by a small press corps. The *Shanghai Daily* ran a modest photo of him getting off his plane on a rainy evening. Our headline: "Wet welcome for Obama."

The *Shanghai Daily*'s coverage always had at least one eye on what the state would want us to say. No matter how interested our readers might be in the fresh American president — the first black president, the first to grow up in Asia — he was never to overshadow Chinese president Hu Jintao. His name was never to appear in a bigger font. In a photo, he could look no larger than the shorter Hu.

Throughout the Obama visit, the newspaper seemed to go to press even later than usual, and JJ and the other bosses seemed a little more on edge than I had seen them before. I could only imagine the pressures — they must have been very nervous of making a wrong move on a story that could so easily upset official sensibilities, yet they knew their readership would want to know everything about Obama in Shanghai and Beijing: how he was received by the Chinese leaders, how he reacted to modern China.

The Chinese media were mum on Obama's schedule, but by checking the White House website, I saw that his Q&A with students was set for 12:45 p.m., Shanghai time. So Ellen and I got on the subway and rode a half-hour over to the Shanghai Science and Technology Museum in Pudong to see what we could of Obamania in China.

There wasn't much.

It was raining hard when we emerged from the Metro Line 2 at the museum's entrance and found a few brave souls with umbrellas standing alongside a lone TV news crew. Some were Australian tourists who had come to visit the museum and found it closed. They didn't know the reason until we told them.

"Obama? Here? Really!"

I talked to a young Chinese woman in her 20s who had heard on Chinese Central TV just two hours earlier that Obama would be speaking at the museum, and she had rushed over to try to catch a glimpse. Someone had told her that the motorcade would be coming from a certain direction, and she invited us to tag along as she went looking for the right corner.

We did, following a line of about a dozen umbrellas. The streets were wide and surrounded by broad green lawns on every side, fronting museums and government buildings.

As we walked, we talked to a young Shanghai man named Chuck. Chinese people like to adopt English names, and he told us that he had chosen his out of emulation for Chuck Norris. He didn't care one way or the other about Obama, he said. He wanted to see the Secret Service. For some reason, he thought the world of the Secret Service.

There were 30 or 40 people on the corner, the only people in sight other than police. The streets around the museum were empty of traffic. It was just this side of desolate.

I saw just one political statement: An Obama pin, worn by a pretty young woman named Ho Yin, who called herself Shirley. She was from Hong Kong. She said she liked Obama. Why? She looked stuck, smiling while she turned her eyes upward for an answer. Then she had one.

"Peace," she said.

And after about 10 still minutes, just the rain falling and the policemen maintaining their postures, the motorcade came by, a couple of dozen dark cars rolling purposefully down the street across a plaza from us. Two limos bore both U.S. and China flags. Obama had to be one of those cars. We waved in the rain and cheered, but didn't raise much noise.

I wondered what Obama thought of the paltry welcome.

Maybe he was thinking: A billion and a half people, and they all must have something better to do.

Maybe: Pretty nice, those folks standing out in the rain like that.

I learned later that, inside the museum, one thing he was thinking was that China ought to loosen its grip on information and opinion.

"In the United States, information is free," Obama told the hand-picked audience of students, in remarks that were televised in Shanghai but not nationally, "and I have a lot of critics in the United States who can say all kinds of things about me. I actually think that that makes our democracy stronger and it makes me a better leader because it forces me to hear opinions that I don't want to hear."

The remarks went unreported in the *Shanghai Daily*. I read them on the website of the *New York Times*.

26
At the Movies

Our favorite DVD seller worked a good corner in front of a convenience store.
Perfectly legal? Oh, sure.

WE TRIED to see "This Is It!," the posthumous movie tribute to Michael Jackson, who died a few months before we arrived in China, at a theater. But we couldn't get in. The crowd was huge. Jackson was possibly more popular in China than in the U.S. He was one American export who, all by himself and although deceased, could possibly even up the international trade unbalance.

The theater was on the fourth floor of the five-story Brilliant Shopping Mall, and the over-bright lobby actually smelled of popcorn, which Chinese flavor with sugar, not salt. None of the theater employees spoke a trace of English, but that aroma unmistakably said "movies."

The other big flick just then was the apocalyptic fantasy "2012." By national policy, the Chinese allowed only around 20 foreign movies into their theaters each year, and so, from America, the public saw a preponderance of Hollywood special-effects and disaster blockbusters. The *Shanghai Daily*, in fact, had just run a story about the high expectations that this end-of-the-world movie had raised among eager young Chinese cinema buffs who cherished the previous Roland Emmerich masterpieces, "Independence Day" and "The Day After Tomorrow."

El and I didn't bother to see "2012," but that didn't stop movie from becoming the all-time box office hit in China. It did not wear the championship mantle for long. Soon it was overtaken by a bonafide world smash, "Avatar." Which we went to see, our first movie-going experience in Asia.

The theater was an Art Deco beauty not far from the Bund — the Grand, dating from 1928 and designed by the Hungarian architect Laslo Hudec back in Shanghai's international heyday. It was exquisitely restored. The main lobby was as big as a ballroom. Any minute, it looked as though Fred and Ginger would come sweeping down the Italian marble stairway, swirling to "The Way You Look Tonight."

We sipped fancy cups of coffee in the sparsely filled house (the 3D version was an expensive ticket for most Chinese) until it was show time. Then we walked through heavily draped corridors into the theater, passing a sign that read, "No stinky or noisy food allowed inside." We soon found out what this meant. Ten minutes into the movie, the family next to us started talking loudly and eating an odiferous something that smacked of vinegar and spoiled eggs. Then they started crunching up their food bags.

A minute later, a woman started talking loudly on her cell phone.

The movie was in English with Chinese subtitles, so Ellen and I were maybe the only people in the theater trying to hear the dialog. But, still.

"Avatar" was an amazing hit. Young Chinese lined up outside theaters for hours. The Hunan Province government renamed a peak known as "Southern Sky Column" in the Zhangjiajie National Park to "Hallelujah

Mountain," capitalizing on the claim that the floating mountains in James Cameron's sci-fi blockbuster were inspired by the Chinese crags (they did look alike, and Cameron crew members had reportedly been spotted location-scouting in the area). Hunan hoped to lure tourists to "Pandora's floating mountain."

But in the midst of the movie's racking up a record gross — $76 million in three weeks — the Chinese government suddenly announced it was yanking "Avatar" in its lucrative 3D versions and replacing it with a state-produced biopic that almost no one wanted to see: "Confucius."

Cameron's most ardent Chinese fans were convinced the switch was political — that the censors had realized that the Na'vi battle for survival in "Avatar" was an allegory. The Na'vi obviously were Chinese small-property owners resisting officials intent on bulldozing their houses for development.

Cooler heads simply credited capitalism, China-style. The state, as it so often did, wanted to protect the home-grown movie industry.

Actually, Ellen and I didn't much care what played in theaters, because so many cheap pirated DVDs abounded all over Shanghai. We actually spotted "This Is It!" for sale in a DVD store on the very weekend it debuted in theaters. Just 12 yuan ($1.76). Which was actually expensive. The street vendor on our corner usually asked 5 yuan per disc. (75 cents.)

We watched everything on bootlegs. Yes, we should have had qualms against the intellectual property theft of it all. But when in Rome …

We watched on a laptop computer, wearing headphones to keep the noise down because we wouldn't start the movies until 1:30 or 2 in the morning, after I'd return from work. Ellen would catnap until I got home and then keep me company as I wound down from my shift. Our life in Shanghai became doubly strange: Alone together on the other side of the world, separated from friends and family and the familiar. And nocturnal.

It was the year of "The Hurt Locker," "Crazy Heart," "Invictus," "Up in the Air" and "Inglorious Basterds," and we saw them all. By the time the Academy Awards rolled around, in fact, we'd seen more nominated movies than we'd ever seen before an Oscar show.

The quality of the discs varied tremendously. I thought "The Men Who Stare at Goats," with George Clooney, was filmed in a very interesting avant-garde style until I realized I was watching a video taken secretly in a movie theater and shot from a seat that was extremely off-center from the screen. When we finally did watch "This Is It!" on our laptop, I was shocked by the poor resolution and wondered why no reviewers had mentioned the amateurish cinematography. Then I saw the silhouette of a guy walking across the bottom of the image. Our DVD was another movie-theater screen-grab. I did what anyone would do. I yelled at my computer, "Down in front!"

But usually the prints were pristine. Very often the movies would begin with the following message: "This video is intended solely for members of the Academy of Motion Picture Arts & Sciences." Clearly, somebody in Santa Monica was doing a very good business in slipping Oscar-consideration videos to a stamping operation and getting them to Shanghai — in days. Hollywood could blame China all it wanted for rampant thievery, but the Chinese couldn't be half as successful in their larceny without inside help in California.

Many foreign-language DVDs would be translated into English by locals, to hilarious results. One R-rated movie began with a careful warning, in perfect Chinglish: "This picture is disgusting."

The very first DVD we bought on the street, in fact, was "Coco Before Chanel," an art-house flick that was playing in a handful of U.S. theaters when we left the States, but on full display in Shanghai's DVD racks, a local hit. The bio-pic was in French, but the street seller, who biked his wooden boxes of discs each day to the corner in front of our local convenience store, showed us a label on the packaging that read, "English Subtitles."

It should have said, "English Sort-of."

Here's an example. Audrey Tatou, playing the young Coco before she becomes the world-famous designer, is sharing a bed with her sister in their struggling poverty days. The sister is trying to sleep. Audrey is reading something.

According to the subtitles, they say the following to each other:

—Finis
—What?
—Reading. I see here is very good-looking design. Do you not take a look at the letter
—I believed in
—Then take a look at / do not look at me put up / good, do not it / yesterday, the style of those things that do not
—Do you think?
—Yes, very good / if I change, might be better to see. But they still

prefer that kind of style they do not agree
  —Yes so it did say
  —Saying that it will not be listening to is, ah, we are responsible for can be a
  —Well, do not want to bar
  —But no I can not sleep / can you fall asleep? Yes, sleepy

The two women break out in laughter and the scene ends.
I wanted my 75 cents back.

27
Back to Teaching

Ellen's blog:
I'VE COME full circle – I'm teaching again.

Every Thursday I take a subway to the other side of Shanghai known as Pudong to teach English.

I've been teaching much of my adult life, so this comes relatively easy to me.

My first teaching assignment, straight out of college, was teaching inner-city first-graders on Chicago's West Side. I wasn't very familiar with the children's lifestyle and customs and their language, nominally English, was often hard for me to grasp.

This new teaching assignment has some of the same feel to it.

I have five students ages 4 and 5 years old, all living in the same apartment complex. Their parents pooled their money to hire an English teacher to augment the once-a-week English classes they have in their school.

We meet each week at one of the student's home. The parents sit at the dining room table and eat and drink tea while I work with the children a few feet away in the living room.

At the beginning of the first lesson, the parents explained that they had been taught in school how to read and understand English, but felt they were weak in oral English. They wanted their children to speak English better than they could.

They said they didn't have any specific agenda, they just wanted their kids to be exposed to an English speaker and to get a chance to practice speaking. Did I think I could help them?

I started out by assessing how much English the children already knew.

They blew me away.

These little kids knew English names for letters, numbers, colors, shapes, animals and food as well as — maybe better than — most American children of the same age.

All this as a second language they study once a week. These kids are scary smart.

Even though class is rather late in the day — from 7 p.m. until 8:30, they pay attention and participate. They love to sing and follow along to "The Hokey Pokey," "If You're Happy and You Know It (Clap Your Hands)," "Itsy Bitsy Spider," and "The Wheels On the Bus Go Round and Round."

The Chinese education system puts great emphasis on rote memory and repetition, so the kids are great at repeating things I tell them.

Sometimes too precisely.

Last class period, I had a tickle in my throat.

I told the class to repeat after me, "This is a round [cough], red apple."

They repeated, "This is a round [cough], red apple."

I started laughing — they started laughing. Then the parents joined in laughing.

I've seen some changes in a few of the kids already. On my first visit, Kalvin was so anxious that he would sit with the group only if his mother sat with him. When she left for a minute he cried and called out for her.

Now when I come to the house he jumps up and down and shouts, "Hello, hello Ellen."

I don't know if I'll be able to make any significant difference in the way the kids can speak English, but we are all getting lessons in American-Chinese friendships. Before I left the States, our friend Jennifer Lin, who has lived and worked in China and has extensive knowledge of the customs, told us, "Chinese people are very friendly, but they don't hug."

Well, after four classes, my students do!

28
Shanghai Christmas

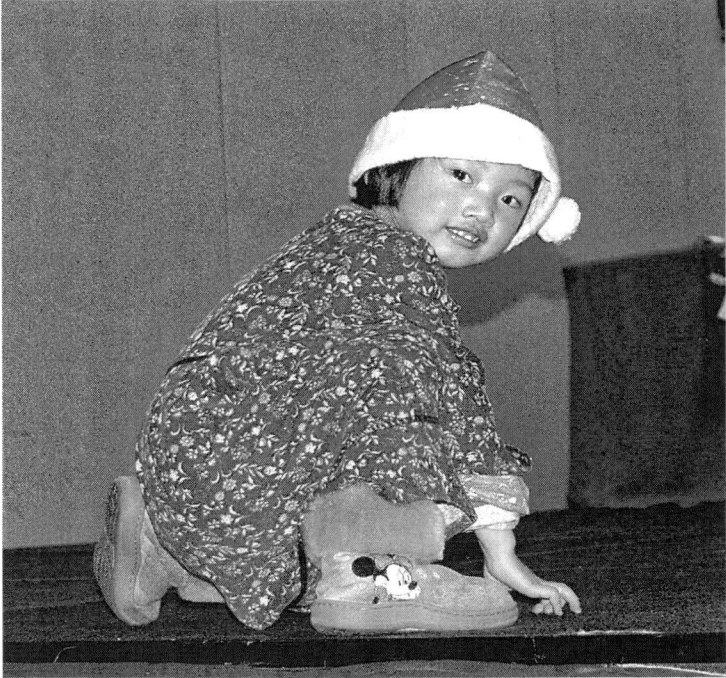

Howard:

YOU'D THINK that if you traveled halfway around the world to an atheist country ruled by the Communist Party, where thousands of years of Confucian, Taoist and Buddhist tradition still showed their heavy imprints, that you would be spared — for at least one December — "The Little Drummer Boy."

You would be wrong.

All over Shanghai, stores displayed Christmas trees, holly, tinsel and pictures of Santa. In any department store, the P.A. system played high-pitched vocal versions of "White Christmas" and "Frosty The Snowman." We saw almost as many colored lights in the trees of Huihai Road, a major shopping avenue, as you'd see on Chicago's Miracle Mile stretch of Michigan Avenue.

But people weren't walking around with arms full of shopping bags. The gleaming, crowded stores did their best to foster the holiday-spending spirit, but Christmas in Shanghai wasn't a big occasion for gift-giving. The Chinese economy did not live or die by the annual volume of Christmas shopping.

Neither did we see any representations of the baby Jesus or the Virgin Mary. No mangers, Magi, angels, donkeys, camels — no trace of the birth of Christ.

The Chinese version of Christmas wasn't religious. Yet it wasn't commercial, either.

I asked my Chinese friends what Christmas meant to them, and they said it was a nice occasion for a party. Young people especially thought so. They'd get together with pals, maybe go to a bar. It was becoming more popular all the time.

The closest analogy I came up with was the way non-Irish people in America embrace St. Patrick's Day. You don't have to be Irish to brighten your March 17 in New York with a pint of Guinness. In the big Chinese city, it was the same thing: you didn't have to be a Christian or feel nostalgic about Bing Crosby to make merry on a winter night.

The Christmas they celebrated in Shanghai, or were learning to celebrate, was the American version, not the European. People said "Merry Christmas," not "Happy Christmas." They loved Santa Claus, not Father Christmas. The music was more Irving Berlin than Handel.

Chinese people loved America. We saw that in every department store. At the jewelry counter, an entirely Asian crowd would be dwarfed by huge glamour photos of American models. Not a Chinese face in any of the advertising.

It was very odd. It was as if Shanghainese were in a rush to adopt big swaths of American culture: the acquisitiveness for consumer goods, the utter compulsion to own an automobile, the fascination with Michael Jackson and Colonel Sanders (his face appearing on so many KFC outlets, all over China, he had to be the most recognizable American in the entire country). They had little use for American-style free speech, free press, freedom of assembly, freedom of religion or ethnic diversity. But they loved blue jeans, Kobe Bryant, Apple — and Christmas.

On a Sunday afternoon in December, Ellen and I walked to the Swissotel Shanghai for the *Shanghai Daily*'s annual Christmas party. It was a non-alcoholic luncheon, and my work colleagues, both Chinese and Western, brought spouses and children — a lot fewer children than you'd see at a company party of similar size in the U.S., assuming your U.S. company still had the dough for a Christmas party.

The party committee did a good job of keeping the speeches short and the laughs rolling. There was a lucky drawing, the winners receiving envelopes of cash. We foreign experts got bottles of Bailey's Irish Cream: glad tidings indeed. The portliest member of the reporting staff dressed up as Santa and posed for pictures with the little kids.

I was asked to get onstage and sing karaoke. In Chinese.

I sported a elf's cap and listened to the lyrics through an iPod and sang gibberish. I was a disaster, but that was the idea.

Then a choir got up on stage. A well-rehearsed choir — a group of reporters, computer experts, advertising representatives and secretaries, making a serious effort to make beautiful sounds. All of them Chinese. All singing "Auld Lang Syne."

They even sang it with the Scottish burr.

It was gorgeous.

29
The Hairdresser

Ellen's blog:
AFTER ALMOST three months it was again time to enter a hair salon.

In preparation, I had been scoping out different shops in the neighborhood. They ranged in style and price from a corner barber shop to a posh salon catering to foreign clientele.

I was intrigued by a shop on my street that seemed different than the others. It was operated by a group of young guys who looked like they cared about style. They wore punk rock clothing and exaggerated haircuts. They reminded me of Japanese anime cartoon characters. I figured they would know how to give me a modern haircut.

I walked in and pointed to a sign in English, "Hot hair conditioning treatment 95 RMB." That was $14. They nodded their heads "yes" and sat me down in a worn orange molded-plastic chair that was probably very stylish in the early 60's.

My hairdresser thumbed through the magazine rack and handed me an expat monthly magazine and a May 2009 copy of "Good Housekeeping." Without asking, he poured a glass of hot water and presented it to me. This was for drinking. It was a common practice here to drink plain hot water, as common as ice water in the States.

A foreign couple, jabbering non-stop in Italian, sat across the room. I could get some idea of what was in store for me by watching their progress.

Instead of a quick wash at the back sink, I sat in my chair. My hairdresser rubbed shampoo into my dry hair and then squirted warm water onto it from a bottle.

The guy then rubbed my hair and scalp until my head was covered in a rich lather. He continued to knead my head, neck, temples and in front of my ears for about 10 minutes. It felt more like a massage than a shampoo.

I mostly enjoyed it, but there were a few moments when it seemed he was going to rub a hole in my scalp.

After rinsing out the shampoo at a sink, he seated me again in my orange chair and applied conditioner. Just as I was settling in, getting used to the process, his assistant rolled a big, portable hair dryer over to my seat, placed the dome over my head and plugged it in.

Before I knew it, a white cloud started coming out of the machine.

After my earlier problems with electrical appliances, I was a little concerned that it was smoke, but since no one else seemed alarmed, I figured it was just steam.

As I sat under the dryer I studied the other customers. The Italian couple had gone and a beautiful Asian woman walked into the shop. She was talking on a cell phone and barely acknowledged the hairdresser as she sat down in the next chair. She continued to ignore him as he washed her hair and massaged her head.

It was especially shocking to see her ignore him while he topped off the hair wash by using a Q-tip to dry all around her ears. I looked around and noticed that none of the customers acknowledged the person who was working on their head — no eye contact — nothing. They just read their newspapers or magazines as if they were sitting alone. This was a completely different vibe than in a U.S. salon, where there is very often a rapport with the stylist. Back home, we talk. How are the kids? What are you doing this weekend? How's business? It's a relationship.

Come to think of it, I couldn't talk to the Chinese stylists anyway. But that was beside the point. The other people, who could have spoken to them, didn't bother.

After 20 minutes came the rinsing, and some more massaging of my head. The Asian woman left — still not having spoken to anyone.

I showed the hairdresser a recent photo of my hair in the style I wanted him to copy. He nodded yes and started cutting. I felt like I was in hands of Johnny Depp in "Edward Scissorhands." He was quick and adept and before I knew it, he had cut and blow-dried my hair. After the long buildup of the shampoo and rinse, the cut took only 10 minutes. It was the shortest part of the process.

I was thrilled with the result and the price: 125 RMB ($18.30). The last time I had my hair conditioned, cut and blow-dried in the U.S., it had cost over $150 with tax and tips.

I was so happy that I signed up for the "pay 100-yuan, get five shampoo/rinses" deal. Less than $3 a visit.

I told myself, I'm going to like it here.

30
Beijing New Year

Howard:
ELLEN AND I rang in 2010 with a thrill, a trip to the Great Wall. It was a true thrill, one of those occasions where you keep saying to yourself: I can't believe I'm here. After seeing it in pictures for a lifetime, a look at the actual thing made us catch our breath.

It is so much larger than any picture can capture. It is there in front of you, snaking across a mountaintop — just one of hundreds of mountaintops — but you cannot believe such a structure is possible. Its placement is so perfect it seems like a natural wonder, an Asian Grand Canyon. And then you reflect, for the millionth time, that it is man-made. Made by manual labor and a minimum of machinery — the labor of thousands, surely tens of thousands. All in the service of a crazy idea: a great kingdom seeking to keep the outsiders forever on the outside.

It was below freezing, but there was no wind and a thin sun was shining, so we were not cold. We had dressed for the Arctic: silk long underwear, extra layers of clothes, parkas. The crowd was light. We had stretches of the wall to ourselves. I closed my eyes to hear the quiet of the mountainsides, and reflected that the same stillness has wrapped these perfectly placed stones for centuries.

The visitors we did meet were from around the world. We exchanged "Happy New Year" with people whose accents carried traces of almost every continent.

It was January 1. The day before, we'd flown up to Beijing from Shanghai and connected with Ben and his college pal Jacob even before we reached our hotel. They were in the city for a five-week program in Mandarin at a Beijing university. After those five weeks, Ben would move to Shanghai to enroll at East China Normal University for a full semester's worth of Mandarin study — and to spend a lot of time with us.

We had just gotten off a subway train with our luggage from the airport on our way to our hotel, and we were hauling our luggage through the swarming subway station in central Beijing, when, to our amazement, we heard someone shouting our names. It was Jacob, whom we'd never met, spotting the two Westerners amid the hundreds of Chinese hurrying back and forth. He and Ben had ducked into the subway ticket-buying plaza just to cross the extremely wide street above. They too had been heading toward our hotel.

And what do you know, in the middle of the millions of souls in Beijing, China, there we were, reunited with Benny, our 19-year-old whom we hadn't seen in two and half months. Big hugs and a lot of "you look great"s and "so do you"s.

After checking into our room we tumbled into a cab and treated the boys to pizza in a wood-fired-oven place that we stumbled into, run by Italians who had recently relocated from Naples. Then we said goodbye, because they had New Year's Eve plans with their new college buddies — Kazakhs, Koreans, Danes. Ben's New Year, we would learn later, involved ice-skating on a rink in a Western-style shopping mall, and a few Tsingtao beers, which must have helped battle the chill of a frigid night. He already had seen the Great Wall with a college group, so El and I made separate plans to visit the wall on New Year's Day.

161

Beijing, we discovered over the next couple of days, was not to our liking — a city of streets half-a-football-field wide, plazas so large they seemed to create their own horizon and squat government buildings that covered whole city blocks. An architecture of intimidation, meant to make you feel small. Albert Speer, Hitler's architect, would have been envious.

We often heard that Beijing was to Washington as Shanghai was to New York City: the political capital versus the financial and cultural capital. This was unfair to Washington. Beijing was more my idea of Moscow, a place I've never been but can well imagine. People wore grimmer expressions in Beijing than they did in Shanghai. The beggars displayed their deformities more ostentatiously. An aura of authority hung over the place.

I usually felt nice and loose when walking around Shanghai, as though the city were made for exploring on foot. In Beijing, there always seemed to be a fence or a guard rail blocking our way. Tiananmen Square contained more security cameras than I've ever seen in any one place.

Undoubtedly the weather had something to do with our mood. On our last morning, we awoke to a heavy snowfall that did not let up all day, piling up as Beijing's worst in 60 years, making it treacherous even to walk and forcing the cancellation of our night flight out.

On the other hand, Beijing actually does make wonderful Beijing duck. The almost 600-year-old Forbidden City still stuns, despite the last century's attempts by the communists — and now the profit-seekers — to cut its mystique and majesty down to size. Across the street, almost mockingly, stood a shopping plaza featuring a Starbucks, a California-theme restaurant and a three-story Christmas tree. We were a couple of years too late to see the Starbucks that had been inside the Forbidden City. The outlet had opened in 2000 at the invitation of Forbidden City managers, but closed in 2007, under fire for being "not globalization, but an erosion of Chinese culture."

The evident triumph of capitalism throughout the Chinese capital made the portrait of Mao over the Forbidden City's main entrance seem badly dated: more kitsch than commanding. The Great Helmsman's body lay in a mausoleum nearby. I wondered if it had rolled over yet.

And we did find kind people. On a subway, we struck up a conversation with a young man of 23, who was carrying a decorative pillow and who had pretty good English. He told us that the pillow was a gift for his mother. We exchanged cards, talked about Florida, and schools (he wanted to go to Stanford someday), and happened to get off at the same stop. When he realized we were planning to walk from the station to Ben's temporary college campus, he grabbed El's suitcase and dragged it through the snow for a good three blocks until Ben met us at the school gate. He gave us his English name: Bruce.

A few days later, El got a surprise email: "Mother, I am your son that met you three days before, in that bad weather. Mind me call you in that way, because you make me feel the mother's love. Are you still in Beijing now? I only want to tell you the temperature will be the lowest in 40 years. Take care yourselves keep warm. I hope I can see you again!"

We never did see Bruce again, but we had his picture, and whenever we looked at how he smiled for the camera, the snow sticking to his horn-rimmed glasses, we remembered how an encounter with a stranger took the chill off a forbidding city.

On New Year's Eve — our New Year's, December 31 — El and I celebrated with a late dinner. We walked along one of Beijing's too-wide boulevards. It was cold, seriously fucking cold, the kind of bitter, painful cold that makes even Chicagoans say, "Mother of Ditka, this is cold." We found a great Japanese noodle place where no one took their coat off but us, the dumb Americans.

After eating, we did what many Beijingers were doing on New Year's Eve. We shopped. We went into a big department store that was aswarm with people, and went downstairs to the pharmacy-grocery section and bought some treasures: Chap-Stick, bottled water, dried apricots, Chinese-made potato chips, Snickers bars and powder for making sesame pudding, a dessert we'd grown fond of. And a French wine, for 82 yuan, $12. A suspiciously low price.

We went back to the hotel room, which was warm, like a room back in the States, with a full-length bathtub and real hot water. And we took a little vacation from the Shanghai perma-chill. We turned on the flat-screen and watched fey Asian pop singers do silly variants of a Dick Clark Rockin' New Year, on channel after channel. The bottle of French wine had a bad cork and gave off the aroma of vinegar: The 82-yuan mystery solved. I opened a miniature Gordon's Gin from the minibar.

An auspicious way to start a new year and a new decade! Ten years before, Ellen and I had stood in Camden, N.J., to watch the '00s arrive with a spectacular fireworks display over the Delaware River, the lights of America's birthplace, Philadelphia, shining in the background. Now we were toasting the arrival of the next decade in the capital of the new century's rising power.

Then it was midnight. On the TV, fireworks were exploding over Singapore. We clinked glasses, El with her vinegary Cabernet, me with my hotel-room-ripoff gin. We kissed: Our 23rd New Year's kiss. Kisses that never got old.

31
Subway Thoughts

SOON AFTER we arrived in Shanghai, El and I walked past the intersection of two busy streets in the former French Concession, Huihai Road and Chengshu Road. And in a sight that seemed typical of the city, two of the four corners were construction sites.

A tall building — maybe two — was going up on one corner. Some undefined activity had turned the other corner into a mess: heaps of rubble and concrete and machinery, and piles of dirt tumbling onto the street. The sidewalk had disappeared. We picked our way through mud and rain puddles at the edge of the street while skirting oncoming cars, buses and motorcycles.

A couple of months later, we rode past that corner in a cab, and I noticed a familiar light pole with stylized red circle and the letter "M." Aha! I got it now. This construction site was going to be a Metro stop some day.

We went by a week later and, by God, that Metro stop was finished.

There was a stairway and an escalator heading underground. There was landscaping — not just sod and saplings, but dozens of flowers, arrayed in perfect lines.

It was flabbergasting. By far, it was the speediest construction of a public works project I ever saw.

It was a stop for the brand-new Line 7, which opened for business just a couple of days after this Chengshu Road station was finished. El — she who was so afraid of the subway when we first landed in Shanghai — rode on it during its first week of operation. She said it was smooth, speedy and spotless.

But then, all the subways we rode in Shanghai were clean and shiny, maybe just not as redolent of the new-car smell as the Line 7. Shanghai's subway cars didn't rattle. Their brakes didn't whine. The stations were

165

brightly lit. Even the wall advertising shone, all backlit with fluorescent lights. There wasn't a trace of graffiti. No tang of pee.

The stations were equipped with LED clocks to count down the arrival time of the next train. The floor of the train platform was outlined with arrows to show you exactly where the car doors would be when the train stopped, so you'd know where to stand as you waited. Trains were sometimes late — we seemed to cover at least one commuting disturbance a week in the *Shanghai Daily* — but I never saw one arrive more than a few seconds past the time predicted on those LED clocks.

Shanghai opened its first subway line in 1995. Just 15 years later, in 2010, we had our choice of 10 lines, with 196 stations and 177 miles of track.

And this didn't include the Maglev, the ultra-high speed train that ran on magnetism, like something out of old science fiction. Levitating above the track, it made the 18.6-mile trip from Pudong International Airport to a transfer station in 7 minutes, 20 seconds.

Now the incredible worker bees of Shanghai were still at it, intending to add yet another line and finish four extensions of existing lines before the 2010 World Expo started in May.

They wouldn't stop there. By 2012, the subway system became the longest in the world, with 270 miles of track. By 2020, if plans held, Shanghai was to swell to 20 routes and 545 miles of track.

In 2001, the Shanghai subway system was not even listed among the world's top 10. By 2011, it was the world's fifth-busiest, with over 2 billion rides that year. It was probably the fastest-growing subway network anywhere.

And the subway was far from the only public-works construction that was going on. Having already built the spanking new Pudong International Airport, the city was busy doubling the runways and constructing a new terminal at the old Hongqiao Airport, turning it into a hub that would connect domestic flights to buses, cars, cross-country trains and city subways. And the city was redoing the riverfront at the historic Bund — all part of $45 billion being spent on the Expo and the city's corresponding spruce-up. All at a time when the U.S. and Europe were cutting spending, vainly trying to fight the recession with austerity.

Five years before, there'd been no such thing in Shanghai as a vest-pocket park, according to an American friend who knew the city at least that long. Now every available sliver between a traffic-choked street and a box-like apartment block had a soothing green buffer: grasses, trees, shrubs.

In early December, tickets went on sale for an almost-finished bullet train that would make the 664-mile trip between Wuhan and Guangzhou — two huge cities — in three hours, instead of the previous 10½. China had opened its first bullet train the year before. Three years hence, China intended to have 42 high speed lines on 8,000 miles of track.

An American had to marvel. For when was the last time we saw a public-works project in the United States that we were proud of? Or that even got done?

But none of this Chinese growth was accomplished without great cost and reckless waste. It didn't take long for one of the two new bullet trains to crash in Zhejiang Province, killing 40 people and injuring nearly 200. In the aftermath, the Railway Ministry was revealed to be a pit of kickbacks, corruption, construction shortcuts and debt, skimming profits and shortchanging safety.

Yet as Ellen and I watched 2010 dawn in Asia, it was a moment of giddy optimism. The *China Daily,* in Beijing, entitled its lead editorial of Dec. 31, 2009, "A Triumphant Decade." For America, this same decade had been a sorry 10 years bracketed by the 9/11 attacks and the Wall Street collapse, between which we saw interminable wars in Afghanistan and Iraq and the shrinking of the middle class. The Chinese thought the '00s were just great — and that more great times were coming.

"Our people are actually among a pretty small few the world over who are embracing 2010 full of confidence and hopes," the *China Daily* crowed.

And in the States? Sixty-one percent Americans believed the country was in decline, according to the NBC News/*Wall Street Journal* poll. With 10-plus percent unemployment and a quarter of homeowners underwater, almost no faction in America was embracing the next decade with confidence and hopes. Despite Barack Obama's campaigning to lead us into a post-partisan age, after one year of his presidency there was no American center or consensus or common purpose, only endless warring between opposite political poles.

After the futuristic airports of Shanghai and Hong Kong, it made an American feel almost embarrassed to return to the United States and alight at cramped, worn Newark International and to ride New York City subways that looked and felt every bit their century of hard use. The U.S. had stopped making great public facilities. The Chinese did just the opposite, flexing their economic muscle to build new transportation systems, parks, stadiums, schools — sometimes, whole cities. Unlike America and Europe, China's response to the recession was to boost spending, even if the spending didn't make sense; lots of those new housing units stood empty for lack of buyers. Some of the new cities were as bare as ghost towns. The strategy helped China dodge the unemployment and economic pain felt in Europe and the U.S.

On the other hand, most middle-class Chinese lived in crowded, unadorned, underheated apartments.Their private spaces were nothing to envy.

It was just the reverse in America, where our homes were our castles, whether large or small — expressions of self in our redone kitchens, living rooms and man-caves, big-screen TVs, yards and pools, three-car garages, book and music collections, shelves of video games, art on the walls.

The public sphere, that's what we let go to hell.

32
Kind People

Ellen's blog:
I DIDN'T have any preconceived notions of what it would be like to live in a country with people I was unfamiliar with.

Would I feel intimidated by the language barrier? Would people be aloof and ignore me if I needed assistance?

Very quickly I found that most of the Chinese people we met were incredibly friendly, curious, happy to lend assistance and make sure we were taken care of.

When, in our first week here, we met Jenny, our real estate agent who became a consistent friend, and Frank and Eva Tam, our landlords who hosted a banquet in our honor, I wondered if this was just "beginner's luck." I soon found it wasn't.

The imported-food store down the street is staffed by very sweet young locals. On several occasions, one of them followed me around the market, holding my basket and intently studying the things I chose to buy. It was as if they felt that by learning my marketing habits they could somehow get closer to understanding what an American was really like.

One day at the checkout counter, one of the young men looked concerned that I had several heavy bags to carry.

"How did you get here? Do you have a car?" he asked me in good English.

No, I said, I'd walked.

"But this is too heavy for you," he told me.

I smiled and made a muscle. "Don't worry. I'm strong," I said, trying to reassure him.

"I'm glad to hear that you are in good health, but it is too much for you to carry," he continued. "I would carry it for you, but I must stay at my station and work."

He seemed genuinely distressed.

We experienced another act of kindness last week. On our way to do an errand, we were trying to find an address and got a little lost. I called the lady we were supposed to meet, but she was not able to speak enough English (and I was certainly unable to speak enough Chinese) for us to communicate.

Just then, a man came walking down the street with his bike-riding daughter, about age 9. I waved my phone and gestured to him to help me with the call. He took my phone and spoke with the lady for a minute, shook his head "yes" to her and handed me back the phone.

"OK," he said, and gestured us to follow him. He told his daughter to stay where she was (we could tell by reading his body language), turned and started walking in exactly the opposite direction of where he'd been headed.

"Stop!" we said, and gestured to him by waving our hands. "We'll be OK."

All we wanted was for him to point us in the right direction.

He shook his head "no" and kept walking.

We walked for blocks, trying to keep up with him. At each intersection we begged him stop and return to his daughter but he refused.

Finally, he deposited us on the corner where we were supposed to meet the lady. Then, and only then, did he seem satisfied that he had fulfilled his obligation to help us.

It was far above and beyond what you expect when you ask a stranger for directions.

I thought that Howie and I might be getting treated extra nicely because we are "old" and the Chinese venerate older people. But no — Ben has also had kindness bestowed upon him.

A couple of weeks ago, Howie and I were sharing a table in a very cozy Bohemian-style coffee house near Jingtao University with a Chinese couple who were listening to music on a laptop. When we heard the ping of Chuck Berry's guitar, we started a conversation.

The man called himself Maxim. He was from Inner Mongolia — the Mongolia that's a part of China, not the independent country —

and from that great distance, at the edge of the Gobi Desert, he had fallen in love with the sounds of blues and rock'n'roll. He played guitar, he told us with a shy smile.

Our son did too, we told him, and he'd be coming to Shanghai soon.

Maxim was excited to hear it, and urged us to let Ben know he'd love to meet him. Ben did arrive, in mid-January, and last week he paid a visit to Maxim. They discussed their shared love of music and took turns playing his guitar. It was raining when it was time for Ben to leave. Maxim did not have many possessions. His apartment was spare. But he insisted that Ben take his umbrella, and none of Ben's refusals were good enough.

From the headlines, you would never know that China is like this. The Chinese government is doing its best to show the U.S. that they're their own boss, not caring how arrogant they appear.

But one-on-one, an American sees none of this in China's most vibrant city. People aren't smug; they're sweet. People aren't aloof; they can't wait to be helpful.

If any one thing makes Howie and me feel great about being here, it's the kindness of the people we meet every day. If any one thing makes us feel great about having made this journey, it's seeing what a marvel the human race is — how much we long to know each other, no matter how geography, politics, economics and borders divide us.

33
Peter's Story

Howard:

ZHANG CIYUN and I are virtually the same age, both born around 1949, a most important year in China, the year when Mao Zhedong's Communist Party won its civil war and took over the country. The birth year of "New China."

But my upbringing in peaceful suburban Chicago and that of the *Shanghai Daily*'s editor could not have been more different. Peter — his English name — was in his teens when China was engulfed by the Cultural Revolution, the infamous purification program triggered by Mao and fueled by the revolutionary fervor of young people who formed fanatical Red Guards, embarking on a 10-year witch hunt that targeted millions of educated people and anyone believed to be a little bit richer than his neighbors — all accused of counter-revolutionary treason.

Teachers, doctors, engineers, scientists were kicked out of their jobs, suffering horrific public humiliations when not imprisoned and tortured. The country fell into chaos. Schools closed and universities emptied. Hundreds upon thousands of students were forced to drop their books and march into the countryside and begin new lives of manual labor.

I started college in 1967, the year after we began seeing television images of legions of young Chinese, all dressed in identical box-like jackets and caps, hoisting small red books of "The Sayings of Chairman Mao" into the air and chanting incomprehensible slogans, although we were pretty sure that "Death to American Imperialism" was one of them. From the looks of it, the closed communist country had simply found another way to lose its mind. China was scary.

All the more reason for the U.S. to get the hell out of Vietnam. Those of us who were beginning to protest the American escalation in Vietnam always had that worry in the back of our minds — did we really want to tempt the Chinese dragon to step into fight on the side of its communist ally Ho Chi Minh? Now we know the idea was ludicrous. The Vietnamese fighters distrusted, if not hated, the Chinese at least as much as they hated us, and they had for centuries.

But our knowledge of the real Asia was thin. What commanded our government's thinking was the Cold War narrative that simplified the world into two large camps, the Free World and the Communist World, with a jumble of nonaligned or vulnerable countries in-between, each of them a domino that if allowed to start falling, would continue to collapse in a line that would bring the Communists directly to the shores of California.

I was in the college generation that rejected that domino thinking and bucked LBJ's war. I marched on the Pentagon and protested the war at the 1968 Democratic Convention, running from Chicago Mayor Richard J. Daley's cops, eyes burning from tear gas on Michigan Avenue. We were the generation that grew our hair long, played our music loud, made heroes of Dylan, Beatles, Stones, Hendrix, Joplin, Zappa, The Dead. We explored freedom with dope and sex and communes and women's lib. We didn't realize how naive we were to think ourselves revolutionaries by wearing hair to our shoulders, dropping acid, joining a protest — pokes in Middle America's ribcage, prodding for a reaction. Real revolutionaries were at work on the other side of the world, smashing their societies to bits while imposing their own orthodoxies.

"Revolution" to us was a cool battle cry. In China, it was a madness let loose, plunging the world's most populous nation into a darkness of misery and bloodshed.

While I was cosseted at Ivy-covered Cornell, Peter was in the Chinese countryside, wrenched from his studies and living hundreds of miles from his family on a collective farm. He has a photograph from that time. It's in black and white. A hay wagon, pulled by a couple of scraggly horses, the hay piled high. Trees in the background, a dirt road at the horses' feet. And three or four children, their white faces a smudge below blurs of black hair. One of the boys looks a little taller than the others. Peter.

The suffering endured during the Cultural Revolution is not an open topic in China. It is barely talked about. Yet its psychic scars must be immense. The writer Yu Hua believes the pain of those years explains why so many Chinese have so fully embraced the current philosophy of chase-the-dollar. They are like the Depression generation in America, the ones who knew deprivation and couldn't wait for the postwar comforts of suburbia. The fervor that drove the Cultural Revolution never really left the Chinese soul, Yu says. That same energy and sense of group purpose hadn't disappeared, just taken a new form — a mad rush for economic development and material success.

But Peter talked openly about his years of rural exile. The long days, the hard winters, the great distance from home. How hard it all was for a bookish boy.

"The worst part," he said, "was they took away your hope. They told us we would never leave, that this was our life.

"It's a terrible thing, to live without any hope."

The Cultural Revolution finally petered out around 1976. And in 1979, with Mao dead, the new leader Deng Xiaoping announced a radical new course. China would open up to the rest of the world, inviting cultural exchanges, visitors and investment. And it would experiment with capitalism, launching several "special enterprise zones" that would encourage work for profit.

With profit as the incentive, the ruined economy might start moving. "It doesn't matter if a cat is black or white, so long as it catches mice," Deng famously said.

Peter somehow re-established his life in Beijing and went to work in 1980 at the *People's Daily*, the communist party mouthpiece, published in Mandarin, helping launch the *China Daily*, the country's first national paper in English. It was an offspring of Deng's directive to open China to the world. How could you do that without a way to let the world in? Hence, an English-language newspaper.

Peter got good at typing up stories in English. He even started taking notes at press conferences in English. His idea of translation wasn't to find a word that corresponded with another word. It was to take the concept he heard in one language and to think of the best way to express that concept in the other language.

His talent was noticed. In 1983 he was allowed the rare privilege of leaving China to attend Stanford University to study journalism. His two years in California were tremendously eye-opening.

"In those days, China didn't even have a supermarket," he told me.

He lived with a host family, who took him to church suppers and meetings of the League of Women Voters — experiences he still talks about, for he had come from a country that lacked both religion and elections. He must have been a talented journalism student as well as a whiz at English because, he said, upon getting his master's at Stanford, the *San Francisco Chronicle* offered him a job as a reporter. He would have been the first foreigner ever hired there, he said, but he felt he had to return to China. Whether he felt pressured to return or if he had decided that his destiny lay with China's opening up, he didn't say. All I know is that he wasn't consumed with bitterness over the way his country had treated him when he was young. Instead, he was determined to carve out a career in which he could better himself and his country, too.

So he went back to the *China Daily*. In 1992, Deng paid a visit to Shanghai and declared, momentously, that he wished he had made the city one of the original special economic zones, but that he'd been able to do only so much in 1979. Now was the time, though, for Shanghai to wake up. And so it did, like an impatient horse charging out of the gate and soon hitting a gallop to join the 20th century. Amid the rush to development, several government bodies decided that Shanghai needed its own English-language newspaper.

And so the *China Daily* started a weekly called the *Shanghai Star*. Peter and JJ, co-workers at the *Daily*, got involved, splitting their time between Beijing and Shanghai. Tensions developed as the two editors grew convinced that Shanghai deserved a daily paper, but the *China Daily* didn't see the need.

In 1996, Peter was appointed deputy director-general of the Information Office of Shanghai Municipality — around the time that top officials said they wanted him to start a daily paper for the city. He said fine, so long as they agreed to his idea of what a Shanghai newspaper should be. It should be aimed at a foreign audience and take some liberties the domestic press would never dare. Not every government pronouncement would be published. Whereas the *China Daily* was a national newspaper, *Shanghai Daily* would be regional, its focus on the city and its surrounding area. Its entertainment pages would list local TV channels and the HBO and Cinemax that foreigners got in their hotel rooms and private satellite hookups; *China Daily* had few listings that weren't the nationwide CCTV (China Central Television). *Shanghai Daily* wouldn't cover city government as its first priority; it would cover business.

The authorities agreed and, much to the unhappiness of the *China Daily*, the *Shanghai Daily* started rolling off the presses.

Shanghai had an English-language newspaper. Not for the first time.

Oddly, the very first newspaper ever printed in China was published in Shanghai — in English. So Peter said. The *North China Herald*, produced by European missionaries, debuted in 1850. A Chinese-language newspaper, a translation of the *Herald*, didn't appear until 1861. The *Herald*, renamed the *North China Daily News* in 1864, lasted 101 years, until 1951. It survived the communist revolution, only to succumb to the Korean War.

The media were changing greatly here, Peter told me.

"Newspapers used to be the mouthpiece of the Communist Party," Peter said. Illiteracy was widespread in the years after 1949, he said, and those few people with reading ability would read the papers aloud. That's how the common man learned what the party wanted him to know.

"It's a different philosophy of journalism," Peter said. "In China, the media exist as an arm of the government, whereas in the West, the media are seen as a counterbalance to the government.

"There are many ways," he continued, "in which a Westerner would be dissatisfied with the degree of information in the media here."

Take the time, a while ago, when a vice premier died in office. The funeral was a big national story. It so happened that the man had also been a powerful official in Shanghai, so the story was especially big here. The state-run Xinhua news agency released one, and only one, photo of the funeral that every newspaper in the country was supposed to run. It showed the Chinese president shaking hands with the widow — only, the caption said that the president, who was named, was shaking hands with "one of the relatives of the deceased." No name. Not even a mention that she was the widow.

The *Shanghai Daily* called Xinhua for more information, but instead of a hard confirmation, all they got was a warning: "You can run the widow's name, but it will be your responsibility."

Peter took the risk. Actually, he said, he wasn't too worried. He knew the information was true and he could argue that he was editing for foreigners. He had his answers ready if anyone demanded an explanation. But no one did. The paper got away with it — stretching the boundaries of permitted information a little bit wider.

This happened many times. Peter was proud to tell me that *Shanghai Daily* was the only newspaper in China whose front page on Sept. 12, 2001, showed pictures of Manhattan's twin towers burning. The headline screamed, in a towering font, "US Attacked!" The *China Daily*, like every other newspaper in the country, led with a Xinhua-issued photo of a national athletics event, the terrorist attacks on the U.S. relegated to small boxes down the page or inside.

Peter had met with a government official beforehand and told him what he intended to do. "I am not going to look silly, not having that on the front page," he said. "This is an historic event." He knew America had never been attacked on its own soil before (Pearl Harbor was U.S. territory in 1941, not part of a state).

"We made you the editor because we trust you," the official told him, asking for just one concession, that the entire page not be devoted to the attacks. So stretching across the bottom of the page otherwise devoted entirely to the screaming headline and a photo of the towers and the gray-black smoke — a page still displayed prominently on a wall in the newspaper's conference room — was a compensatory, ho-hum item about China.

Shanghai Daily developed a reputation for offering more real news than most Chinese media, partly because it was geared toward foreigners who wouldn't buy a propaganda sheet and partly because the English in which it was written was beyond the ken of most censors. *Shanghai Daily* helped push other Chinese newspapers to be more modern, Peter said — for instance, by being the first to use color.

Contrary to my impressions, there was no in-house censor, Peter said. The local propaganda office would know that an uncomfortable story was coming because the topic was already in the news or reporters had been asking a government office for an interview. When the censors wanted to put a stop to a story, they'd make a rash of phone calls or send a blast email to the city's editors.

But it was a murky process. Editors never knew the exact line that defined what was permissible to print and what wasn't. Nor did they know the punishment for crossing it. It was a useful vagueness. Left to guess what the government might not like, most editors tended to be extra cautious. The government had a powerful censoring effect simply by getting into editors' minds this way. No doubt Chinese journalists played many stories softer than they had to, because they could never know when the government would stomp its foot.

Except for JJ, all the editors at the *Shanghai Daily* were picked by the government. The paper was owned not by the state directly but by a company called Wenhui Xinmin, which published two or three other newspapers in Shanghai in Chinese. JJ always referred to Wenhui Xinmin as a private company and noted that the *Daily* had to earn revenues through advertising and subscriptions. Many people at the paper believed it was a state-owned company, but no one was entirely sure. In the absence of hard evidence, we looked for the circumstantial. The company cafeteria was government-subsidized. And Bernie, my fellow polisher, a savvy Australian, pointed to a loutish man who often accosted us foreigners just outside the office doors as we were coming in to work, asking us to edit his compositions in English — childish two-page stories about meeting beautiful women on tropical islands and wishing he could touch their beautiful long hair.

"The only reason a guy like that can be here is because the government insists on hiring a quota of the handicapped," Bernie said. "No way he'd be here if this was really a private company."

Who owned, truly owned, the *Shanghai Daily*? It was the most basic of questions, and in this opaque society I was never sure of the answer.

As proud as Peter was of the newspaper, he knew it fell short in many ways. He knew that his reporting staff needed more training. They were young and smart, "but they don't think," he said.

"They don't choose good ledes," he told me one day over a coffee in the lobby shop. "They're not selective. They spend too much time writing or thinking about what to write, instead of boiling it down to a simple sentence, like you'd use to tell your best friend what just happened."

He couldn't use the more experienced, foreign members of the staff for reporting because the government wouldn't allow him to. It wouldn't countenance non-Chinese snooping around official offices, prying for information. Peter could assign us foreign experts to write features or business stories, but to cover city or national offices would be out of the question. And even if one of us did receive a hard-news metro beat, we'd be competing against Chinese-language papers whose reporters, in some cases, had held the beat for a decade or more.

"The only way to improve the paper," he told me, "is to improve the staff we've got."

He asked if I'd help him do that. Would I make it a priority to undertake more staff training?

Of course, I told him. For starters, how about we make the reporters stick around while I was editing their pieces? Their habit was to leave the office as soon as they turned their stories in. I was reduced to calling them when they were on the subway to clear up all the confusing sentences they'd left me to read. My idea was, if they knew they had to be edited before their day ended, they'd start handing in their stories earlier, making them more efficient, and they'd see the reasons that we editors were making the changes we made, giving them the opportunity to learn. Peter agreed, but if we couldn't institute that reform, at the least I should sit down with reporters the next day to talk about the reasons for specific edits and rewrites. This itself would be a huge change. Incredibly, few reporters seemed even to read the edited copy when it appeared in the finished newspaper. No wonder they kept making the same writing mistakes again and again. I suggested writing a list of common errors and how to avoid them. Peter liked that idea. And he asked me to lecture to the staff from time to time.

I wrote that guide. A copy went to every staff member. But I never saw anyone ever pull it out and use it. I gave a lecture, comparing American and Chinese press practices, and I had a roomful of attentive listeners. But the idea of reporters sitting at my side while their stories were edited, or even huddling with them after the stories were published, never became part of the routine. I'd work with reporters in that close manner only rarely, almost always with the same couple of particularly ambitious young ones.

This turned out to be one of the themes of life at *Shanghai Daily*. Veteran polishers had warned me. Each of them, it seems, had made useful proposals in past years to improve the reporters' output. Each proposal had been respectfully received, and then quietly ignored.

So it went with mine.

34
'A Joyous Journalists' Party'

I COULDN'T eat the lavish dinner in front of me — not the baked cheese lobster, not the braised sliced abalone with Japanese mushrooms. I could barely touch the baked beef fillet with black pepper sauce, the stewed partridge with fig and almond. Toasts of wine were being offered, but I didn't risk a drink. I was feeling dizzy enough already. My appetite had fled, run off to wherever my confidence had disappeared to.

I asked myself why I'd ever agreed to this: to perform in a little skit at "a joyous journalists' party."

There was nothing little about it.

Ellen, Ben and I were in an enormous ballroom at the Shanghai World

Financial Center, then the third-tallest building in the world, maybe the handsomest skyscraper I've ever seen, a subtly curved triangular tower that seemed to change shape as you circled it, a rhomboid cutout through its top floors giving it the nickname "the can opener building." A dozen round, white-table clothed tables filled the floor space, wedding banquet-style. A enormously long stage stood at the front, dressed end to end in communist red, equipped with a high-tech video backdrop and bathed in professional stage lighting. Four video cameras on dollies were aimed at it. Theater-quality microphones and loudspeakers were magnifying every syllable with a rich velvet clarity.

All the other "journalists" on the program were TV personalities. Extroverts who were used to the camera, the limelight, the attention.

The skit and song I had prepared and rehearsed with El and Ben were scaled for the living room.

I was pretty sure I was going to be sick.

I got up from the table while an opera singer who looked like Paul Robeson was channelling Verdi or Puccini. A performer with actual talent.

An aide waved me toward the direction of the men's room. Then another aide, and another, their hands making the palm-sideways gesture that Chinese people use for pointing. The Shanghai World Financial Center teemed with people whose job was to extend a palm-sideways hand to guide you. From the instant we entered the building's front door, then walked through a corridor to the elevator, and then out the elevator to another corridor, and then further down the corridor to the ballroom entrance, there was a man or woman in uniform with a smile and the sideways palm. The decor was high-corporate wood and gloss. Everything smelled just-built. I felt like royalty. Like Ray Liotta entering the Copa through the VIP kitchen entrance in "Goodfellas."

Nobody ever did this for us in an American skyscraper.

But China was nothing if not wealthy in cheap labor. Even here, in the most modern and beautifully appointed of office buildings, we saw an unreal ratio of useful labor to make-work, proof that an occupation could be found, no matter how minor, for every breathing soul (until age 60, anyhow).

In the sparkling bathroom, I washed my hands and face at the automated tap and gave myself a "you can do it" squint in the mirror.

The face that looked back at me was pale.

THE SHANGHAI Daily always took part in this big party that the city put on before the Chinese New Year for the city's local and foreign journalists. A little presentation of talent, my boss Jiang Jianjun had called it as she ambushed me when I walked into work one day: "Howard, Howard, come here, we have something special we want you to do."

The paper wanted me to perform at a party, she said. I should include Ellen. Ben, too, since he'd be in town by then. We can decide what to do: A song. A few jokes. A game for the audience. Maybe something related to the World Expo.

How perceptive it was of JJ to have spotted my latent stage talent, last seen in "Yellow Feathers," the occasional Palm Beach County journalists' revue. A couple of years ago, I had wowed 'em as Professor Harold Hill, singing a parody of "76 Trombones" to lampoon a big tax giveaway for biotech firms.

Or maybe Sarah, one of the veteran polishers, had it pegged.

"They always pick the new people for this," Sarah told me. "They know the rest of us won't do it."

As JJ propositioned me for stardom, she introduced me to two sharp young women who handled community relations for the newspaper, Michelle Qiao and Lesley Chen. They seemed very anxious about this party.

Michelle asked me to start thinking about what kind of performance we'd put on.

"Maybe a song," I offered. "Ben will be here, and he can play guitar."

Michelle liked that idea.

"And maybe he can say a few words in Mandarin at the start," Michelle said, knowing Ben was studying Chinese in college. "Introduce yourselves, because there will be some people who do not speak English."

She assured me that no matter what we did, people would love it. They'd love that we were here in Shanghai as a family: the journalist, the teacher, the student.

"Just be who you are," Michelle said, "a charismatic, happy, harmonious family."

Sounds great, I told her. We'd think about it.

Ten minutes later, Lesley was back at my desk. She had her pen and a notebook out, like a waitress ready to take my order. She was a woman with a job to do — nail down the entertainment — and was determined to nail it as soon as possible.

"So," she asked, "do you know what your skit will be?"

"JUST DO the kind of entertainment you would do at a joyous journalists' party," Michelle had said.

But that couldn't be right. In the States, our idea of a journalists' party was skits and sketches to mock the political hacks, buffoons and powerhouses we were forced to cover seriously the rest of the year. An occasion for satire.

No, the political leaders of China would not put up with needling from reporters or anyone else. Any entertainment from us would have to be kind and gentle.

The entire event was just the opposite of a parody night put on by an American journalists' group, like the Gridiron dinner. Here the government was the host — playing up the conceit of being the press's friend and fatherly guide. The journalist "colleagues" were the honored guests.

As told by the Information Office of Shanghai Municipality, we were all working together — newspapers and government, journalist and bureaucrat — to convey the amazing story of the growth of Shanghai. Or as the Information Office's website put it, "to showcase the glamour of the Oriental metropolis of Shanghai to the world."

And to celebrate that partnership, the information office held this annual party — in a party-like atmosphere such as only the Party could devise.

I hated caving in to this political fiction, but I had to say yes. It was a matter of face for our company: our editor in chief, Peter, was also a major executive in the Information Office of Shanghai Municipality. He was a journalist and a city publicist at the same time, a dual role that captured the contradictions of the little journalists' party itself.

So I came up with a cute and harmless idea: a skit tied to the overall theme of the upcoming Expo.

I took the old, funny country song, "I've Been Everywhere" ("Reno, Chicago, Fargo, Minnesota / Buffalo, Toronto, Winslow, Sarasota...," sung as fast as a mouth can move) and applied it to the dozens of countries putting on exhibits.

El would play a *Shanghai Daily* reporter at the Expo, and I'd play the tourist. She'd ask whether I'd seen much of the Expo, and I'd reply that I'd seen the pavilions of absolutely every country. In song: "Samoa, Togo, Congo, Burkina Faso / Belgium, Bangladesh, Luxembourg and Mexico..." Ben would read words of welcome in Mandarin at the start and play guitar when I sang.

Michelle loved the idea, and after she'd received approval from the banquet's organizers, I went to work on the lyrics. When Ben arrived from Beijing, we figured out the music. After a couple of rehearsals and a lot of help from Lesley on Ben's translations, we were set to go.

I was full of confidence and completely casual about the whole thing. Then the day arrived, February 3, 2010, and we were driven by luxury car to the Shanghai World Financial Center. We were ushered into the big ballroom and I saw the huge stage, the theatrical lighting, the array of cameras, the people running around with clipboards and headsets, and I felt the tremble of terror: "Oh my God. This is a big fucking deal."

FIRST CAME speeches.

This must have been a familiar ritual, because the room was completely silent and still, 130 people at banquet tables not even playing with their silverware.

The vice chairman of the Information Office, a pretty woman in sophisticated dress named Wang Jianjun, stood at a lectern behind a bevy of flowers, welcoming us all. The remarks took a long time because she had to pause every few sentences for a translator to put them into English.

The director of the Information Office, a button-down fellow named Song Chao, spoke next, reading a list of his office's accomplishments for the year ("The Information Office gave 23 press conferences and answered 134 questions").

Then we heard from a truly important person: Yang Zhenwu, Minister of the Department of Publicity of the Communist Party of China Shanghai Committee — in other words, the chief government censor for this part of the world. He'd been recently promoted after a high-ranking career at the People's Daily, the government mouthpiece paper in Beijing.

The stilted speechmaking went on for at least half an hour. The basic message to us — reporters and executives from local papers, correspondents from Agence France-Presse, the Wall Street Journal, China National Radio — was that the coming year would be huge for Shanghai, what with the World Expo and the expected 70 million visitors. Luckily, our great friend the Information Office stood ready to guide us in every way possible.

At last, one of the apparatchiks raised a glass of wine and said, "And now let the party begin." Just like that, hubbub arose. At every table, people hoisted toasts, made conversation, shook hands, exchanged business cards.

Waiters swooped in to deliver food with the precision of a marching band at halftime.

A Mongolian band played music.

Then a kids' karate class got on stage to perform martial moves and acrobatics. An English-speaking local TV personality — a guy from South Carolina turned Shanghai TV regular — roamed the room, playing game-show host, his questions all Expo-related. The opera singer performed an aria or two. A team of foreign translators came onstage to enact a prolonged game of telephone in a mixture of languages — a total bore for the audience as the "action" occurred entirely in whispers.

All the while, my stage fright mounted. I wondered if it were possible to collapse from flop sweat before actually getting onstage.

Finally, the Chinese announcers were speaking our names. It was time to go on. I hid my nervousness and climbed up there with El and Ben, who started things off with a recitation in Mandarin. I watched proudly. It was like reliving his bar mitzvah. He was speaking in an ancient language that he'd recently learned, pausing every now and then to explain himself in English, and a big crowd gave him props for making a nice effort.

We went into our skit and then the song. And miracle! Our upbeat tune was the liveliest thing all evening. The audience started clapping at once.

I spotted Mr. Song Chao in the audience with a wide grin on his face, slapping out the beat.

We were a hit. We finished to a wash of applause and climbed down the stage to a swarm of handshakes and congratulations.

"You were the best!" exulted Michelle with obvious relief, "and I say that objectively."

I felt great. I'd hammed it up and been showered in praise. No wonder people go on stage.

And I realized I'd had a one-of-a-kind experience. I'd be able to tell my grandchildren that, once upon a time, I caused a leader of the Chinese Communist Party in Shanghai to break into a smile and clap along to a country and western song.

(photos: Information Office of Shanghai Municipality)

35
Ben, the Intern

BEN ARRIVED, his trip from Florida by way of Beijing a miracle of logistics over college-student disarray, and it was great. He quickly acted at home in the huge, unfamiliar city, jumping on the subways and riding the buses like he knew where he was going. He started an internship at the *Shanghai Daily* his first week, and it turned out to involve a lot more than fetching coffee and practicing his Mandarin with the Chinese staffers. They assigned him to write stories, something he'd never done.

Yet there he went, out with Bob Wang, the reporter on the Expo beat, to a press conference given by the Portuguese government, which wanted to describe all the wonderful things that Portugal was going to show off in its pavilion when the World Expo started on May 1. Ben came back to the office and spent a couple of hours writing a kind of encyclopedia entry about the prospective pavilion. What he wrote was clear, it was accurate, it was complete — but it wasn't a newspaper story.

I told him he needed to do it differently. He needed to choose the most interesting or surprising thing that he'd learned that day, and start off with that. This was news to him; he'd never thought about the necessity of a lede before. While we spoke about the basics of news writing, Bob took Ben's information and turned it into a few publishable paragraphs and bam, the byline Ben-Darrow Goodman appeared in the next day's newspaper.

The following day Ben went out with Bob to the Italy press conference. This time, he did a better job of telling a news story, but he got stuck in generalities. I gave him lesson two: be specific. And then on the third day, he was sent out on his own, to the Russia presentation. Our cub reporter had a few uneasy moments because the press conference was conducted in Russian and Chinese. But he persevered and came up with enough material — and enough specifics — to write a few serviceable, even colorful, paragraphs for the metro pages.

By Ben-Darrow Goodman
Giant strawberries, flowers and trees will feature in the Russia Pavilion to show a comfortable city as seen through children's eyes, an official revealed yesterday.

Visitors will travel along the path as if in a fairy tale, said Vladimir Strashko, Russia's commission general for the Expo. Along the way, they will meet giant foods and plants. The path will move through five sections highlighting progress in different areas of Russia's development...

Benny grabbed an empty desk in the corner of the newsroom assigned to the metro staff, the lone Caucasian in a cluster of young Chinese who were folded into computer cubicles, many with pots of tea on their desks, along with vaporizers hissing moist air to combat the dryness of China's infernal indoor heating units. He seemed perfectly at ease, making fast friends and accepting invitations to lunch with the group.

Between the English they spoke and the patchy Mandarin he could understand, he got to see his co-workers in ways that most of us Westerners didn't. He found out that most of them, 20-somethings going on 30, lived at home with their parents because they couldn't afford apartments of their own. It would be shameful to marry without the means to support a wife and family, so many young lives were on hold. The conversations could be tricky to follow. Some of the reporters would speak Shanghainese instead of Mandarin — a significantly different tongue — or slide into other dialects when talking to others from the same region.

Ben loved nuances of language, and even as he spoke to the others about shared interests — bands, movies, TV shows, video games — he could see that his new peers were grounded in a very different culture. One of the reporters, he noticed, would never speak in Shanghainese with the man who was his immediate editor, though they were the same age and contemporaries in every respect; the hierarchy had to be observed, even at lunchtime, and this included the speaking of the more formal Mandarin. If they had been of equal rank in the company, they probably would have relaxed and spoken Shanghainese between the two of them.

One day Ben started thumbing through a book that had been left on his otherwise empty desk. It was a mimeographed version of The Elements of Style, by William Strunk, Jr., and E.B. White. In one of those small-world coincidences, it had been left by my predecessor Sue Hill, who in a fit of optimism long ago had placed copies all over the office in hopes that the Chinese reporters would write better English. By coincidence, Sue and I had at different times attended the same grad school, the University of California at Berkeley Graduate School of Journalism, and had been mentored by the same professor, a veteran political reporter named Edwin Bayley, who imparted a reverence for "the little book" to his students. Now, with no prompting from me, Ben was discovering Strunk & White. And loving it as Sue and I had.

"I've always been able to tell when some writing is good and some writing is bad, but this book shows you why that is," Ben said, excited to have unearthed some secret wisdom. "I never knew there was a guide like this."

What Ben was learning was that the great bulk of what he'd learned about writing in high school and college was shit. Strunk & White taught, in a quick 85 pages, that good writing shows, not tells. It's concrete and specific, not vague or wishy-washy. It uses the active voice. It prefers simple words.

He began to take a close interest in how I edited stories, sitting at my elbow as I rewrote and improved a night's worth of copy: why I cut this word out and added that one, why I moved a paragraph up or down. For me, it was a kind of bliss to have my son at my workplace, taking so close an interest in the knowledge that I had acquired over years as a professional, and wanting it for himself. I felt I was connecting with him in some ancient paternal rite, the way hunters passed along the ways of the forest or craftsman conveyed the secrets of the tool bench. And how extremely odd that Ben and I should be making this connection, this delving into the hidden laws of English composition, in China.

The paper sent Ben on more assignments — and we both learned new things about Chinese media. He attended a press conference called by the Spanish Consulate to discuss plans for their country's Expo pavilion (highlight: the outer walls would be covered in baskets) and came back with a few bottles of Spanish wine. Compliments of the consulate.

Another day, he accompanied a reporter covering an actual news story. A group of workers had been denied their pay on the very eve of Chinese New Year. They needed the cash to travel home to celebrate with their families, a holiday obligation. A government ministry had stepped in to save the day with an envelope of money for each worker. Now the ministry wanted to publicize its beneficence. Ben and the *Shanghai Daily* reporter drove to a factory and a government office at the city's outskirts to hear the officials' boasts and talk to some of the workers who were getting set for their holiday journeys.

When he returned to the paper, Ben held a squat cardboard box filled with three dozen eggs. It was a gift of the Agriculture Ministry. Every reporter had been handed a box just like it.

Taking a gift like this could be a firing offense for a reporter in the United States— assuming any government agency would think of offering it. At the *Philadelphia Inquirer* and *South Florida Sun Sentinel,* reviewers bought their own movie tickets. When taking a newsmaker to lunch, reporters paid for their own meals. The reason: You didn't want the newspaper to be the least bit beholden to people or institutions you wrote about. You didn't want even the appearance of a conflict of interest to cross a reader's mind.

But in China, gift-giving was part of the culture. For many press conferences, business events, auto shows, musical performances or art openings, reporters received *hong bao*, or "taxi money," envelopes of 200 to 600 yuan (about $30 to $100), along with the press release. A story was expected to follow.

The newspaper played the game with enthusiasm. In my first days at the paper, JJ told me that while she couldn't pay me better, a few perks were within her power to bestow. Every now and then there'd be free theater tickets, she said. (And in fact, Ellen and I did see a spectacular performance by a touring London symphony orchestra on a pair of these giveaway tickets). And let's say we wanted to fly to Hong Kong or Singapore or Yunnan Province. JJ said to let her know, and the paper could get us a free flight — just by doing the airline the favor of running a small ad for free.

Without any embarrassment, she let us know that the paper was on the take. Which made things just about perfect. Not only was the *Shanghai Daily* subject to censorship from the Communist Party, it also bent to the petty corruptions of capitalism.

The wine? The eggs? They were terrific.

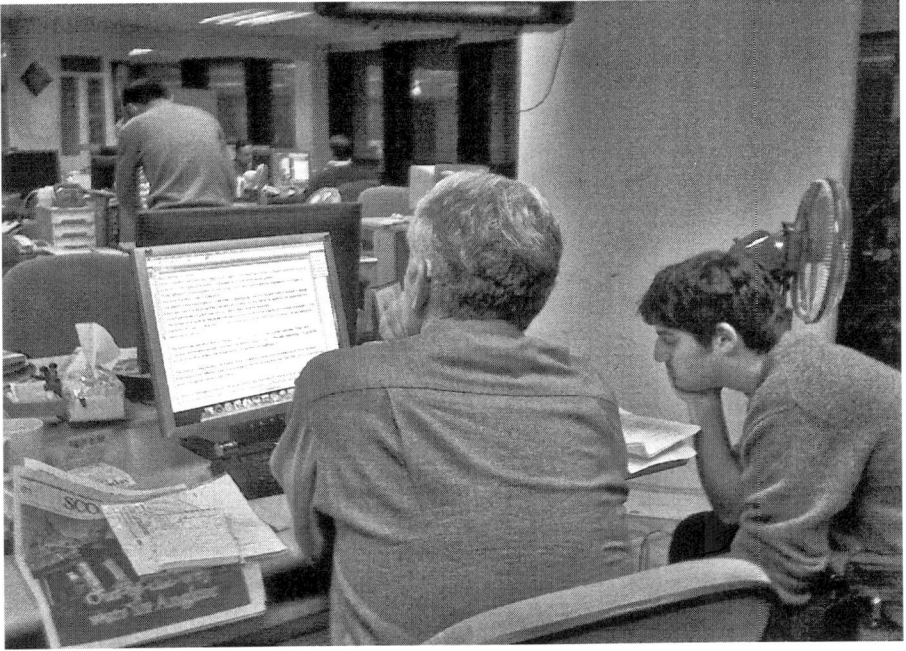

36
Year of the Tiger

A RIOT of noise and color and motion.

Mostly noise.

It was Chinese New Year and the city night was exploding all around us.

The eruption came at midnight, and it was beyond anything we had imagined — the intensity of fireworks going off all over the city, near and far and in between, filling the horizon with brilliant bursts of light and color and then the heavy smoke of gunpowder.

The noise of a million explosions like a single seamless snare-drum roll. Hour after hour.

And a steady rumble, a subwoofer hum, shaking the building like a nervous condition.

We had an incredible vantage point. Our 18th-floor balcony gave us a panorama of a big swath of the city. This was no distant spectacle. Some of our neighbors set off rockets on the driveway just below us, and those babies exploded within reach of our railing. A few hit our glass doors.

This wasn't seeing fireworks — it was being rocked in the middle of them.

Duck! Get back in the house!

Ben stood on the balcony, serenading the crazed noise of the city with his saxophone.

Ellen, out there with him, her face flushed and beaming, was yelling as loudly as she could against the thunder: "Bring it on!"

In the din and the flashing colors, we shook loose all the uneasiness and uncertainties we'd felt since my layoff, as if refuting our foreignness in this strange behemoth of a city, as if declaring our intent to make a brave new life for ourselves.

Fuck it!

Yes!

THE EXCITEMENT of the holiday had been building for weeks.

They call it Spring Festival, and it was like Thanksgiving, Christmas, New Year's and the 4th of July rolled into one folksy, patriotic blow-out.

It was called the world's largest annual human migration, hundreds of millions of people frantically trying to go home to visit their families, most leaving jobs in the big industrial cities to travel long hours to the hinterlands. The railroads alone were expecting to handle 210 million passengers over a five-week period. Imagine two-thirds of all Americans cramming train stations and passenger cars, hoisting suitcases or plastic-wrapped bundles and battling short schedules to get back.

The seven-day Spring Festival was the one essential holiday of the year, and those who didn't go home to see family risked the unthinkable, a loss of face. This time it was Year of the Tiger, and according to the lunar calendar, it fell on Sunday, February 14, same as the Western world's Valentine's Day, which, yes, the Chinese did celebrate — at least the younger people. The *Shanghai Daily* had a good story, asking people whether they were going to celebrate with their families or with their lovers. The answers were studies in agony.

The city quickened as the day approached. Decorations went up everywhere: Red and gold lanterns, good luck signs, fireworks. Many, many cartoon tigers. People cramming candy stores to buy sweets as presents. Holding pre-holiday lunches, dinners, toasts. Hurrying through piles of work they needed to get done before they could leave their jobs for a week. Even the *Shanghai Daily* — the daily newspaper! — would shut down for a few days.

Lunar New Year travelers at Shanghai railway station
(Photo: Shanghai Daily)

THE HOLIDAY arrived, and it was strange. By day the city seemed empty. Streets yawned. You could get a seat on any bus. Everyone had left town to see Granny.

But the fireworks returned every night. Who was even around to set off those thousands of explosions?

NOW IT was the fifth night of Spring Festival, the city erupting once again with color and noise — almost as many fireworks as on the first night. It was amazing, the bursts rising from every distance and at every point on the panorama as we watched from our living room window and balcony.

Imagine the wildest drummers you can think of — Ginger Baker, Keith Moon, Buddy Rich — all soloing at once, going on for hours: smacks, snaps, cracks and booms, unrelenting, blurring into a raucous drone. That was the sound of Chinese New Year in Shanghai.

Ben asked a question that sounded funny, given the all-encompassing sensory experience, the free-for-all of it: Did the municipality sponsor these

195

displays? I saw why he asked. In America that's how we do it. But here, no. The city didn't do fireworks. The sound and light were purely expressions of individual initiative. Any street, any sidewalk, any driveway, any vest-pocket park was a launching pad. Any space above the trees or between buildings was a potential canvas for an erupting ball of red, blue, yellow, white.

A building just in front of ours housed a nightclub — a Chinese-only establishment with a mobster vibe, filling late at night with gangster-looking guys and eye-candy women dripping with noir glamour. Tonight, those folks were shooting off dozens of rockets that exploded over their building, just like everybody else. They were setting them afire right in front of our window.

Boom shocka locka. Boom shocka locka.

We drank it all in. It made us delirious.

We knew we'd be spoiled for fireworks from here on.

The fireworks on Chinese New Year, the eve of Spring Festival, were meant to scare away ghosts that might haunt you, bother you or curse you in the coming year.

The fireworks on the fifth day of Spring Festival were supposed to greet the god of good fortune. This god is particularly partial to noise, lots of noise.

How, I wondered, do the ghosts and the god know which fireworks are meant for whom?

37
Is This an Intervention?

Ellen:
THAT SAME wild night of Chinese New Year, I had to make a difficult phone call home. I had to tell my parents that the time had come for them to have a caregiver.

I hadn't expected this. When I'd agreed to move to China, I thought the toughest part would be leaving my children and grandkids. I didn't realize my biggest concern was going to be my aging parents.

Gertrude and Martin had always been very independent, always in great health. They had travelled extensively, even taking a trip around the world. A photo of my very-short mother standing next to a very-tall Masai tribesman hung in their den, flanked by photos of the Rock of Gibraltar and my father kissing the Blarney Stone. One of their favorite vacations had been an anniversary cruise where they had the ship's captain renew their wedding vows.

They had met as teens in Staten Island and eloped before the Marines sent Marty off to World War II. He could be a hellion and was court martialed twice for battling authority. After the war he began work at the growing electronics giant RCA. Beginning as a TV technician, he worked his way up the corporate ladder to become a company vice president, each step up requiring us to move to a new city, a dozen moves by the time I hit high school. All his life he was meticulous, well-organized, self-confident and keenly proud of his executive abilities. Even on his off-hours, he couldn't help telling us the best way to do everything, from how to shop for an air conditioner to how to pour milk and coffee — the best way, of course, being some method he had discovered.

He left RCA for a second career as a consultant, which left him comfortably retired. He kept himself busy by volunteering, first as a court guardian for troubled teens and later as a mediator for Palm Beach County courts. Mom was a 1950's style housewife in the tradition of "Father Knows Best." She had no ambitions and was happy to sit home, watching TV, waiting for Mart to return. She always left the thinking to him. Even as a child, I knew it was strange that when Dad got transferred to a new city, he chose the house without Mom ever seeing it. He liked taking total control, and that was fine with her.

A few months before Howie and I left for China, Dad's steady, predictable behavior started to slip. He began shopping extravagantly: buying Mom very expensive jewelry, getting a brand-new red Cadillac despite owning a Cadillac that was only two years old. When he told me he had paid the sticker price in the spring of 2009, when the bankrupt GM was desperate for any sales, I knew he was not in his right mind.

Mom had been seeing a neurologist for quite some time for her memory. He'd given her a prescription for Aricept to help slow her loss of recall. When Dad asked me to join him on a visit to see the doctor I was happy to tag along, thinking we were going there for my mother. I was shocked to find that this was a follow-up appointment for him. Concerned about his own memory slipping, he had seen the doctor six months earlier. Dad too had been prescribed Aricept, but hadn't filled the prescription. I sat with him while he struggled through the tests. After the testing, he was given a brain scan. The diagnosis was Alzheimer's.

I wasn't surprised by the diagnosis after having seen, in one of the tests, that Dad was unable to draw a picture of a clock.

That was his last visit to the neurologist. He refused further treatment because he didn't like the psychologist who had performed the tests. This was pure Marty. He often changed doctors if he perceived an insult or felt in any way embarrassed. And it didn't take much to set him off. He could be extremely stubborn and ornery, even violent. Family legend tells of times he lashed out verbally and physically to relatives he felt had crossed him. He had an unpredictable temper. We were all terrified of it.

I was devastated by Dad's diagnosis, but what could I do? I had already agreed to go to China and I knew it was the best thing for Howie and me.

I tried to think of all the things that would need doing while I was away. Dad, such a meticulous bookkeeper for so long, would no longer be able to handle the family finances, so I arranged for their bills to be paid automatically. My brother Scott and I went to my parents' lawyer and made sure the attorney would help them with legal matters while I was away.

Man plans, God laughs, as the saying goes. And in this case, our plans unraveled fast.

Less than three months into our move to Shanghai, I got an anxious email from our daughter Rachel. She said she had just come back from visiting my parents and things at their home were not as they should have been. She was especially concerned that they weren't taking their pills properly.

> Dear Mom,
>
> I had a conversation with Grandma today trying to figure out if they were available for a visit tomorrow and she was completely confused.I am now emotionally exhausted from the experience so I don't really have the energy to write a perfectly articulate email to you about the matter but basically it's this:
>
> Grandma and Grandpa have declined to the point that they need more than just me popping in every 7-9 days. It's just not enough and it's not fair to them or to me. They are really not competent to be the ones to tell you that they don't need help. The choice must be taken out of their hands.
>
> I do agree that in a sense this is not my place as the Grandchild, but I don't see a choice until someone else steps up to the plate.

We needed a nurse, a caregiver, a something. I'd known this would happen eventually, but not this quickly. Suddenly it was time to tap into Mom and Dad's long-term care health plan from Genworth, the mega-insurance company they'd been paying into for years. They had been very proud that they'd thought ahead to take out this type of coverage when they were fairly young. They'd felt so strongly about it that they insisted that Howie and I get policies, too, so "we would not become burdens on our children."

I called Scott from Shanghai and asked him to find out how to initiate a claim for home health care. Scott called back with news of a catastrophe. He had spoken to Genworth and they told him my parents no longer had a long term health plan.

"There must be a mistake," I stammered.

I quickly called Genworth. A woman said Mr. and Mrs. Rubin no longer had a policy. It had been cancelled in October.

According to her notes, Genworth had called my father to ask if he wanted more insurance, and he told them no. In fact, he didn't want or need any insurance. He was going to live forever, he announced. Well, that's fine, Mr. Rubin, Genworth said, we'll just cancel your long-term health plan and how about we refund your latest premium balance — $2,000? We learned that both parents signed and cashed the check. Dad was thrilled; he thought he'd made money off the big, bad insurer. And as far as Genworth was concerned that was it. If we wanted to get the policy reinstated we were going to have a long fight ahead of us.

That sickening feeling was my sense of security being completely pulled out from under me. How were we going to afford the help Gert and Marty needed without that policy? First Howie loses his job while we have a kid in college, we have no health insurance of our own, and now this. I had always figured that if things got really bad financially, I would be helped by my parents. Now it was looking like Scott and I were going to have to be the ones to support them. How the heck was that going to happen? I didn't know the answer, but I knew something had to be done quickly. With or without insurance, my parents needed help.

On Chinese New Year, with all of Shanghai celebrating, I was torn between the exhilaration of the moment and my obligations to my family back home. I dreaded the thought of telling my parents that the time had come for them to have a caregiver. Would they accept it or put up a fight?

The phone call went surprisingly well. Luckily, Dad didn't come to the phone as he usually did. And Mom, after a slight hesitation, agreed that some small form of assistance might be needed.

So we got an assistant. Amy came to the house once a week to aid with Gert and Marty's medications, doctor appointments and family finances. I felt so relieved. Now, I hoped, I could fully enjoy living in Shanghai with my parents taken care of, the burden lifted from Rachel.

My relief was short-lived. Amy soon started to tell us about other concerns she had. The most urgent was that Marty was still driving. Dangerously.

I thought it best to tackle this in person. With Ben in Shanghai, I felt it would be all right to leave Howie and make a trip back home for a visit. I wanted to meet Amy, see how my parents were doing, and try to mend fences with Rachel.

My daughter was very angry about our leaving. Phone call after phone call, she had plenty to say about how I'd abandoned her to look after my parents — an accusation I rejected — yet had no interest in anything we were doing in China. I just hoped it would get better.

The trip turned out to be exhausting. It took 24 hours to get from my apartment in Shanghai to Rachel's guest room in Florida. I hadn't considered how debilitating the jet lag would be. My body made the trip in a day, but my mind, like lost luggage, didn't arrive.

It was a joy seeing my family, hugging my grandchildren, visiting friends, but I walked around in a fog. Conversation was difficult and decision-making nearly impossible. Still, my parents and Rachel were overjoyed that I'd come. I realized that frequent visits were the only thing that might keep the family on an even keel, and I promised everyone that I would see them every three months, jet lag be damned.

I kept that promise. Over the next few months, I traveled so frequently that Continental Airline deemed me platinum status, allowing me into the exalted atmosphere of the VIP lounge and, on one glorious trip, upgrading me to first class. Hopping halfway across the planet was becoming my routine.

But not even the frequent visits put an end to the family crises. How do you get your father, a stubborn ex-Marine with a wicked temper, to stop driving when you can see that what he is doing is unsafe but he cannot? At this stage of the disease, Marty was acting like an angry teenager. Trying to tell him almost anything would precipitate an argument. He'd scream, "I'm going to kick your ass!" Given his history, that was no idle threat.

For months my brother and I vacillated between ignoring the

situation and groping for a feasible plan. If he found out that we had anything to do with his losing his license, we knew there would be hell to pay. Did we really want to risk his not speaking to us? And what would that do to Mom? But what if we didn't act? What if he killed some innocent person because we were too lazy or weak to stop him?

Many of my Shanghai nights — daytime back in the States — were spent talking on Skype with Scott, Rachel, Amy, my father's doctors, the Florida Department of Motor Vehicles.

We managed to get his doctor to send a letter to the DMV stating that he no longer was competent to drive. The DMV, in turn, wrote to my father, saying that if he wanted to keep driving, he'd have to get a doctor to attest that he was competent. Now, his faculties may have been failing, but Marty was still very canny when it came to the rules about keeping his license. He doctor-shopped until he found a guy pliable enough to fill out the necessary form declaring him fit to drive. Fortunately, I was in town then, and met with the doctor. I explained that Dad had run a few stop signs and gotten lost when driving in the neighborhood. I suggested that he reconsider what he wrote, and he agreed. He said he would rewrite the form and I could pick it up the next day. When I went back to pick up the revised copy, the office was closed. I soon found out why — the quack had been arrested for writing phony drug prescriptions. Dad had found a true bottom-feeder.

So I returned to Shanghai with Dad still driving, the problem worsening. Marty behind the wheel was becoming the stuff of legend; people in my parents' high-rise were talking. They'd seen him running a stop sign or parking in restricted zone or leaving the car while the motor was still running. Scott, Rachel, her husband Tal, Amy and I cooked up plans for an intervention. Tal, my hefty son-in-law, would block Dad while somebody else got ahold of the car keys. It was like a football play. At the last minute, Scott and I called it off: we were only going to get one shot at getting the keys and this sounded too risky. We didn't want anyone getting hurt and we needed Amy to remain welcome in the house. We decided to wait for a more opportune time.

I wish I could say that all our hard work and planning paid off, but that isn't what happened. Stubbornness was what finally ended

Dad's driving. He refused to fill a prescription for a urinary tract infection, and landed in the hospital. By the time he was released he was too weak to drive. While I was on one of my trips back to the States, Scott came down from North Carolina and we took Dad's beloved red Cadillac back to the dealer. His hospitalization had another benefit besides ending his driving. It allowed us to get a full-time health-care provider. And now we could afford it. Through Scott's persistence, the Genworth long-term-care policy had been reinstated.

Although my parents were now being looked after, their decline continued. And so did my sense of responsibility. Calls to home got more and more depressing. Dad hardly ever got on the phone and Mom complained of loneliness. She cried and said that she missed me and wanted me to come home. I was racked with guilt. How could I plunge into an adventure in Asia when my happiness caused so much pain?

I felt conflicted, and the feeling never left me.

38
Coughing in Xi'an

Howard:

EVERY VISITOR knows that to see the glory of ancient China, you must go to Xi'an, in the center of the country. We did. The antiquity was incredible. The modernity was unbreathable.

Xi'an is the place from which the emperor Qin Shi Huang unleashed his armies and unified the country of warring kingdoms for the first time, back around 220 BCE. Qin (pronounced Chin) was one of history's pioneers in mass organizations. He divided his realm into 34 units (same as now; the modern People's Republic has 34 provinces, or provincial level divisions). He created a uniform system of axle widths (to simplify road-building) and innovated in a lot of other ways to cement an empire.

Unfortunately, he was also a crazy tyrant. He burned most books and if subjects didn't do things his way, he simply buried them alive.

He's the emperor whose underground remains were "guarded" by the terracotta army, thousands of life-size statues in full battle dress who lay buried and undetected until 1974, when a farmer digging a well found one of the figures. That led to the unearthing of one of the great archeological finds of the 20th century and the founding of a flourishing tourist industry. Qin's court historian left records indicating that 700,000 workers toiled on the tomb, its contents, and the soldiers at its periphery. The tomb itself is still yet to be excavated. It is said to hold incredible treasures for some future archeologist to find — "models of palaces, pavilions and offices as well as fine vessels, precious stones and rarities," the ancient historian wrote.

The Chinese have built a museum around the archeological pits, so you can see many terracotta figures as they were found in shards and pieces, others that restorers were still patching together, and yet others all assembled, standing in serried ranks, 1,000 strong: foot soldiers, cavalrymen, charioteers.

It was mind blowing. In my school textbooks, it was Greece and Rome that produced the artworks of the ancient world that looked convincingly human; the realism was one of the markers by which we moderns held these civilizations to be advanced. But ancient Chinese statuary was every bit as realistic. And astonishingly prolific. The thousand soldiers on display were just a vanguard. Another 6,000 were yet to be pieced together and restored. The work would take years because the statues originally had been colored in a kind of paint — paint! Now the colors vanish as soon as an unearthed statue is exposed to the air; scientists were trying to figure out how to excavate the still-buried while preserving their hues.

Each of three main pits was surrounded by walls, roofs and climate control. We had a guide named Jenny, who spoke good English and for 100 yuan ($14.60) spent more than three hours with us, explaining it all. First we saw a 360-degree movie that put us back in the time of Qin and explained how the warriors were made. Then we went to the three sites, each a little different from the other because the army was arranged with the martial logic of their era: foot soldiers over here, horsemen over there, support staff somewhere else.

When we were done, Jenny walked us through a lengthy mall of souvenir shops and food stands — a whole economy in the middle of former farmland, based on clay statues buried two millennia ago; terracotta-soldier candies, terracotta-soldier chess pieces, terracotta-soldier playing cards. No one was shy about the marketing of the terracotta soldiers. On our way out of town we saw small buildings with models of the soldiers in front of them, looking like suburban lawn ornaments, the buildings with names like "Xi'an Cultural Terra Cotta Duplication Factory." No question about it, Emperor Qin and his legions did achieve a form of immortality.

Before we left the site, Jenny led us through the Terra Cotta Soldier Jade Factory and Store — jade being plentiful in the nearby Black Horse Mountains, its presence one of the reasons Qin liked the idea of spending his eternity here. A store clerk gave us a well-practiced spiel on telling good jade from the so-so, the so-so from the out-and-out fake. I listened with the polite resistance I'd last used on an Orlando time-share sales team.

Ellen, though, got the real sales pressure.

Let her tell it:

"After about 10 minutes I was ready to leave, and that's when the salesgirl really tried to put on the pressure for me to buy something. She explained to me that her manager would want a reason why she had not been able to complete a sale 'after spending so much time with you.'"

The Realtor in her knew how to handle this.

"I told her that I would be more than happy to speak directly to her manager about it. And that seemed to shock her into ending her pleas.

"All I can say is that watching a sales pitch can be really amusing for a person who is herself in sales."

We extricated ourselves from the clerk — although El did break down and buy a very pretty jade bracelet at another shop. It broke in half only a few months later.

Then we walked through a souvenir store. An immense place, filled with terracotta-soldier take-home goods.

Near the entrance was a table with a large stack of coffee-table books about the soldiers. For 300 yuan ($45) you could get the book, the accompanying CD — and an autograph from the farmer who discovered the first of the figures back in 1974.

The farmer was sitting right there, a slightly pudgy man with jet-black hair who was probably in his 60s, his farming life long since over, now dressed in city clothes and spending his days signing autographs for the world's tourists who come to look at the Eighth Wonder of the World that he had stumbled upon as a peasant in the midst of the struggling days of the Cultural Revolution.

His discovery had created all this: an enormous museum complex, a thriving shopping mall, a surrounding town. I wondered how many times he stopped and smacked himself on the forehead and marveled at the whole damn thing.

The terracotta soldiers were world-famous. But nobody seemed to know about another mass of relics, less than an hour's drive away in a burial site called Han Yanling. It was a smaller site than Qin's but perhaps even more astounding. Here were figures surrounding the tomb of an emperor who ruled about 100 years after Qin, named Jingdi, of the Western Han dynasty. Unlike the hard-ass Qin, Jingdi believed, as his deceased father had, in the new Taoist thinking: You didn't make war on your enemies, you pacified them with diplomacy. You didn't overly torture wrong-doers. You didn't crush your subjects with taxes. These policies brought peace and prosperity, but Jingdi is not to be confused with a hippie. Archeologists recently found a graveyard for 10,000 mausoleum builders in Han Yanling. Jingdi, apparently, took the same view of employee relations as Qin Shi Huang did, murdering the help to keep his tomb a secret.

But whereas Qin's tomb was peopled entirely by terracotta soldiers, Jingdi's was populated by terracotta musicians, women on horseback, women with parasols, eunuchs, livestock ... a society engaged in lots of things besides warfare. A society with elaborate court protocols and complex agricultural life.

The figures were the size of dolls — lifelike dolls with expressive faces, instantly relatable.

We saw them first in a museum, where thousands of pieced-together figures were displayed in glass cases. Then we drove a short way to the underground site where archeologists were extracting more of them from pits. We walked over these pits on a glass floor, looking below our feet at the ancient things. It was amazing.

Outside, the air was thick and hazy, and over the flat farmland we saw mounds of other burial sites — hundreds of years old, no doubt, for many other emperors had made Xi'an their capital besides Qin Shi Huang and Jingdi.

And we saw the blurred tops of cooling towers of Xi'an coal-fire plants. We could not miss them, nor the airborne shit they produced.

The air in Xi'an was terrible. It was gray and granular and it had an acrid smell, like a combination of a spice and a metal. On the first night of our stay, I woke up in the middle of the night with tightness in my lungs, a stabbing in my lower back, soreness in the back of the throat.

My eyes were red. I had trouble falling back asleep.

After that, I wore a surgical mask whenever I was in the city, for the first time since arriving in China. Ellen and Ben did, too. Almost nobody else on the street had one one; masks were rarer than bike helmets. The locals rode their bicycles, did their morning tai chi, and ate the street food with complete unconcern for the exhaust spraying up from the avenues and the gray-brown blanket that hung overhead like the curtain over a stage. Maybe our family had a certain allergy that made us especially susceptible to the pollutants, because I couldn't fathom how the average person in Xi'an was able to breathe — let alone smoke at the same time.

Xi'an did show signs of former glories. The old city was surrounded by a tall brick wall, some 600 years old, that makes a perfect square, 8 1/2 miles in perimeter. There are huge old Buddhist pagodas and public buildings, and a Muslim mosque whose construction began only about 100 years after Mohammed started the religion. In those days Xi'an was the Chinese terminus of the Silk Road, a place where caravans from the Middle East and the Caucasus came and left their imprints.

Now those remnants of the romantic past were swallowed by modern city streets that showed their wear and tear, cacophonies of traffic, buses bulging with crammed-in passengers.

On the ride in from the airport, we saw row upon row of half-finished apartment buildings, enormous things, 40 stories or so — all in the exact same stage of incompleteness. It was as if all construction in Xi'an were paced by a giant metronome.

And so much construction! In Shanghai, we had gotten used to seeing incomplete buildings, hearing jackhammers, dealing with dust: the city was pushing to look its best for the fast-approaching Expo. But Xi'an was a revelation: Shanghai was by no means unique. Hundreds of miles into central China, the country was in similar eruption. New superhighways, new railroads, new power plants, new apartment blocks, new factories, new shopping centers, new towns.

It all made the air grayer and stinkier — an especially unfortunate blight for Xi'an, a place already sufficiently plagued by annual sandstorms swooping down from the deserts of Mongolia.

All in all, there was a lot about modern Xi'an that we'd sooner avoid. Our tour guide, Jenny, who is from the area, recognized this. She told me she'd studied tourism at university before becoming a guide at the terracotta site. She'd had the government job for five years, and she was proud to say it had once given her the opportunity to take a group to Hainan Island, in the extreme south of China. Something like a Chinese Florida, Hainan was rapidly being developed as a luxury resort destination. It was the most distant place Jenny had ever been, it seems, and it left a deep impression on her.

When she got back home, she told her parents that she intended to earn a lot of money and buy them a house in Hainan, far from the sandstorms and pollution.

Her father wanted none of it. I suppose that every place, no matter how awful an outsider might find it, is someone else's home, cherished and irreplaceable. This was his. He would not leave Xi'an.

His tone
further discussion.

"The emperors," he said with finality, "were here."

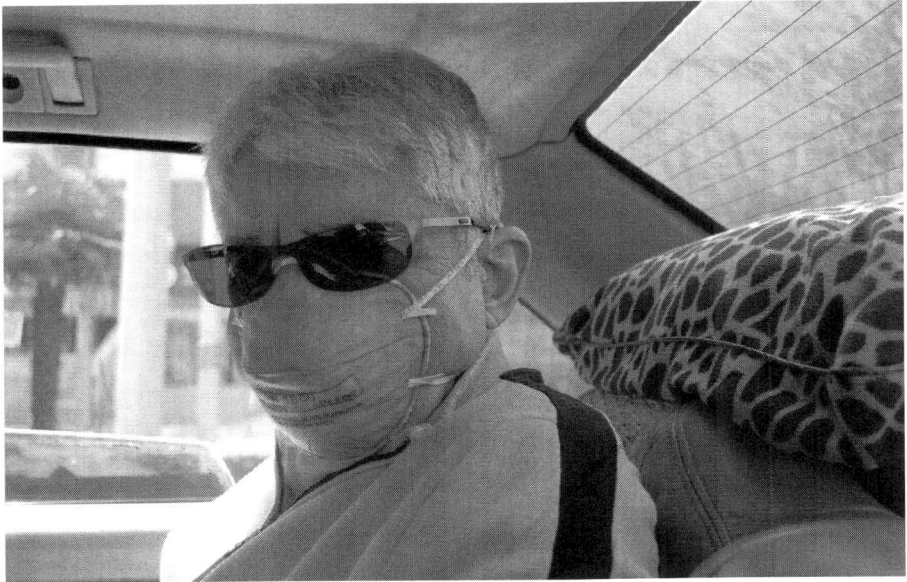

209

39
Crowded at the Top

WE WERE in a speeding car outside Xi'an, wondering how much it would cost for the driver, whom we'd hired for the day trip to see the terracotta warriors, to take us to Hua Shan, a famous mountain peak 60 miles away. We asked Ben, who was in the front seat, to find out.

It turned out to be the a-ha moment when the kid's Mandarin skills acquired a spine.

The business of comparing prices, times, and availabilities caused the halting language student to quit worrying whether he was about to make a mistake in pronunciation or vocabulary, and just barrel ahead and try to make himself understood.

El and I watched from the back seat, happy for him. He was

conversing, actually conversing, with the man whose name, Ben learned, was Han Juin Li, a wiry fellow with a lanky build and extraordinarily long fingernails on his pinkies. These trowel-like nails doubled as tools for ear-cleaning and as status symbols: they declared his liberation from manual labor. Mr. Han also had an avid smoking habit that he graciously kept in check while we paying customers were in his nicely maintained sedan.

He drove like a madman. Which is to say, he drove like everybody else on the road.

As author Peter Hessler put it in his terrific book about China, *Country Driving*:

"People drive the way they walk. They like to move in packs, and they tailgate whenever possible. They rarely use turn signals. Instead they rely on automobile body language: if a car edges to the left, you can guess that he's about to make a turn. And they are brilliant at improvising. They convert sidewalks into passing lanes, and they'll approach a round-about in reverse direction if it seems faster... Drivers rarely check their rear-view mirrors. Windshield wipers are considered a distraction, and so are headlights...

"It's hard to imagine another place where people take such joy in driving so badly."

Our man was fully joyful. He leaned on the horn as if that were the instrument that made the car accelerate. He swerved from lane to lane as if empty asphalt were his enemy. He tailgated at every opportunity, leaving the butt end of the forward car only to pass. He drove onto the right-hand shoulder to pass. He drove into the oncoming car lane to pass — no big deal, except when we were sure we could see the whites of the eyes of the oncoming driver.

Whenever lacking immediate opportunities to pass, he straddled the center line.

"This is like a Disney ride," Ellen said, all gallows humor. "With consequences."

The only time we felt safe was when we all got out for a gasoline stop. Han, suddenly all pious about safety, made us leave the car during fill-ups — probably a good idea, considering how many of the drivers had cigarettes in their hands. Ellen brought up the gas station scene in Hitchcock's "The Birds."

The drive was as endless as it was harrowing, because Han got lost, and rather than consult a map, he stopped every 10 minutes or so to ask directions. We drove for many kilometers on two-lane roads in the Chinese countryside, passing one-story buildings and muddy front yards along the curbless highway, with bricks and other construction materials in stacks along the way, as if waiting for a handyman who was long overdue.

Many residents sat in front of their houses with bottles of soda on little tables, a frenzy of competing lemonade stands. Just a few years ago, these places must have been quiet farmlands. But the automobile — conquering here as it did rural America 100 years ago — was bringing noise and movement and people past rural doors, and there was no sense in sitting idle when you could sit and make a few yuan at the same time.

Some entrepreneur put up his own idea of an irresistible roadside attraction: a pyramid, five or six stores tall, with a sphinx in front of it. Just in case you had the urge, when driving along the outskirts of Xi'an, to see an ersatz Egypt.

It took three hours for Mr. Han to get us to the village at the base of Hua Shan. We wanted to go to this place because we had seen it — or its like — in countless ancient Chinese artworks: cone-shaped rocks softened by horizontal mists and undulating strokes of calligraphy. Peaks amid the clouds, the inspiration for generations of poets, philosophers, religious ascetics.

We boarded a tour bus, which took us up a jostle of hairpin turns to a cable-car station. We stood in line 50 minutes. And then the cable car carried us high, high above an enormous gulch. When we got off, about 5,300 feet up, with much more height to climb, we were at the mountain. But there weren't mountain paths. There were stone steps and concrete walkways. There was a hotel. There were souvenir stands. Up we went, on an enormous outdoor staircase. It's not to say that the experience was entirely domesticated. In many places, the only thing between us and a precipitous drop from a cliff was a metal chain to grab. The steps were sometimes little bites out of a stone wall; you had to walk straight up or down, as on a ladder.

We were three people among hundreds, maybe thousands. This was a wilderness getaway, China-style. It sounds nightmarish — but it was great up there. The air was clear, the sky blue, the peaks glorious. We saw Taoist temples, still in use, and marveled at the determination and lung power it must have taken to build them in the pre-cable-car centuries. We saw Chinese hermits who had the vagabond look of the men on calligraphy scrolls. They might have been enlightened. They might have been crazy.

To get back down, we waited in line for the cable car, a snaking, patient mass of men, women and children way up on a mountain peak that once was a place for solitude and contemplation, and that still exists that way in artworks. It took us an hour and 45 minutes to inch our way to the cable car.

Finally we got on a tour bus for the ride down to the village. We swayed from side to side as the bus hugged the hairpin turns, the road to our right dropping sharply to a rocky brook far below.

Our bus driver, of course, felt compelled to pass the identical tour bus in front of us. A thoroughly pointless maneuver, as we were both going to the same drop-off point. He moved into the oncoming lane and sped up at the same time he was taking a sharp curve and careening downhill. I pressed my foot to the floor in front of my passenger seat, a reflex, willing the damn bus to brake.

The bus arrived safely, one more daily miracle of the Chinese road, and we met up with Mr. Han for the drive back to Xi'an. This time, he managed to find the expressway that he had missed on the trip out — a brand-new plane of beautiful asphalt — but it was night and very dark. Not a street light to be seen. At high speed, Mr. Han tailgated big trucks, and cars behind us came right up to our rear and tailgated us, and —

OH JESUS!

Sorry, but that was close. Mr. Han thought it was a good idea to pass a truck by using the right shoulder, but before he could get past it, the shoulder began to narrow because there was a disabled truck up ahead, and now he was trying to squeeze in front of the moving truck on our left but there was less and less room in our disappearing lane and — omigod! — the driver of the disabled truck, standing in the shoulder, saw us coming at him and jumped up the steps of his cab to scramble inside just in time as Mr. Han pounded his horn and made a quick move to the left and regained the road inches in front of the moving truck. We made it. We had passed another vehicle. We were momentary winners in the never-ending Chinese game of road warrior.

Mr. Han did not pause to savor victory. He simply stepped on the gas some more.

Not quite getting away from it all

40
Isolated

ONE SPRING night, I flagged down a cab on Hengshan Road to get to work.

I got in the front seat and with hand gestures showed the driver the direction I wanted to go.

"Shanxi Lu," I said, pointing my hand to the left, "And Weihai Lu," pointing right.

"Right."

He said it with perfect diction.

I was floored. In all the cabs I had ridden in Shanghai, I had never had a cabbie speak to me in English, other than to say "OK" and "Bye bye." And very rarely had I heard any Chinese correctly pronounce an "r".

"Your English is very good," I said.

He looked at me. "Only a little."

"No, no, you speak very well."

He didn't reply and we drove in silence, weaving with Shanghai taxi-driver recklessness from lane to lane on the upscale avenue lined with 1920s-like apartment buildings. Hengshan Lu always reminded me of Sheridan Road in Chicago.

We had to slow down when the road merged with Changshu Lu. Another cab intruded into our lane in front of us, nearly hitting us. My driver wagged his finger in disapproval. Now the driving was choppy: the street was all bumps and dips, torn up from construction.

"It's a mess," I said, pointing to the road in front of us.

"Expo," the driver said. "Shibohui," he added in Chinese.

"Yes, everything is Expo," I said.

"Where are you from?" he asked me.

"America."

"Ah, America," he smiled and nodded.

This was the longest, fullest conversation I had ever had with a

Shanghai cab driver. I felt like I had broken through some isolation in which I didn't even realize I'd been enveloped. All of a sudden I noticed how little I normally communicated with the environment. When you don't speak the language, being in China is like wearing noise-canceling headphones. You hear the interior dialogs of your own head, but you're deaf to the things people around you are saying and you almost never expect to converse. You're at a remove.

I was so unaccustomed to speaking with a random Chinese man that it didn't even occur to me to ask his name. But I studied his taxi ID card. He was 29815, a short, round-faced man with straight black hair haphazardly framing a large forehead.

We turned onto Yan'an Road, a double-decker street illuminated at night with eerie blue neon lights.

"*Lan se*," I said, trying out my Chinese 101 to take note of the color that now cloaked the cab.

"Blue," 29815 said in his perfect English.

"You really speak very well," I told him again.

He gave me a rueful look and shook his head.

"I like English. I love English. But I have no time to learn."

"Oh, I see. You're always driving."

29815 nodded. Then he said: "Of all the taxi drivers in Shanghai, I am the only one with English."

I wondered how he could possibly know that. Then I wondered how it had happened that I'd stumbled upon his cab. Then I got a strange feeling about being in Shanghai. A feeling of comfort.

I was having this conversation, however basic, and for the moment China felt not nearly as foreign.

But I knew the feeling was going to last only a moment. I envied Ben. He was learning to communicate here, meaning he could feel at home here in ways that I knew I never would.

I wanted to ask him how he'd learned to speak as he did, what he thought of Shanghai, what he thought of America, what his working life was like, but I hesitated. I was afraid my questions would exceed his vocabulary to answer. And by now we were at the destination.

He stopped in front of the newspaper tower. I paid my 16 yuan and opened the door to get out.

"Bye bye," I said. "*Zai jian*."

"Good bye," he replied in the perfectly articulated enunciation one would expect from the only taxi driver in Shanghai with English.

41
Jian the Grocer

Jian, left, in her habitat

Ellen's blog:
HOWIE AND I just cooked the most delicious beef stir-fry thanks to a lady named Jian.

On one of my first strolls down the local market street, Wulumuqi Lu, my Australian friend Jacinta steered me to a small stall filled to the brim with fresh fruits, vegetables and eggs. Unlike every other stall on the street, this one had a wall piled high with items like olive oil, pasta and pine nuts. And a refrigerator filled with imported cheeses, chicken and beef. Foods that wouldn't interest the locals at all.

Jacinta explained that the owner, Jian, was a very savvy business woman who catered to foreigners. She stumbled onto her specialty by asking foreigners if she could peek into their shopping bags to see what they had purchased elsewhere before coming to see her. She'd study the purchases, nod her head, and the next time you went to her shop, you would see the same products. For less!

There must be a dozen produce stalls on Wulumuqi Lu, each about as narrow as a tool shed, the fruits and vegetables tumbling in rows down to the sidewalk, each Chinese apple carefully wrapped in its own soft white webbing. But there's only one that also has Heinz ketchup, Progresso black beans, Kraft parmesan cheese and Hershey's chocolate syrup. We doubt that Jian knows exactly what cooks do with these things, but she stocks them.

Who is this woman, I wondered? She looks to be in her 30s with bright, intelligent eyes and a shock of unruly black hair sticking straight up. There's a weather-beaten look about her, like many of the millions of workers who've migrated from the country for the better opportunities of the city. Although she is not very big, she has very large chapped and calloused hands that show a lifetime of manual labor. Like many country people, she looks to have never been to a dentist and has a mouthful of rotten teeth. Even with that, she's got a great smile. I'm not sure where she's learned her English, but she speaks pretty well. Like many Chinese, she adds an "a" to final consonants. Beef is "beefa."

She has an assistant or two, but they never make small talk with the customers as Jian does or hustle over to make sure that everybody gets some attention. With Jian, there's no such thing as self-service.

I'd been warned that you can get very sick from eating food from the markets, so I started out slowly at Jian's, just buying foods that seemed "safe," like bananas, broccoli and carrots. Each time I went, I saw foreigners filling their baskets and speaking in thick British or French accents about how great the selection, prices and service were. Over time, I got braver and bought more and more of our food at Jian's rather than at The Pines, the local expat grocery with expat prices.

In January I saw that Jian's store was boarded up. I feared that

219

she was going out of business or moving to another location. Turns out that she was *expanding*, doubling the size of her store. Her business was booming.

My Mandarin-fluent American friend, Amanda enjoys talking with Jian. The other day we visited Jian's store and asked her why she had two different baskets of eggs. "Cage-a, No cage-a" was her answer. Then in Mandarin she asked Amanda how she should say it. Now when Jian is asked about the two baskets, she proudly says "Free range-a eggs." She is such a quick study. I envy her ability to learn new words so quickly.

On Sunday night Howie and I strolled up Wulumuqi Lu after going out to dinner. It was almost 9 o'clock and most of the vendors had closed for the day. Not Jian.

On the spot, we planned a stir-fry dinner and bought all the ingredients. Jian looked tired.

"You work very hard," I said.

She smiled brightly, put her hand on her hip. and proudly explained that her days start at five and she works EVERY day until nine. In the entire time I've been here, she's only closed the store for three days. That was during Chinese New Year. Most of that time was spent on a train going back and forth to visit her family in a distant province.

As always when she saw us pausing on the sidewalk to look at her produce, she came over and put a plastic basket in our hands, a smart merchandiser's move to get us to fill it up. We put in a green pepper, some apples, Chinese greens. When she heard us mention cheese, she waved us over to her refrigerator case and pointed to a big wheel of cheese.

"Gouda," she said. This time the final "a" sound was phonetically correct.

We bought a pie-slice worth. The whole basket came to about 36 yuan: $5. Half the price was for the cheese.

As we were finishing paying, I remembered needing something else.

"Ah, cilantro!" I said.

Jian scurried back to the refrigerator, pulled out a big bunch of cilantro, separated about a third of it and stuck it in our grocery bag.

No charge.

42
Quiet Happiness Road

Howard:

I COULDN'T tell you the day that I realized that I loved Shanghai. No single special event jumped out. It was the whole of it, the panorama, that got me.

I walked out the lobby of our apartment building. It was a cold day, so naturally the front doors had been left wide open, because what else do the Chinese do in winter but let the frigid air blast the inside of the house? I waved goodbye to the doorman. Then to the door woman. Then to Mr. Chou, the handyman. Then to another guy who was always hanging around, acting official and barking at any car that rolled into the front driveway and blocked the door. He was a handsome fellow, with the chiseled looks of a Chinese Jack Palance. Vain, too. I once ran into him at the barber's, getting his hair dyed in a new coat of shoe-polish black.

This same cast of characters hung around our front door at all hours in one combination or another, lives spent lingering in our lobby and guardhouse.

I waved hello, and they waved and smiled back.

They didn't speak English and I couldn't say much more in Mandarin than to greet "*Ni hao*." Ellen and I knew they were well aware of us, virtually the only Caucasians in the building. (We heard there was one other American, but we never saw him.) We seemed to be amusing curiosities. When a package arrived for us, that was a big event — much waving of the arms and nodding of the head and rushes of words we couldn't understand, but we would catch the gist, and walk over to the front desk. The doorman looked so happy when we picked the package up, as if he or she had consummated a crucial international transaction. We smiled and nodded, too, grateful they were looking out for us.

Past the door brigade, I was on the street, Anfu Lu, taking in the sights.

A pair of urban hipsters was walking toward me. They had just left the theater in the next-door building. A young man in a suit glided by on a bicycle. A pack of parents waited for children to emerge from the elementary school down the street, and tour buses — enlisted as school buses each afternoon around 3 — were parked in a long line waiting to fill up with kids going home. A delivery man rode by on his bicycle, an enormous wall of boxes piled on the bike's rear, high over his head. A motorcyclist zipped the wrong way down the one-way street. A woman walked her dogs, each fussed-over pooch in another silly outfit.

Anfu Lu was like a street in Manhattan or Georgetown, except that it was in China, which made it as strange as it was familiar. Our block was a long one, at least as long as the blocks between avenues in Manhattan, and it was a parade of dissimilarities. We had a little CD store through whose wall-size windows I almost never saw a customer (and which would go under after a few months, replaced by an even more mysteriously patronless clothing shop); a barber shop where I got a quite credible haircut for U.S. $1.50; our dry cleaner, a man and wife who were at work over their ironing board until long into the night in a shop that was open to the street in all weather; a shop for UGGs, the Australian-made wool-lined boots — the smallest stand-alone store I have ever seen, too small to accommodate both customers and stock at the same time, so the customers tried on the boots on the sidewalk, which was genius salesmanship when the weather turned cold and frigid toes instantly warmed up in the boots under consideration.

There was the ornate but ill-heated theater for live plays, where one night we tried to watch a production in Chinese of "Sleuth," but got our money back at intermission when we told the manager and the sheepish young woman director that we couldn't understand the action because the English subtitles were out of synch; a nightclub that opened for business around 10 p.m., wreathed in an aura of big-city sin, as cigarette-flicking valets and costumed usherettes, all fur collars and mesh-stocking legs, lined up at the door waiting for sleek cars to deposit women in sexy dresses and ultra spike heels, eyed by men in suits, dark glasses, and lips pressed with menace; a couple of good coffee shops; two or three expensive wine stores frequented by foreigners; a good wood-fired pizza place; two convenience stores where, besides buying our milk, Coca Cola and Dove bars, we could pay our water, electricity and phone bills; an amazing regional restaurant where English was scarce and the buttery fish in the boiling pot came covered in hundreds of chilis and the chicken was deliciously smoked in bamboo thatch envelopes.

And opening onto the street were mysterious lanes and doorways that led to snaking alleyways and rough apartments, each an indigenous world of its own — an old, old China we knew we'd never penetrate.

Workmen were busy on the street at least 12 hours a day, rehabbing buildings, repaving sidewalks. Always by hand. Even through the weekends.

"Anfu Lu" means something like "Quiet Happiness Road" and that's just what it was to us. The busy, exhaust-filled city was only a few blocks away, but our street was a refuge from the cacophony; trees shaded the street and the pace was calm. But the street is full of life.

Jane Jacobs, the great advocate for lively cities, who decried zoning laws and urban renewal and who extolled dense, diverse, unique neighborhoods such as the Greenwich Village of the late '50s, would have been right at home here. I never before lived anywhere which so closely matched her ideal.

Behind one old wrought-iron gate stood a particularly beautiful old villa, surrounded by a stately lawn and ringed arrangements of flowers. It was now the home of an American education enterprise, and when El went over to introduce herself in hopes of a job, she learned that the property had been the home of the mayor of Shanghai before the 1949 communist revolution. Ever since, our neighborhood was one of the very few sections of the city to be spared the relentless tearing-down of old lanes and houses and the putting-up of cookie-cutter residential high-rises.

Later, we fell into conversation with a young Australian guy who had been in Shanghai awhile. "Anfu Lu," he said, "is the best street in China."

We believed it. The mayor wouldn't have lived just anywhere.

ELLEN MADE a whirlwind trip to the States for a few days to take care of some family business. She brought back a copy of the *Sun Sentinel*.

"Jobless Rate At 35-Year High," the front page blared.

Florida's unemployment had hit 11.9 percent for January 2010, much higher than the U.S. rate of 9.7 percent.

The rate for Palm Beach County was worse yet: 12.5 percent.

"Florida has lost 926,100 jobs since 2007," the story said.

This was me. One of those jobless.

On almost the same day, the *Shanghai Daily* led with "China Economic Boom Continues."

"China's economy found yet another gear last month," our story said, "with industrial production, investment, retail sales and trade all on an upward spiral."

One side of the world seemed to be shutting down, the other rising up.

This was why we were in China. We wanted a time-out from the bad times back home.

And we wanted it to last for as long as it could.

43
The Kindness of Strangers

Ellen's blog:
A COUPLE of nights ago my Internet connection stopped connecting.

It was 11:30 at night, and I had just been reading an email Rachel had sent about my father's poor health. I needed to call her on Skype, my computer phone, so I ran across the street with my laptop to a cafe that has Wifi. This is a place Howie and I seldom go to because it is usually smoky and filled with Asian bohemian types. It has a Greenwich Village decor but doesn't encourage a Western clientele.

Even though the door was open, I could see the place was closed. The chairs were stacked on top of the tables and a man was counting out money at the cash register. I asked him if I could possibly use my computer to make a quick call. He told me he was going to be busy for a few more minutes and that I was welcome to come in.

One call led to another. I apologized to the guy and explained that my father was in the hospital. He assured me it was OK to stay longer.

When I finally finished, I thanked him for his kindness. Instead of being irritated that I made him stay late, he smiled and said, "Don't worry about it. I hope your father will be all right."

I started to leave, but he wasn't done.

"I'm going to lock up, but if you want to sit on the steps outside, you can still use our Wifi," he said. "Or you can go to the convenience store next door. They have Wifi. I'll tell them you need it. They'll set you up with a table and chair outside."

No, I told him, I really didn't need that.

But I was overwhelmed once again by the extreme generosity.

225

44
Better City, Better Life

THERE WAS no bigger show than the Expo.

The Chinese meant it to be larger than every other World's Fair in history.

They piled on the superlatives. Their expo hosted the most countries and international organizations (250). It was spread over the largest area (1,305 acres on facing sides of the Huangpu River). It cost the most money (almost $2 billion in operating costs alone). It drew the largest crowd. China predicted that 70 million people would show up over the six-month run, and you could bet they would hit that mark, if they had to bus in millions of school kids or pad the numbers to demolish the existing record of 64 million in Osaka, Japan, in 1970.

Most of the world couldn't care less about World's Fairs, large or small. In the age of global Internet and satellite communications, nations don't need mammoth events to show off new wonders like the telephone (Philadelphia, 1876), ice cream cone (St. Louis, 1904) and television (New York, 1939).　　　But this didn't deter the Chinese leadership, who plastered the country with wall-to-wall advertisements featuring a goofy blue mascot called Haibao and the tag line, "Better City, Better Life." They even sponsored a float in the Pasadena Rose Bowl Parade on New Year's Day 2010 in hopes of stirring up some international interest.

The ploy did not work. The Shanghai Expo attracted few foreign visitors. More than 95 percent of fairgoers were mainland Chinese, many of them hayseeds from the countryside, provincials from smaller cities, folk who had never seen Shanghai.

These folks were as agog at the modernity of their country's financial capital as they were unaware of how to behave in it. We saw old men use their time in queues to pluck their nostril hairs with tweezers. We saw several mothers lift their infant children over litter cans so the kids could pee into them. One supervised her son as he urinated into a fountain.

The Expo authorities posted signs to tell the multitudes how to act while queueing up:

Polite Language and No Noising
Waste Sorting and No Littering
Polite Sharing and No Challenging

But the enthusiasm of these millions was moving. For most people on the mainland, this look at other countries' pavilions was the closest they'd ever get to the outside world. Foreign travel, while less restricted than it used to be under Chinese Communist Party rule, was still in its infancy for the vast Chinese public.

The Expo meant long lines, sore feet, too much walking, too much waiting, too much hot weather, too many sudden rainstorms.

Our friend, Michelle, from the *Shanghai Daily*, told us how much her mother treasured the Expo, regardless. A lively woman in her 60s, Michelle's mom was a career officer in the Chinese air force. To the government, she possessed too much inside knowledge to ever be allowed

— or trusted — to leave China. She'd never get a visa.

"The Expo," Michelle said, "is how my mom is seeing the world."

Of course, the Expo didn't show its visitors what Arabia, India or America were really like. It was no more genuine than Disney's Epcot. It hardly mattered. The hunger for contact with foreigners and foreign cultures was palpable. Ellen and Ben and I were constantly stopped by strangers who used sign language and smiles to ask us to pose for pictures with them. As Caucasians walking around the grounds, we were stared at like the Mickey and Minnie characters at Disney World.

Every country you can think of was at the Expo, and some nations were highly creative about it. Great Britain covered its pavilion in a porcupine-quill sheathing, a modern art statement called "The Seed Cathedral" which announced a Britannia that may no longer rule the waves, but was pretty damn cool. Spain cloaked its outside walls in baskets. The Netherlands, apparently tired of being the lowlands, built high — a curving ramp for showing off quirky artworks that could have been built by Seuss. Japan's pavilion resembled a massive insect. In purple. Denmark hauled the "Little Mermaid" statue from its harbor home in Copenhagen and built an alabaster house for the Chinese to see it in.

The reason for all the effort was obvious. Every country wanted to make nice to China and show why it could be a great trading partner with the great emerging economy.

Every country except the USA.

Congress had passed a law in the 1990s forbidding the use of federal funds for international exhibitions. That left the U.S. with one of the only governments playing no role in World's Fairs. We came close to insulting China by ignoring their Expo. But then a business group with ties to the U.S. Embassy and the Bush Administration rattled the doors of corporations, begging for money and promising dozens of sponsorships.

The result was slapped together: a building that looked like a metallic Best Buy and an exhibition that made America seem like the Land of Lockheed and IBM — forget Lincoln, freedom of speech or human rights. When Secretary of State Hillary Clinton came for a look shortly after the Expo opened, she gave it a review that El, Ben and I have cherished ever since as a model of wan politeness.

Her quote: "It's fine."

Our pavilion made us embarrrassed. As an abdication by government and a branding opportunity for Chevron and GE, it said all too much about where America was at in 2010.

But polls showed that the Chinese liked it. What saved the day was a diverse, enthusiastic group of American 20-somethings who served as hosts and greeted the visitors with a little stage act.

"Hi, I'm Bobby," a guy would say. "And I'm a typical American. You know what that means. I eat hamburgers at every meal!"

Jokes like that. Got laughs every time.

Then came a short film in which a number of American celebrities such as Kobe Bryant said simple things like, "Hello, it's nice to meet you," in Mandarin — mangling the language badly.

Ben, who visited the pavilion without Ellen and me, watched this and cringed. But the Chinese all around him found it hilarious.

In the end, they gave us Americans high marks for friendliness, youthfulness and being multicultural.

The USA did send over some fine entertainers. One night, Ellen took in a performance by New Orleans singer and pianist Harry Connick Jr. Another time, the city of Chicago sent a delegation of blues musicians. That gave me the chance to see an old high school buddy I hadn't seen in years named Barry Dolins, the long-time organizer of the Chicago Blues Festival.

El and Ben and I made seven or eight trips to the Expo, several hours each time, and even then had no hope of seeing everything.

But we did draw some strong impressions:

Most outrageous contrast: North Korea versus South Korea. The North Korea pavilion offered a peek inside the mindset of one of the most closed-off countries in the world. And that mind was absurd. The exhibit's centerpiece was a large, faux-classical fountain circled by statues of frolicking nude bathers — not Asian, but some comically bad rendition of classical Europe.

There must be some kind of law: The more egomaniacal the dictator, the more awful the kitsch.

South Korea, on the other hand, was colorful, youthful, energetic, optimistic, high-tech and bubbling with people. Thanks to Ben, we got the VIP treatment. A friend he'd made at his college in Shanghai, Johnny Cho, about 26, from Seoul, worked as a guide and showed us around. The building was a cheerful collection of boxes and circles bedecked with Korean characters on primary-color tiles. Inside were all kinds of interactive toys and games on the benefits of going green. One wall-size computer screen showed how Seoul had torn down a riverfront expressway and replaced it with a tree-lined riverfront park.

We all left the pavilion thinking, South Korea — what a great place. Who knew?

Gaudiest: Saudi Arabia. The Saudis had set off a diplomatic dust-up by trying to build the largest pavilion at the Expo, an affront to the Chinese. So they built the next-biggest, a humongous thing that looked like Noah's Ark if Noah had had money. On the roof was a big artificial oasis with palm trees. Inside, it might have been the world's largest hotel lobby, all marble and crystal and exquisite carpeting, crowned by the world's largest IMAX projection. In front of the movie, you glided along on a conveyor belt past scenes of gigantic sand dunes, men at Muslim prayer, oil refinery pipes — projected below you, above you, at eye level. At times you felt you were flying.

People by the thousands waited for hours in some of the longest lines of the Expo. We got right in, thanks to another VIP connection of Ben's, again a classmate at his Shanghai college, this one claiming to be a Saudi prince. We didn't quite believe him until Ben called him on his cell phone and handed it to a stern-looking fellow in full, flowing Arab dress, from keffiyeh to sandals. After a few seconds of listening to Ben's friend, the guy stood up a little taller. Then he handed the phone back with an air of respect and ushered us through a velvet rope and up a back elevator.

Despite the royal treatment, we were underwhelmed. We looked at each other when the IMAX movie ended: That was it? We'd seen a lot of money on display, but very little human life.

We had come hoping to learn something about Saudi Arabia. Maybe we had.

Doing the most with less: Israel. A very small pavilion, dwarfed by nearby China and Saudi Arabia. But elegant: it looked like mating sea shells, one of glass, the other stone.

The Israel you met inside was absent all talk of the Promised Land, Palestinians, Zionism, intifadas or the Holocaust. The theme was innovation. A multi-media show told you that this tiny country was the home of stents, high-tech irrigation systems, flash drives, a camera that one swallowed like a pill for medical diagnoses: things China could use.

From our experience, people in China knew very little about Jewish people — and why should they? Lacking a history of hundreds of years of Christian-Jewish conflict, they also lacked the prejudices that darkened Europe for centuries. They didn't obsess about saving Jews' souls, resent

Jews' business success or wonder where Jews hid their horns.

If they thought about us at all, the Chinese respected us. Sometimes for odd reasons.

At my newspaper office, I worked across the desk from a young Shanghai woman named Qing who was as smart as she was pretty. Fluent enough in English to understand our jokes and puns, she was now studying French. She had received two masters degrees in London. Qing was worldly.

One day, I mentioned I would be late to work because I would be attending a Passover seder, explaining that it was a Jewish holiday, and she perked up.

"Jewish!" she said with a huge smile. "I know Jewish!"

You do?

"Yeah, yeah, Jewish!" she said. "'Sex in the City'!"

There it was: 4,000 years of Jewish history, culture, religion, philosophy and anxiety reduced to a plot line about Charlotte, the WASP career woman who couldn't marry the bald, warm-hearted Harry unless she converted to Judaism.

Qing looked at me in a new light after that, as if I were something special.

I met a guide at the Expo pavilion named Mengyao Wang, born in China but raised in Israel and a convert to the Jewish religion. A Mandarin-speaking Israeli, she said most of the Chinese who visited the pavilion had a very positive view of her adopted country. "They think Jews are smart, good at inventing things, good at business."

If you're going to be stereotyped, you could do worse.

Most enticing: Italy. A wall of pasta. An olive tree rising from the floor. Wheat growing down from the ceiling. A red high-heeled shoe, six feet tall. A Ferrari. A custom suit-maker at work in a glass case. A marble model of the Roman Pantheon, in perfect antique symmetry.

Italy looked irresistible.

Best celebration of the simple things of life: New Zealand. You walked through a maze that showed you photos and flooded you with sounds of daily life on the island nation. Commuting to work, going to school, caressing the sheep ... just kidding about the sheep. Finally you found yourself on a rooftop rainforest.

And realized you'd probably feel right home on a visit to New Zealand.

Most overly friendly: Pakistan. We finished a little dinner of halal beef and noodles with flatbread at the pavilion's food stand when Ben excused himself to go to the men's room. While he was in there, a Pakistani employee approached him and handed him his card with his phone number.

Ben scurried back out and said we had to leave right away.

We did.

THE EXPO was bound to leave a big mark on Shanghai, long after the six-month run was over, the 70 million visitors had come and gone, and nearly all the buildings and exhibits had been torn away. The Chinese pavilion, a huge bright-red inverted Asian pyramid, would remain as an art museum and reminder of Expo glory — like Seattle's Space Needle — and so would an enormous state-of-the-art arena that was partly owned by the NBA, which was going to book it for pre-season games for the next 10 or 15 years. The Expo grounds, a former industrial wasteland, would become a new business and residential area, on streets and utility pipes that had been laid with the intention of becoming part of the city grid after the Expo was over. Elsewhere, the city had miles of new subway, tens of thousands of freshly planted trees, a massive improvement of The Bund waterfront.

This Expo was filled with a lot of pious talk about creating a greener planet, and participants indeed made a few gestures in that direction: Some buses ran on electricity or as hybrids. One Chinese province showed off the wonders of indoor hydroponics by creating lush gardens and waterfalls that were almost musical.

Shanghai actually cleared the air during the Expo, moving some factories out of town and imposing restrictions on city driving, much as Beijing had done two years earlier for the Olympics.

The results were dramatic. One day, the *Shanghai Daily* ran an illustrated feature to educate readers about those strange formations they were seeing in the sky. These were clouds, the newspaper explained. Cumulus, cirrus, stratus.

Yet China remained one of the most horribly polluted places on Earth, its factories, coal-fired power plants and throbbing automobile traffic spewing exhaust from Beijing to Guangzhou. Within months, Shanghai's own skies returned to their former gray-brown haze.

"Better City, Better Life" — if not a bad joke, an impossible ideal.

But who could tell what was spinning inside the minds of the millions of people who came to the extravaganza and tasted the foreign foods, gawked at the new technologies, took pride in so many of the world's countries paying tribute to China's new eminence? The Expo site itself was being redeveloped into a "sustainable" office zone with indoor trees, water features, courtyards and hanging gardens; the results would be ready in 2015.

Perhaps we would learn in years to come that a generation of green-energy engineers had been inspired by the red solar cells that encased the Swiss structure, the recycled shingles on the Finnish building, or the water-saving model home in the Shanghai pavilion.

It was easy to get irritated by the Expo. The grounds were too large, the throngs too intense, the machines that were supposed to dispense timed tickets to help you bypass the queues were always on the fritz. By day, it was too hot or too rainy. By night, your feet were sore.

I didn't care. I thought it was grand: All the world's countries, putting all that money and effort into a celebration of creativity. What a great thing for the nations to do.

And how amazing that this was taking place in China, only a few decades ago so mired in poverty and so fenced-off from the world.

That old China sometimes still showed.

To cross the Huangpu River from the one side of the Expo grounds to the other, you could walk across a footbridge, or take a subway built for the purpose, or go the scenic route: by ferry. We took the boat once.

Our ride was preceded by a long wait in an open-sided shelter. We joined a line of hundreds of Chinese in a cheerful stockyards of a holding pen, many of them opening small collapsible chairs and unpacking hand-wrapped snacks; they were experienced at long waits. Operators kept count, and when the number in line reached the next boat's capacity, they would starting herding people into a different pen. So you knew that when the boat landed, everyone in your pen was assured a seat on board. The boat approached and people folded their portable chairs, put away their food, and formed a nice, even queue.

Then the gates opened, and the race was on. The queue instantly dissolved as people ran frantically across the gangway and crammed the entry to the boat. It was a senseless competition to win an already guaranteed spot on a 15-minute ferry ride that was taking every single person to the same place at the same time.

In the city of tomorrow, it seemed that yesterday's mindset still held. Generations of Chinese had grown up with scarcity. They had learned from their parents or their own hard experience that unless you cut corners, or drew a favor from a party official, or ran ahead of your neighbor, you might very well go hungry.

This, too, was on display at the Expo.

45
Shanghai Folk-Rock United

Ellen's blog:
BEN IS really thriving in this city. Just turned 20, he's growing up fast. He's living in a dormitory at East China Normal University, about 15 minutes from us by cab, studying Mandarin and making pocket money teaching English.

He's making friends with people from all over the world: Saudi Arabia, Korea, Kazakhstan, Sweden, England, Japan, and Portland, Oregon. In this low-crime city, they hop cabs to jazz bars, music clubs and other late-night places, embracing big reaches of Shanghai like it was their hometown.

He's writing and playing music on his guitar, and last Friday I went to hear him perform at a small local club. He was one of four musicians playing that night — two Americans, two Chinese.

I arrived a few minutes before he was scheduled to open the show and was warmly greeted by Liu Jian, the organizer of the evening's performance. (Howie couldn't attend. He was working, poor guy.)

We had met Liu at — of all places — a seder. My friend Jackie hosted about 15 people with Jewish connections to celebrate Passover. Among them was Rebecca Kanthor, a young American living in Shanghai and doing reports for CNN.com. Liu, 32, is her boyfriend. He speaks no English, but he plays guitar and has written two novels and published one, about his experiences in the Chinese army. Ben and Liu made a quick connection that evening at the seder and agreed to get together to play music.

Liu is a go-getter, and puts together shows, asking musicians to take part in programs and finding a bar where he can stage them. It didn't take long for him to ask Ben to be a part of one of his programs.

They made a good pair. Although Liu writes his songs in Chinese and Ben writes in English, their subject matter is often similar, both writing about the city and how it affects the people who live here.

Liu opened the show by saying it was a special night, with Ben Goodman's mama in the audience. Then he pointed to me and smiled.

Everyone in the room looked around to see who he was talking about. I'm not sure if I was more flattered or flustered. But I lifted my bottle of Tsing Tao to the applause.

Ben performed four songs that he had written and I can say — with great objectivity — he was terrific. He has an easy-going stage presence and he sings his songs with heart.

Many of his college friends came to cheer him on. There were lots of photos taken and, at the end of his set one friend handed him a bouquet.

It would have been enough of an achievement if Ben had just performed in a show, singing songs that he had composed — but he had also written about the show for the newspaper.

A week before the performance, he had interviewed the musicians, in Mandarin and English, about their musical careers and the inspirations for their songs. On the day of the performance, there was a full-page news article in the *Shanghai Daily* on Shanghai's indie music scene. Byline: "Ben-Darrow Goodman reports."

The page was taped to the window of the club.

I kvelled.

City indie music folks really rock

Shanghai's small indie music scene is multifaceted and growing, both above and underground. There's a new label just for city bands, plus music collectives and a folk-rock community passionate about telling stories. Ben-Darrow Goodman reports.

Shanghai's indie music scene is growing. An increasing number of bands and musicians, such as Pinkberry (above left and center) and David Warner (above right), give regular performances and release new albums. — Linnea Backstrom

Armed typically with acoustic guitars and stories to tell, Shanghai's folk-rock musicians are individual singers and songwriters who are establishing a community within the indie scene.

A notable folk-rock personality is guitarist Liu Jian, who started playing when he was 16. After being expelled from high school for playing punk music in the school, he joined the People's Liberation Army.

It was in the service that he began writing songs.

Now 32, Liu is both a musician and published author. He has written two novels, "Out of the Army" (2008), a sequel to his first work, "Rock Soldier."

The debut novel is a semi-autobiographical portrayal of young and restless musicians who enlist in the army after being expelled from school.

Liu wears several creative hats. He is a music organizer as well as singer, songwriter and author.

In 2005 he formed Shanghai East District Power, a collective of 10 folk musicians from eastern parts of the city. The group has played many shows and released a CD, "Shanghai East District Power Unplugged."

He recently formed a second collective, Shanghai Folk Rock United.

"The difference is more people and more diversity," Liu says. The original team was only 10 individual acts all from eastern parts of the city, but Shanghai Folk Rock United now has more than 20 musicians from throughout the city, including suburbs and rural areas. He expects the group will soon number around 30.

The idea is to have many Folk Rock United shows, each featuring four or five artists.

Folk Rock United performs tonight at 696 Livehouse near Hongkou Football Stadium. The next show will be on May 28 at the same venue. In both shows, Liu will play alongside three fellow singer-songwriters.

"I think folk suits Shanghai," says Liu. "The weather here is mostly comfortable. The people here prefer their food sweeter, unlike Sichuan's spicy fare."

One of his fellow musicians and story tellers is New Yorker David Warner who arrived in Shanghai three and a half years ago and mixes Chinese and English in his lyrics.

"I studied Chinese back in high school, and it was my major in college. I always knew I would end up in Asia," Warner says. "China is the mothership."

Warner, like Liu, started playing guitar around the age of 16.

"The difference is more people and more diversity ... I think folk suits Shanghai."

Liu Jian

"I try and mix it up, half and half. If you don't understand both, you won't understand part of who I am.

"In my opinion, Shanghai is going through a salon art movement as France did in the 1800s," he says.

"There is an underground scene and it is actually underground, we've stumbled on shows up on the third floors of unmarked buildings."

He sees a real and sizeable city folk scene. Sometimes the songs are stories, sometimes they're performance.

Information about the shows can be found at www.douban.com/ event/11852821/ or www.eeera. info/index.php/-shows/details/22-shanghai-folk-united-5.

(Writer Ben-Darrow Goodman is a young musician in Shanghai Folk Rock United.)

Banding together under fresh label

MANY people are intrigued by Shanghai's underground and indie music scene and want to know what's really going on. It's multifaceted, expanding and changing, and a fresh indie label is suggesting some answers.

Started just five months ago, the label Zhu Lu He Feng is strictly for Shanghai bands. The name comes from a classical Chinese poem describing the breeze over lotus flowers.

One of its strengths is bringing the diversity of Shanghai music to a wider audience.

The label is headed by drummer Lezi (Andy Yan) from the heavyweight band Sonnet. He's also an organizer, promoter and general man-about-town.

"Our goal with the label is to promote and develop local rock and indie bands and to help record and promote their CD and tours, not only in Shanghai, but also eventually in cities like Guangzhou (Guangdong Province), Hong Kong, Suzhou (Jiangsu Province) and Hangzhou (Zhejiang Province)," Lezi says.

The label has signed seven bands so far: Pinkberry, Sonnet, 21 Grams, JoKe, MR (a female singer), Man Ban Pai and Shen Zhi Wu Zhi (which translates as "Who Knows God Know").

The bands are touring, and the label showcases the diversity of Shanghai music. The signed acts include rock, punk, folk, electronic, dance, and in Shen Zhi Wu Zhi music that's very silly and fun.

Recently, these bands have been on a three-university tour in Shanghai. Man Ban Pai will record a CD this summer.

The idea is that Zhu Lu He Feng bands perform along with local college bands.

The next stop on the Zhu Lu He Feng university tour is Fudan University on May 31.

City music blogger Jake Newby sees the label, and its rapid development in a short time, as a good model for organization in the Shanghai scene.

"Hopefully this is a sign to other bands and collectives in Shanghai that this stuff is possible," says Newby.

"Taking the bands to campuses will bring the underground music scene to a wider audience and help previously unaware people discover that really interesting things are going on with Shanghai music."

The newest Zhu Lu He Feng release is "Go! Boom!" from Pinkberry. The CD release show was at Yuyintang Shanghai.

Guitarist Tony says they worked on the album for around two months.

"But we are already thinking about the future. We want to change up the instruments on the next album and give it a more electronic sound."

The group says they love NoFX and other punk, as well as some pop and rap like American singer Keisha.

"We have been excited about university shows," says lead singer Yoi, noting they also played the Yixian Camping Music Festival in Hebei Province early this month.

Read more about Zhu Lu He Feng and the bands at www.zlhfmusic.com or www.douban.com/label/zlhf/.

You can also follow Jake Newby's articles on Shanghai underground music at www.kungfuology.com/jakenewby/.

A member of Sonnet, which is one of the seven bands joining Zhu Lu He Feng

46
A Good Day to Dry

Howard:

I LOOKED out the living room window shortly after waking up on a summer day — shortly before noon, my usual time — and could tell the weather had changed.

The sun was shining and laundry was hanging from the clothes lines and hanging rods outside people's houses.

It was the first laundry I'd seen outdoors for days, I realized. And I knew it had to be a good day out there.

Shanghai is very modern in many respects, but the laundry dangling everywhere makes it look like a place that jumbled up the decades. An office tower near our flat was right out of 1990s Midtown New York, but the laundry blowing across the street was New York, 1933. On several very nice days, we actually saw laundry hanging on the office building's plaza. Somebody needing dry skivvies had declared the space for himself. The cops wouldn't let children run on the grass in a park, but nobody minded if you appropriated the private space in front of an office tower for your wet laundry.

As befitted a city vying for world respect, self-appointed citizen groups were trying ardently to rid Shanghai of provincial customs deemed hick, such as the habit of Shanghaiers to wear pajamas in public. The debate was hot. PJs as street wear: Civic disgrace or local charm?

There was a similar campaign to ban the public drying of laundry. But it had little effect. Quite the opposite. Shanghai people were very righteous about laundry-hanging. According to our first Shanghai friend, Jenny, Chinese people were taught that laundry that dries in the air is healthier than laundry that dries in machines. Which, of course, made perfect sense to us. It had to be all that fresh city air permeating the fibers that made the clothes so healthy.

Jenny had also told us that it was essential to take down the laundry before sundown. If we didn't, ghosts might get into the clothing.

Then there was the small group of *Shanghai Daily* reporters and editors who took a six-week trip to the Washington, D.C., area soon after Ellen and I arrived. One of their first dispatches back to China was to tell how one of the guys had ruined all his clothes by putting it — horrors! — into a dryer, a machine apparently unknown on the mainland.

As editorial writer Wan Lixin, put it, "Here in America I found we have to roast our laundry for about one hour in an electricity-powered drier."

Wan went on: "One trainee in our group said that the roasting had ruined two of his shirts. One originally fit for people with a height of 190 cm (about 6'3") had shrunk to one for 170 cm (5'6") after being dried, and one female colleague had similar grievances."

Roasting one's clothes was more than a waste of good top wear, Wan continued. It was a sin against the planet: "We all know the wear and tear on clothing and the energy costs if all Chinese began to use this method to dry their clothes."

On this score, Wan was utterly correct. The Chinese may have been copying the American appetite for automobiles, but the world would be better off if they stuck to their habit of dripping their wet clothes from limbs of trees, balcony poles, electrical lines and the iron rods that protrude like porcupine needles from some apartment buildings expressly for the purpose.

As Wan wrote, "hanging laundry outside in the sunshine ... is probably the only green way to dry the laundry on earth."

"In George Washington's enormous plantation at Mount Vernon there is a room where his many slaves used to wash the family laundry and then dry the laundry on the grass and shrubs in the courtyard," Wan added, referencing a time in American history that seems kinder to the planet than to human beings.

I became quite fond of the sight of laundry dangling around Shanghai, and Ellen and I got used to living dryer-less. Our apartment was frequently redolent with the scent of moist detergent, as wet socks and blue jeans hung from a portable rack in the dining room or draped over the portable radiator in the bedroom. The soggy textiles added welcome humidity to the dry heat in our building. On calm, warm days we hung the laundry outside, on built-in clothes racks on our balcony that moved up and down as needed, like theater curtains.

None of our unroasted shirts ever shrank.

Note from Ellen:
THIS SYSTEM was not without complications.

Due to a division-of-labor agreement based on work schedules and Howie's discomfort at being on a balcony 13 floors up, I was the point person for laundry drying. I accepted the assignment, studying other people's clothes-hanging techniques and making a practice of looking for extra-strength clothes pins when shopping at the local sundries store.

All was well until one day when I went out to the balcony to retrieve some shirts and realized that one of them was missing. I looked all around, and then down. A gust of wind had picked up Ben's shirt and sent it sailing down to the balcony of an apartment below ours.

OK, I thought. Good excuse to meet the downstairs neighbor.
I hopped the elevator down and knocked on the door. No

answer.

Now what? I went back to our apartment, got the camera and photographed the errant shirt, which was resting on the ledge below. Camera in hand, I went down to the lobby to ask for help. I showed the doorman the photo and pantomimed the shirt blowing off the line and floating down. He nodded, but I couldn't be sure he understood me.

And yet, 15 minutes later the helpful doorman knocked on our door and handed me the flyaway shirt.

Problem solved.

On our balcony

47
Teaching My Girls

Ellen's blog:
"TEACHER, TEACHER, Let me try," they're chanting.

"I want a pink-a pig-a," says Nomi.

"This is a black-a boot," says Liu Liu.

"Okay everybody — let's do 'Rain, Rain, Go Away' — again," I say.

I'm sitting cross-legged in front of a dozen 2- to 5-year-old Chinese kids at a preschool in the new Pudong part of Shanghai, teaching them English in the way I like to do it — by making up games that grab their interest. They are completely lovable. It's only Wednesday.

And already I'm exhausted.

I haven't had this job long. Howie was asked by a woman at the paper if I might be interested in a teaching post. A college friend of hers named Janet was helping run a private preschool for Chinese children. She needed a native English speaker to teach a few hours each morning.

A few days later I visited the school and was impressed with how beautiful the facility was and how adorable the children were.

I accepted a position, teaching four groups of small children from 8:45-10:45 each morning.

"No sweat," I thought. "I can teach for a few hours in the morning, return home and visit with Howie and then go out to my tutoring jobs later in the day."

I had forgotten how tiring little kids can be.

By Wednesday I was really dragging. By Friday I had to admit to myself and Janet that I just couldn't continue to teach both the morning preschool and my evening students.

I'm finding that at 61, I just can't do the Hokey Pokey as I used to do.

But it's a shame because I really enjoyed being around such sweet little people and seeing the world through their eyes. They never seemed to get tired or bored. They were always ready for one more song or game.

I also enjoyed my interactions with the Chinese teachers and assistants who were studying my teaching techniques. I soon got used to looking up and seeing several of them writing notes or taking pictures.

I was lucky to have Janet sit in during most of my lessons and help interpret for me. One day as I was saying good-bye to the class, one of the little boys started to sob.

"Oh my gosh Janet, did I say something wrong? Why is he crying?" I asked.

She laughed. "He's crying because he likes you and he doesn't want to leave."

Wow, that had never happened to me before as a teacher.

So it was with a heavy heart that I quit those morning classes. I'm content now to tutor my three private students four afternoons a week from 4-6 pm, in their homes in different parts of the city.

On Mondays and Thursdays I teach 7-year-old Monica, a very sweet little girl with a shy smile who has some delays in language and reading comprehension. She eagerly answers the door when I arrive and rushes into the study to begin our lessons. Even though the assignments are sometimes difficult for her, she never complains or gives up. Her best friend is her little apricot colored poodle named Tian Tian who patiently sits outside the closed door waiting for our lessons to end.

Wednesday takes me to Vicky, a 10-year-old who was born in America and whose parents want her to speak English without a Chinese accent. Not easy for a Chinese girl living in Shanghai.

Vicky is very outgoing and little interested in doing her lessons. She often tries to steer our conversations towards the things she's cares about.

Here's an example: Last class, we were reading a book that talked about a man with a mustache. That led into a discussion about the difference between a mustache and a beard — neither are very common in Shanghai. To illustrate what a beard looks like, I took out one of my family pictures and showed her that Howie and my son-in-law, Tal, have beards.

Vicky pointed to Tal's picture and suddenly jumped up and started talking about Lady Gaga and how lots of boys and girls go to see her.

With big arm gestures she started to pantomime Gaga's fans jumping up and down. And then she put her arms out to her sides like she was holding back the crowd. "Not the police, but ...." she tried to explain.

It dawned on me. She was trying to tell me that my rather large son-in-law looked like Lady Gaga's bodyguards!

I never know what she's going to come up with next.

Friday is my favorite day because I teach Judy, one of the smartest children I have ever known.

She is a true bookworm and has a wall full of books in English, ranging from the Harry Potter series to the Bible. Judy's parents lived in Erie, Pa., for a year when Judy was 6 and she attended an

245

American elementary school for first grade. If you spoke to her on the phone you might not even know that she was Chinese — or 10 years old.

Her parents don't have an agenda, they just want Judy to get experience working with a native English speaker. Together we read the *Shanghai Daily* and discuss current events in English. After lessons in reading, spelling and writing, we cap off the session by reading a chapter of Jules Verne's "20,000 Leagues Under the Sea."

The other day we were reading about Lance Armstrong and how he overcame cancer. Judy wanted to know more about the disease and how people contracted it.

She got very quiet and then asked if I thought too much homework could give you cancer.

I told her that I kind of doubted it. She replied, "Well, if it did, then the teachers would have to stop giving us so much."

Couldn't disagree with that.

I think I enjoy my visits more than she does.

48
Held Up at the Bank

Howard:

THE NUMBER of millionaires in China was growing faster than anywhere else on Earth. Like everyone else, I wondered just how long it would be until the country overtook the United States and Europe to truly dominate the world's economy.

But then came an encounter in everyday banking that made me realize any worry was exaggerated. China had a lot of things going for it, but common sense and efficiency were not high on the list.

I did something dumb. I left my debit card in an ATM machine after withdrawing 1,000 yuan ($150). A couple of days later, I discovered that the card was missing from my wallet. I kicked myself for my stupidity, but, hey, it was no big deal. I'd go to the bank branch where I'd opened my account and get a new card. For a day or two I'd be unable to take money out of a machine. A small inconvenience.

The branch of the ICBC (Industrial and Commercial Bank of China) was right in the lobby of the *Shanghai Daily*'s office building. It was where the paper automatically deposited my pay each month. They knew me there. I was the silver-haired *laowai* who worked at the English-language paper upstairs.

They might have known me, but that wasn't going to help me get a replacement bank card.

The gentleman at the customer relations desk wore a starched white shirt. He used his rudimentary English to tell me I needed my passport before he could even start the process for a new card. I had with me a photocopy of the passport. A perfect, full-color reproduction. That wouldn't cut it.

"No, no," he said, giving me a smile, a shake of the head and an apologetic laugh, "you need-a passport-a."

Never mind that they already had my passport information stored in their records. Never mind that Mr. Customer Relations knew very well that I worked in the same building as he, and that my company added money to my account in his bank every month like clockwork. Never mind that he was looking, at that very moment, at my account information on his desktop computer screen and could see, to the yuan, how much of my money ICBC was holding.

"No, no bank card today," he said.

I came back the next day with the passport.

"Ah, ah," he said, nodding briskly. He seemed very much relieved that we were no longer dealing with a photocopy of a passport and were back in the familiar terrain of names, numbers and dates of birth printed in a little stapled booklet.

He pulled a bunch of forms from his desk drawer, tapped many keys of his computer, and placed the passport under a scanning device. The scan could join all the previous digital copies of the passport in the ICBC data bank. He filled out each form with care, as a second bank employee, a woman in prim white shirt and red scarf, stood at his elbow. At the right moment, she pressed each page with a little red stamp. She was the branch manager. For the 15 minutes that he took to fill out the forms, her sole function was to stand there and make sure he spelled my name right and copied my account number correctly. And then, satisfied with his execution of those tasks, she stamped her approval.

At last I signed my name.

We seemed done.

"OK," Mr. Customer Relations said. "You have card in seven days."

What?

Seven days? It was going to take seven days for the bank to approve a replacement card for a customer who'd been keeping his money with them for months, whose identity they had no reason to doubt and who, until he lost his previous card in one of their very own bank machines, had been in every respect a perfectly reliable patron?

Correct.

I told myself to keep calm.

"This is very inconvenient," I said. "I guess I'll take my bank book up to the teller window and withdraw some money because it's going to be a long time before I can get to a bank machine."

His gave me a regretful smile that looked almost genuine.

"No," he said. "We can't do that. You don't have a card."

"I need a card to go to the teller window? I've never heard of that."

"Bank rules. I am sorry."

"You know," I said slowly, "in America I would get a bank card in one day. And you know what else? I would be able to get my money that same day."

He looked thunderstruck, as if he'd never dreamed of such efficiency. He squinted at his computer screen, seeming to search for the ICBC regulation that would allow him to grant an exception to an American customer who was accustomed to a better way of banking.

He gave up.

"America and China," he said apologetically, "are very different."

But how was I going to get to enough money for the next week? How could I go without the means to buy things?

He thought a minute.

"Do you have friends? You could borrow from your friends."

What?

"Or, ask the *Shanghai Daily* to give you some money."

He had to be kidding.

"Look" I said. "I'm not going to borrow money from anybody. I have money. I just want to get my own money. It's in your bank. I want to get my money out of your bank."

He shook his head.

"No card."

This wasn't funny, I told him. I couldn't do without money. How was I going to eat?

He suddenly smiled. Something was amusing.

"You need to eat? You can come over to my house. I'll make you a dinner."

There it stood. I wasn't going to prevail. I had logic on my side. He had the stronger hand. He had the bank's rules.

Then my boss intervened.

I told JJ the story of the thwarted card. The next day, she came downstairs with me to the bank branch, and she gave the branch manager a good barking-to. That did something. The bank reluctantly agreed to speed things up.

I could have the card in six days, instead of seven.

The six days elapsed. I showed up at the appointed time. But I was asked to wait. First, the customer relations man and the branch manager had to study the forms they'd filled out six days before. They did this very carefully. I watched as they filled out more forms. Once again, they took my passport and scanned it into the computer.

This would be the third time they captured my passport. At least. I couldn't understand this at all. It wasn't as though the information had changed since they'd scanned it last. My passport photo looked exactly the same. I was getting older all the time this was going on, but my picture wasn't aging.

The two bank employees seemed very anxious. Everything had to be approved by a supervisor at some central ICBC location. In fact, because they were granting me the new ATM card in six days rather than the usual seven, they needed the approval of two bank supervisors.

As we waited for all the approvals, closing hour arrived. The customer relations man shut the glass front doors and dimmed some of the lights. Behind the counter, clerks tallied up the day's deposits and withdrawals. One bank employee took a stack of 100-yuan notes — the currency's largest denomination, each note worth about $15 American — and tied it with string, like it was an old-fashioned package for parcel post. The block of bills was as thick and as squared-off as two bricks laid one on top of the other. In the age of electronic fund transfers, this was the reality of banking in the world's second-largest economy.

We were nearing the end of the procedure, but they told me about a complication. Because they had shut off my previous card, and hence my previous bank account number, my *Shanghai Daily* pay for the coming month could not be deposited. They would be sending money back to Miss Guo, who handled the newspaper's payroll, and Miss Guo would have to resubmit the pay under my new account number.

All this, because of a moment's inattention — leaving a goddamn ATM card inside a goddamn bank machine.

Finally, they gave me the unobtainable. The new ATM card.

"And I can use it today?"

"Yes, yes," Mr. Customer Relations said, nodding and smiling.

The bank manager, standing at his elbow, smiled and beamed too.

They seemed so pleased to share this modern miracle with me.

After all, it had been only about a week since I'd first walked in to ask for a new ATM card. I'd only had to come back three more times.

This last visit took only 55 minutes.

Whoever said time was money? At the Industrial and Commercial Bank of China, time and money were absolute strangers to each other.

49
Wrestling with Choices

NO ONE was spitting in public. No one was blowing hockers onto the sidewalk.

We were in Hong Kong, and it was almost like being back in North America. The city looked like Vancouver, all harbor and mountains and office towers. A Vancouver with a hell of a lot more Chinese people than the one in Canada. And with an intense business vibe. A Vancouver where people scurried as they do in New York.

There was English everywhere. We never felt we were going to be confused because we didn't know Chinese. We could look at a magazine rack and actually read what was there, instead of scanning the unfamiliar publications in vain. In Shanghai, we were illiterates. In Hong Kong, we knew how to read again.

Hong Kong taxi drivers drove cars with automatic shift, and knew how to drive them. They didn't grind along for the whole ride in a second gear that was pleading for mercy. Passengers had to secure their seat belts, by law. In Shanghai, not only was it uncustomary to wear a seat belt, I once had a driver look terribly insulted when I attempted to put one on. So I didn't.

There were no bicycles in the Hong Kong streets, let alone pushcarts. Barely even a motorcycle. Instead, the streets rumbled with luxury cars, double-decker buses, diesel-spewing trucks.

We were visiting on sparkling summer days. There was much less haze and soot in the air than we'd known in Shanghai. The buildings looked better built. The windows were clearer. In Shanghai, everything had been built very fast and soon looked old. In Hong Kong, half the city still looked new.

Officially, we were still in China. The British, who founded the colony in the 1830s and ruled it for about 150 years, handed it over to the Chinese in 1997. Beijing agreed that for 50 years Hong Kong would retain its Western ways. Thus there were opposition political parties, a free press, freedom of assembly, and plenty of protests. There was a separate currency, a separate flag, a separate stock exchange, and one of the most open free markets in the world. "One nation, two systems," was the slogan that explained the schizophrenia.

In Hong Kong, we could access the whole Internet. For the first time in nine months we could look at YouTube and Facebook. I quickly abandoned the latter; there was too much catching up to do. But in our hotel room we gorged on Sixties rock videos on YouTube.

At the top of a big indoor mall called Times Square, we walked into the best book store I'd seen in almost a year. Thousands of titles in English. And yes, we found a camera store with a great price for digital cameras.

We rode the Metro, a fast, spotless, on-time, easy-to-navigate subway that many people thought the best in the world. It was indeed pretty darn good, and obviously the model for Shanghai's. But the riders of Hong Kong didn't push or swarm. They queued.

We spent most of our time in downtown Hong Kong, ultra modern and ultra money-conscious. In no other corner of the world had we ever been so relentlessly surrounded by advertising for luxury goods.

But bus rides to the other side of the island took us to scenes of great natural beauty: lush green hillsides dropping precipitously into ocean bays, small islands glimmering in the near distance. Picturesque beach towns. The Peak, the mountaintop where crowds gather at sunset to watch the lights go on throughout the glass and steel density of the Hong Kong skyline unfolding below you.

We took ferry rides to the foot of the skyline, the office towers rising starkly from the shoreline with mountains fast behind them. We inhaled the smell of sea water. We ate sumptuous meals, courtesy of our host, Frank, the landlord of our Shanghai apartment, who lived in Hong Kong and insisted that his feelings would be hurt beyond repair if we didn't allow him to pay our way.

And I paid a visit to the *South China Morning Post*, the excellent, 100-year-old English-language newspaper that seemed to cover fully and insightfully a great many stories about mainland China that the *Shanghai Daily* had to censor. In Shanghai, I'd started a habit of reading the Post, which would arrive by mail (you couldn't find it on newsstands on the mainland), and admired it. An introduction from an old *Inquirer* colleague got me an appointment with the editor, a veteran of the *Wall Street Journal* named Reg Chua. I arrived to discover that Chua had looked over my resume with some care and had already called one or two of my references. Our conversation went well, and within a few weeks he told me he had a job in mind, if I were interested: chief rewriter. He said he wanted his paper to run plenty of long, in-depth stories, and he had reporters who were very good at amassing reams of facts, but pretty bad at making them read well. My job would be to turn these lengthy messes into engaging stories for Page One and other prominent spots in the paper.

It was a very nice offer. My one-year contract with the *Shanghai Daily* would expire in October. I was sure to be asked to renew: the Shanghai editors kept giving me larger responsibilities. By now, I was handling all the editing for the *Daily*'s Page One and the two other main news pages.

But how did I like Hong Kong? Hard to say. It was so Western that there'd be little culture shock. Living there would be easy in that sense. But the city seemed to lack the soul, the funkiness that we saw everywhere else in China — the weirdness and discomforts and dislocations that made living in a foreign place so interesting.

This could be a hard decision.

And then it got harder. On a short trip back to the United States, I was offered an opportunity to work at a newspaper in the quiet Florida city of Fort Myers. It would be my smallest newspaper since the *Oregon Statesman*, back in the 1970s. The town was in a conservative patch of the state: Bible-believing, Tea Party country. But the editors I met were terrific, and the work situation seemed sweet. I'd be writing and editing in-depth pieces for the Sunday paper. I could depend on the job lasting a good five or six years, I was assured; the paper's finances were pretty sound. We'd be only a few hours' drive from friends and family.

By this time, Ellen and I had hoped we'd see an improvement in the U.S. economy. But that wasn't bearing out. Our house in Delray Beach was costing us $18,000 a year, despite the rent we were getting from tenants, and continuing to lose value. Our lawyer friend Michael gave us blunt advice: Sell it. We quickly faced facts and put the house on the market — leaving us with the prospect that we would soon be propertyless in America. It seemed almost unpatriotic. Also scary.

Soon after we returned to Shanghai, I wrote an email to my sisters about what we'd just experienced back home:

> All in all, our trip to the States was heavier than we expected.
>
> We thought it would be all about tending to El's parents, spending time with Mom and seeing Ben off to college, but what dominated was the unexpected realization that we have to unload the house.
>
> Our initial idea coming over to China was that we'd spend a year outside the States and hope that the recession would brighten enough for us to come back and pick up where we left off... but housing values are still declining in Palm Beach County, where the courts have a backlog of 55,000 foreclosures. We were smacked with the reality that we have to dig in for a longer period of flux.
>
> We'll be ecstatic to be rid of the financial drag that the house represents, but we do find ourselves with a sad sense of loss to part with that beautiful place, and something deeper too: a feeling of drift. We won't have a home in America to come back to.
>
> That's not the way this adventure to China — or wherever — started last October. It was a lark then. Now it's, like, our life.

I wrestled with the choices for weeks. Head back to the States, where I'd have a semblance of security — but in a sleepy, out-of-the-way city? Jump to Hong Kong, where the newspaper tackled one of the biggest stories on earth, the rise of China, but where the job was unlikely to offer much permanence? Or stay in Shanghai, a city we were loving more with each passing month, but where the 1 a.m. hours were wearing me down and state censorship made a joke of good journalism?

Central Hong Kong

50
Farewell, Shanghai

WE DIDN'T want the adventure to end. We opted for Hong Kong and the *South China Morning Post*.

Life would have been easy in Fort Myers. But we weren't ready to leave Asia, and the chance to see it from the vantage point of Hong Kong, that great crossroads, was too enticing to pass up.

With regret, I told Peter and JJ that I wouldn't seek to renew my contract when it expired in October. Generously, they said they understood.

"You'll like Hong Kong," JJ said. "It's much better than here."

And so we wrapped things up. Sold a bunch of household goods on ShanghaiExpat. Saluted our pals in round upon round of farewell drinks. Hosted a farewell dinner at our favorite Uighar restaurant, a splash of Chinese Muslim culture where the waitstaff pulled you by the hand to get on stage with them and belly dance.

It was sad to leave Shanghai, a place that had seemed so strange and impenetrable 12 months before. But then, a melancholy often attached to the city in early October, the month when the weather was always best and the Mid-Autumn Festival and the National Day converged. Many residents used the five days' off to travel. Anfu Lu was uncharacteristically quiet, with stretches of long minutes before we'd see the next bicycle or hear the next car. At work, people passed around Moon Cakes — little, decoratively wrapped, disc-like paperweights with red bean paste and an egg inside, symbolizing the full moon and not tasting anywhere close to as good as they looked. They were like tokens of kindness. JJ took a great interest in finding how well I liked them.

We went to the city zoo with Ellen's 10-year-old student Judy and her parents. We saw pandas as we stood amid a thick crowd of young and old, some holding China's red flag as though they were making a patriotic pilgrimage to the animal. Judy's father had a white-collar job at a chemical company and drove us in the family car. He and his wife were in college during the 1989 Tiananmen Square rallies, where students (and then others) demanded wider freedoms, and which Deng Xiaoping's government crushed with tanks and bullets.

One day Judy's father let us in on an amazing confidence. He had been there, on the rally's fringe, when the shooting started. He jumped over a fence and a pack of parked bicycles to escape the violence. He then went a long way around to get back home, out of range of the noise and the bloodshed, skirting an event that China has tried, Orwellian-style, to shove down the memory hole ever since. That he felt comfortable telling us this story seemed like more than a guy making a personal connection. It showed a yearning to keep a truth from being forgotten. To be telling that story to us, two Americans, expressed a desire that China should become a normal country, that its citizens should be free to expose its faults and shortcomings, as people do in the West.

On one of my last nights at work, on October 12, I arrived to find that CNN was off the air.

"Because of the Nobel Prize," an editor told me.

The peace prize had been awarded to dissident Liu Xiaobo, and the Chinese government was shutting out the news.

"So none of the Chinese media are going to run it," I said.

He nodded. So did another editor. They were young and smart Chinese men. They looked a little embarrassed.

"It's not on our website?" I asked.

The editor shook his head.

"And it probably won't be in the paper?"

More head shakes.

"But lots of people know. They're looking at websites," he said.

"It's really a shame," I said, "that the government acts like the people are children who shouldn't hear about certain things."

"Yeah," he said, "but the children are finding out what's going on anyway."

His words have stayed with me.

As the next day's paper took shape that night, Adam and JJ said they wouldn't be allowed to run the news of the Nobel committee's announcement. But they were very cagey. They decided to leave space open on the bottom of the main news page.

"We're hoping the Chinese government says something," JJ said.

If so, the *Shanghai Daily* could then write a story about the government reaction to the award, and let in the news from Oslo through the backdoor.

That's just what happened. Around midnight, the Foreign Ministry denounced the award and its host country Norway, and Xinhua's English-language service ran a story about it. The fact that the award had gone to Liu was held back till the third paragraph, slipped in as background to explain the ministry's fury, but it was there.

I slapped on a headline: "Norway criticized for Nobel Peace pick."

JJ looked at the AP story that was read the world over — everywhere but China. "There is nothing wrong with this story," she said. "It is objective. It says Liu Xiaobo won the award, and what he did to win it. And says that China is mad. And says what Norway says.

"And look at Xinhua…"

The Xinhua story described Liu as a criminal who was convicted of agitating against the government, but didn't try to explain what that "agitation" was — not a word about his complaints about the government, and certainly nothing about how the government had swung the hammer against him.

She smiled, as she always did when she knew that her smarts and knowledge and journalistic instincts could not stand up to the weight of the regime, and made a humorless laugh. There was nothing to do but run the Xinhua.

But at least our readers would know the next morning what the vast millions of China would not: that a writer and professor who had called for the end of single-party rule and was serving his fourth prison term had become the first Chinese to win the Nobel Prize (unless you count the Dalai Lama).

A few nights later, I was working on the National news page. We had a story about a fake housing project in southwest China that attracted more than 2,000 buyers and allegedly swindled nearly 300 million yuan ($45 million) in half a year.

Another story saying that vocational schools in the central province of Henan were pushing students to take internships with Foxconn, the giant electronics maker where a dozen workers committed suicide because the working conditions were so awful.

We had a story from Guangdong Province about a father and a grandfather who allegedly hired people to bury living newborn twin girls because they couldn't afford to treat the babies' heart disease and brain disorder.

A story about a hospital in east An'hui Province that was under fire for refusing to save a woman who, after seeming to die in labor, had miraculously regained consciousness after an hour — wouldn't save her despite the tearful pleading of her husband, who fell on his knees in anguish.

But nothing about Liu's wife, who had tried to visit her husband in prison, and was promptly placed under arrest.

Ellen's blog:
YESTERDAY ON my way home from teaching I made a conscious effort to really look at all the amazing sights I have already started to take for granted.

I stopped and watched about 50 older local residents doing some dance aerobics to a bouncy rhythm on a boom box. They do it every night the weather allows.

I passed by a bicycle carriage that glided along the street next to a big SUV.

I watched a street vendor grill kebobs right next to a bicycle repair shop where men were taking apart a motor on the sidewalk.

The street is used by everybody — for dancing, pet walking, driving, bicycling, cooking, fixing, cleaning, peeing, spitting, sleeping ...

It's so alive.

I'm really going to miss it here.

Exercising in the street at twilight

51
Rough Landing in Hong Kong

Howard:

SOMEHOW, WHEN we had visited Hong Kong on vacation, we missed the polluted version.

Now that we had arrived to live here for a year, the true nature of the city was all over us. The airport bus had plopped us at a hotel in a teeming commercial section called Causeway Bay. An exotic name, redolent of faraway ports of call, stately ships bobbing in the water, seamen on the prowl, drinks on the verandah, a palm tree swaying in a seductive breeze. The actual place was all grimy concrete, glaring neon signs, double-decker buses, elbow-to-elbow humanity, and a blanketing veil of diesel exhaust.

"My God, this place is almost as crowded as Times Square," we kept saying. In fact, as I would discover on my next trip to New York, we had it wrong. Times Square isn't nearly as mobbed as Causeway Bay.

I went off to work right away, slaloming through the dense sidewalk crowds to my new office at One Leighton Road, a curved building fronted by a huge billboard for luxury watches, leaving El to find us a place to live. The *South China Morning* Post (SCMP) had given us only one week of free lodging at the Rosedale Hotel (in Shanghai, the Daily had given us a month at La Renaissance), so she'd have to work fast.

Unfortunately, the real estate market in Hong Kong was like Manhattan's. Everything cost way too much and was way too small. For hours, El rode bravely and alone on trams from one end of the island to the other (the best bargain in Hong Kong; you could ride for miles for 23 cents), looking at unspeakable flats. She showed me a couple of the more promising examples, and they made my heart sink — confining, run-down places. Those which we thought we could afford were the farthest away from the office, meaning I'd have a longer commute and that El would have to spend more time alone. She had no idea how she'd spend that time. She made a few calls to schools, trying to line up teaching work, but they all told her they wouldn't be hiring till after the holidays. This was November. The holidays didn't mean just Christmas and New Year's, but also Chinese New Year's.

So she was looking at late February, early March before the teaching job market would open. And some schools were talking about hiring for the coming fall — almost a year away.

Ellen's blog:
HOWIE'S HOURS at the paper have turned out to be not all that much better than in Shanghai. He came home (if you can call it that) at 11 last night. I've got to tell you that I am not loving it here yet.

The rents we will have to pay, even for a very tiny place, are about half of Howie's salary and I am starting to wonder if we can afford to live here. I've been looking in different parts of town with different realtors, and all I've seen is one place worse than the next.

The apartments are grimy and tiny, in areas where I didn't see a single westerner, with insane traffic just outside the windows. I absolutely can't imagine myself living in any of these places.

I feel like I'm trying to do a giant crossword puzzle. I need to get the first word and then I might be able to work off of that and complete the rest. I need the first piece: either a place to live, or a job for myself, or a neighborhood where I can see myself living ... some one thing that feels right, that I can build the rest of a life upon.

I miss Shanghai, where at least I had a nice apartment and friends to spend time with until Howie got home.

Hope I will have better news in my next note.

Far from home: The only redhead in Causeway Bay

Howard:

ELLEN AND I hit bottom as we sat over big cups of cappuccino in a second-floor McDonald's.

We had moved into a serviced apartment in a building called the Regent Heights, one room without a kitchen that was going to cost us a frightening amount to rent for a month. We'd had to leave our hotel after a week and the Regent Heights was the best alternative. It was only a block away. A porter had piled our bulging suitcases onto a luggage cart and pulled it through an alley and over the sidewalk to the new address, like it was the Joad family's overloaded jalopy.

Money was really troubling us. The SCMP hadn't paid El's airfare (as the *Shanghai Daily* had) and we were watching our small reserves emptying fast. The search for a reasonably priced apartment was going nowhere. So was El's search for a job. We were not having anything close to fun. We were wondering, amid the frenzy of Causeway Bay, if coming to Hong Kong had been a terrible mistake.

The McDonald's next door to the Regent Heights was a refuge. As we sipped our coffees, I reached for a napkin and wrote down our options. Maybe it was time to admit defeat and cut our losses. Go home. But if we returned to the States immediately, I'd have to repay my airfare to the SCMP. The contract said I had to work for at least three months.

So the logic was clear.

"You should go back home," I said. "Live with Rachel or your folks for a few months. I'll stay here and make enough money to at least break even for our trouble in getting here."

It hurt just to say it. But I kept on.

"It makes sense," I said. "If you're back there, you could get your parents straightened away and maybe get your real estate going again. And when I get back, maybe I can still get that Fort Myers job."

Our hearts sank as we looked at that little piece of paper. We had never separated before, never even thought about it. We couldn't imagine what our days would be like if we were apart, how forlorn we'd feel if the other were on the other side of the Earth.

No, we said. We won't do that. Not yet, anyway.

We scrapped that piece of paper.

And kept going.

It was soon Thanksgiving, but it was no holiday. No one at the SCMP would think of taking off for the American feast day. We were too new to know where to find a turkey dinner. But an editor named Ting Shi, who had lived in the States and gone to UC Berkeley ("Go, Bears!" she chirped as we compared biographical notes at the China Desk), invited us to lunch at a restaurant near her apartment, where we could have an approximation: duck sandwiches on baguettes.

That afternoon, our luck changed. Just after finishing our makeshift Thanksgiving lunch, El rode the tram to an as-yet unexplored neighborhood. It had the goofy name of Happy Valley, but it looked much less awful than most of the others she'd seen. Feeling frayed, she stepped into a cubbyhole of a real estate office, let the agent know that she, too, was in real estate, and begged to see nothing but good, clean flats at reasonable prices.

The agent's name was Linda Lo. She had lived in Vancouver and spoke great English. Ellen poured her heart out. "I've been so frustrated. If I see one more horrible place, I might run out of here crying!"

"Well, I don't want to see you cry," Linda Lo said.

What do you know? Linda Lo had something to show — an apartment that Ellen liked. And when I saw it, I liked, too. Within a couple of weeks, we moved in to our 15th floor flat in Horace Court, a residential tower surrounded by other residential towers, with a partial view of the famous Happy Valley Racetrack if you looked through a couple of the windows at a certain angle.

The place was tiny: 450 square feet, with a narrow, tubless bathroom, with a toilet so weak that you had to fill the tank with water from the shower-head hose before you could get a good flush. The narrow kitchen was too small for the two of us to be cooking at the same time and it lacked an oven (though it did have a washing machine). But the apartment was equipped with loads of built-in closets — rare in Hong Kong, where the abiding home decor seemed to be stacking boxes of your goods all over the place, as if your apartment were also your attic. It even had an under-the-bed storage space for hiding our huge collection of luggage. It was painted in bright oranges and yellows and shone with wood floors — it was almost hip. There was a flat-screen TV with surround sound, a red leather couch and a white formica desk for two. There was no dining area, but what the hell, there were plenty of places to eat in Hong Kong.

Happy Valley was located at the end of a tram line, which gave us access to the rest of the city. It was about a 20-minute walk to the newspaper, so I could stretch my legs on nice days.   And it took us out of Causeway Bay. Not that we were moving to some bucolic village. Happy

Valley loomed with tall buildings. We heard trucks, buses and cars grind their way up the steep hills all day and night. There were live, doomed chickens for sale at an outdoor butcher shop a block away. There was a video store that was fully stocked with movies and TV shows from America and Britain. Within a few minutes' walk of our apartment were a good international grocery store; the warm aromas of an egg-tart bakery; a community center with squash courts and a public library; the race track, which doubled on off-hours as a park for soccer and field hockey, jogging and power-walking; a first-rate private hospital; a Chinese diner that served a mean dish of Singapore noodles; a Subway sandwich shop; any number of dog groomers; and at least three British-style pubs, including one that became our favorite place to eat a late breakfast or sip a Hoegaarden, the Happy Valley Bar & Grill.

Linda Lo met with the landlord — and managed to negotiate a cheaper price for us. We moved in on December 14.

Ellen's blog:
SO, AFTER a near freak-out where I seriously considered running back home in defeat, things are finally falling into place and I think we're going to be OK now.

Next on the agenda: a job for me. And FRIENDS.

52
A Great Job, But ...

Howard:

REG CHUA was true to his word. He set me up with a post on the Hub, the desk through which he intended all the paper's main story to flow before going on Page One or to lead the Metro pages. I was thrown into the deep end on my first night, forced to make sense of a complicated apparent scandal involving government favors and commercial real-estate prices. I think I looked like a fool in the eyes of the city editor, Quinton Chan, with my basic questions about Hong Kong politics and property values — interconnected subjects that proved to be the very heartbeat of Hong Kong news. But later I found out he had other reasons for being surly.

There were lots of smart people on the paper. The first time I sat in on a news meeting, listening in as the various editors described the stories that were being prepared for the next day's edition, I was bowled over by the casual intelligence on display. The city editor would mention a policy change by a city official, and two other editors would be thinking ahead to what the next day's story ought to be, and the story after that — and what Beijing's reaction was likely to be, and how some Southeast Asian neighboring countries would react to that. I hadn't seen that kind of collective brainpower at work in a news organization since the *Philadelphia Inquirer* in the 1990s. I felt lucky to have been admitted to the group, and knew I'd have a lot to learn to keep up.

I was seated next to great people. Chow Chungyan was my immediate boss. A strikingly tall man, he knew only Mandarin until he was a teenager. He grew up in Yunnan Province, so isolated from the outer world that he didn't realize other languages existed. Whenever a world figure appeared on television, like Henry Kissinger, the foreigner would be dubbed into Mandarin. But here he was, just in his 30s, and so wicked smart that he held a major editing position at Southeast Asia's foremost English-language newspaper. I held Chungyan in great respect and soon learned he took a similarly lofty view of my editing abilities. One night we were at a company party at The Derby, the go-to pub across the street from the paper, and someone asked him just what it was that I did at the SCMP. "Howard," he said, "turns shit into gold."

Then there was Niall Frasier, a Scot who had been living in Hong Kong and Thailand, his wife's home country, for some 15 years. He was a classic city reporter, possessing a Rolodex of police sources and a persona on the phone that was pure brusqueness. When I closed my eyes, I thought I was listening to Sean Connery. But there was nothing suave about Niall's appearance; he was all working-class stubble. He'd been put in charge of young metro reporters, a job that demanded a patience and a tolerance for others' shortcomings that weren't in his arsenal. A working day for Niall was a progression of mounting frustration. I'd watch his face turn redder and redder and hear him slam the phone down harder and harder as the shift went on and he seemed more and more besieged. I was sure that someday the poor guy would collapse at his desk with some horrible heart attack.

"Niall," I said on one of my first days there, "I'm going out for some coffee. You want any?"

"Cyaw-fee!" he cried, breaking into a huge smile. "Cyaw-fee! I love the way you say that! You sound just like a cop show."

Oh, I see. I'm the one with the funny accent. It became a running joke, Niall asking me if I was enjoying my cyaw-fee.

Niall didn't hear much American around that office. About half the staff were Chinese and the other half were from Commonwealth countries, their writing steeped in British-style journalistic conventions, their mouths heavily accented in Irish, Scot, Australian and London.

The *South China Morning Post*, like so much else about Hong Kong, was an invention of a British colony. It showed in the language. We wrote about Victoria Harbour, the city centre, television programmes, savoury sauces, school enrolments. Apartments were flats, government plans were government schemes, pay raises were pay rises. In the legislature, lawmakers would "table a bill" when they wanted to talk about it — just the opposite of the American phrase, where tabling a bill means letting it languish. I caught on to the spelling changes quickly enough, but I resisted using Brit-style phrasings. They were too much in the passive voice and slowed the stories down — yet conversely, the stories and headlines often jumped to hyperbolic conclusions. A lot of the rewriting I did was to put the reporters' work into plainer, snappier English, the reporting on safer, more substantiated ground. Often I'd open the paper the next day and find that one of the copy editors — or as they were called, sub-editors, or "subs" — had followed up by putting the writing back into Brit-speak.

My best friend was Alex Lo. Brilliant and perpetually disheveled, Alex was a columnist as well as an editor. He was born in Hong Kong but went to high school in Toronto and to college at St. John's, in Annapolis, Md., where he majored in philosophy and studied the Great Books. Alex liked to read philosophy tracts and physics texts for fun, and tried to sneak as many cheap sex jokes into his columns as he could. He was hugely well-read and an extremely fast writer. We established a friendship on my first day, as soon as he found out I'd worked at the *Philadelphia Inquirer*. It was the paper he'd read in college, believing it was then the best in the U.S.A. My stock soared further when I told him I'd been to Woodstock, the 1969 music festival.

"When I heard that we were getting this new hire from the *Shanghai Daily*, I thought, oh, Jesus, we're going to get some kind of party functionary guy," he told me. "And then you show up!"

Alex and his wife Jojo, a former newspaper reporter, had two children and four dogs, which were Alex's obligation to walk, mornings and evenings. His car reeked of dog, its upholstery itchy with dog hairs. His desk at work, possibly the messiest in China, smelled of wet dog. He came from a brilliant family. His parents, long divorced, had money, and Alex took ample advantage of his father's memberships at the Japan Club and the Hong Kong Jockey Club, treating us to fine lunches. One sister was an important person at the U.N. Another lived at Hong Kong's outskirts, with farmlands in back and a view of the hilly border with mainland China. El and I visited one day and gratefully inhaled deep breaths of fresh air — fresher, at least, than what we breathed back in the central city. Alex became my go-to guy when I needed a beer and a men's night out. He would discuss the latest discoveries in quantum physics one minute and the SCMP's sexual history the next; to hear it from Alex, the staff roster was a casualty list of randy relationships gone wrong. He and I shared much the same politics. At adjacent computers, we'd read the news and make daily fun of the Republicans in Washington.

Reg was a dapper man — the anti-Alex — and a true cosmopolite. He was constantly checking his BlackBerry for emails, and spent much of his time in New York, where his girlfriend worked as a journalism professor at Columbia. He had been the SCMP's editor for a little over a year, its fourth in a seven-year span, and he didn't sound terribly optimistic about staying long. I arrived as he was trying to change the newsroom's work-flow. The Hub was part of his reconstruction. I soon learned that editors on the City Desk and the China Desk saw the Hub as a threat; as the Hub grew in power, theirs lessened. And I was one of Reg's people. As the year went on, I'd find that at least one editor, the none-too-friendly Quinton Chan, would be trying to undermine Reg by balking at his changes of direction and complaining to higher-ups, even to the extreme of bad-mouthing him in a rival newspaper, the Chinese-language *Apple Daily*.

At the same time, Reg was facing pressure from the publishers, a prominent Malaysian family with huge business interests in mainland China that made them reluctant to stir up trouble with Beijing. The family wanted to be regarded as peers of Hong Kong's most rich and powerful. This made them reluctant to blare bad news about the tycoons who ran the city. Both these attitudes got in the way of objective news gathering. It was obvious that sooner or later things would come to a head. Either Reg would trim his journalistic conscience or he would have to leave. An early departure was a good bet.

I saw none of this in my early days at the SCMP. I was very proud that the paper handled the Liu Xiaobao story exactly as the *Shanghai Daily* could not. There was no need to sneak this story in. The SCMP sent a reporter to Oslo and ran major pieces about the Nobel Prize every day for a week. On the day of the awards ceremony, we led the paper with a huge, damning photo of the empty chair that had been set out by the awards committee in honor of the imprisoned Peace Prize winner.

Later, I took pride in editing an ambitious investigative story by Fiona Tam, a sharp reporter, who revealed that mainland Chinese hospitals were profiting from specious, and probably dangerous, operations involving stem cells acquired from induced abortions — a story that won a first-place prize from the European Commission. "The expose has generated intense discussion in China's blogosphere," the jury said, and called it "very brave."

I was equally proud to have a hand in ushering into the paper a fine, long story that showed how mainland authorities had harassed and imprisoned lawyers whose so-called crime was to defend people accused of dissident activities.

Only much later did I learn the disturbing news that the writer, an ace freelancer named Paul Mooney, had tried for weeks to get that story into the paper while it languished with no clear explanation for the delay. It had been held up on the China-news desk, run by a former *China Daily* hand named Wang Xiangwei.

A few months after I left the paper, Wang became the SCMP's editor. He declined to renew Mooney's contract, despite Mooney's enormous skill in navigating news sources in the mainland and several Human Rights Awards in Hong Kong.

And Wang soon plunged the paper into a hugely damaging controversy by seeming to scuttle news of the death of Li Wangyang, a Tiananmen Square democracy activist who was found hanged in his mainland hospital ward in the summer of 2012. The authorities ruled suicide, but the family suspected foul play, given that Li was blind, hobbled and nearly deaf. The story got extensive play in Hong Kong's Chinese-language media.

The SCMP ran a full story in its first edition of June 7, 2012, but

Wang ordered a remake for the second edition. Li's death became a 101-word brief.

A veteran subeditor whom I knew, Alex Price, a colorful guy who habitually came work dressed in motorcycle gear, asked Wang by email, politely, for an explanation.

Wang responded: "I don't have to explain to you anything. I made the decision and I stand by it. If you don't like it, you know what to do."

In following days, the SCMP ran front-page stories on Li, but the appearance of self-censorship sparked an uproar in the newsroom and across the city. Protesters gathered outside the paper's front door. The *Wall Street Journal* said in an opinion piece that Wang had "built a reputation as the newspaper's in-house censor since he became China editor in 2000" and pushed stories favorable towards Beijing.

A clearly startled Wang insisted to the AFP (Agence France-Presse) it was "never my intention to downplay that story and try to exercise self-censorship."

The SCMP was left under a cloud that would take months to dissipate.

Alex Price left the paper.

53
Snapshots

Howard:

THE TROUBLE with Hong Kong was, we'd gone halfway around the world, and all we'd done was come to the world's largest jewelry store.

That's what I thought when I walked around Causeway Bay with its miles of display windows filled with Swiss watches. Or when I stared at the gleaming headquarters of banks, 40 and 50 stories tall, that canyoned the Central waterfront. Or rode through the curving streets of Mid-Levels, carved into a steep hillside and anchoring high-rise apartment houses with awnings and doormen that looked no different than Manhattan or Chicago's Near North Side.

It didn't feel foreign enough. I wanted the Hong Kong that James Bond prowled in "Thunderball" with a Victoria Harbour filled with Chinese junks. I wanted the Hong Kong of The World of Suzie Wong, all tropical humidity, slit-gowned women and imperialist gilt and guilt.

I was decades too late. The junks were all gone except for a few, available to rent out for a party cruise for yourself and your clients. By now, Hong Kong had completely achieved all its ambitions of developing into a simulation of a Western city.

But the skyscraper architecture, the lavish advertising were a veneer. Underneath breathed a Chinese soul and a hybrid uniqueness. The place had characteristics that couldn't have existed anywhere else.

If I stepped out of my office and turned left, weaving through the density of pedestrians along Canal Road with its streams of double-deck buses coughing out diesel fumes while more traffic thrummed overhead on the street's upper level, I'd pass small shops selling incense sticks and metal Buddhas, hole-in-the-wall noodle houses, aisle stores displaying neatly boxed candies, bins of flowers that overtook the sidewalk and curb with long stems and colorful petals, and then a side street for fruit sellers and fishmongers, their arms shiny with fish slime, their tables red with split-open fish and severed heads, the unblinkable eyes still staring.

I'd usually be out for the best coffee in the neighborhood, which happened to be in the second-floor McDonald's across from a towering mall called Times Square. One of the only *guailos* in the place, I'd be served my McCafe Latte by the same pretty young woman who every time gave me the same half-smile. I liked to imagine that the smile got warmer as the year went on, but knew the smile was strictly a formality. I loved the name on her name tag: "Corsica." Or I'd be meeting Ellen for a quick dinner at a Vietnamese place we found on a narrow side street off Canal, called Tang Lung Street, which had a row of unassuming restaurants. Some of them (not ours) put their tables right into the street at night for al fresco dining interrupted by the occasional minibus and surrounded by the upheavals of redevelopment. Those buildings still standing on Tang Lung Street were being allowed to crumble, just waiting for the day to be torn down for more office space, hotels and high-end shopping.

We were in the heart of the modern, striving city. But what was that drumming sound?

It was coming from Canal, echoing under the overpass. Here, the street was a city block of concrete above and below, a clangorous underbelly where long lines of passengers waited to board buses to get home, their faces looking the wearier under a dull-pink pall of dim fluorescent lights. The sound was an irritated *thap thap thap*. The sound of the curse ladies, or villain-hitters.

These were old women, squatters on plastic stools, who took your money, $6 to $12 American, and beat pieces of paper with an old slipper while chanting in a hoarse sing-song. For the small fee, these women cursed your enemies. It was part of the folk religion of Guangdong Province. There must have been plenty of people in competitive Hong Kong whose thirst for revenge outweighed their disbelief — the cuckolded, the dumped, the swindled, the sued, the demoted, the laid off — because, day or night, the drumming and chanting never seemed to end. I gave some thought to buying some curses myself, cheap catharsis for losing my job, my house, my savings. But I couldn't attach a villain to my misfortunes. Part of my curse was that I had no one to blame.

THERE WAS another, much larger, group of women who spent a lot of time sitting on the sidewalk. We'd see them every Sunday throughout downtown Hong Kong's parks, plazas and staircases. They staked spaces with blankets and hung out all day on their patches of ground, socializing, eating, dancing, talking, sleeping — vast numbers of women in colorful foreign plumage carpeting the surfaces as completely as the creatures in "The Birds."

The financial area around the landmark HSBC tower belonged to the Filipinas. Around Causeway Bay were the Indonesians.

All of them were nannies and housekeepers — the servant class that made Hong Kong comfortable for the well-off.

It took a while for us to figure out what was going on: These women, who worked a six-day week, slept in tiny rooms in their boss's apartments. Sunday was their day off. Hong Kong's public spaces were their default living-rooms. That's where they met their friends and enjoyed some time to themselves. It must have been the thing they looked forward to each week.

It was lovely to watch the women dancing, playing music on boom boxes, joking with each other. Touching to see them napping on each other's shoulders. And altogether poignant to realize the humanity behind Hong Kong's peculiar socio-economic social ladder. The city was flooded with these cheap workers who came by the tens of thousands, the cooks, the cleaners, the carers of children for the people in the nice apartments. The domestic helpers needed the work because however low the pay, it was better than anything they could find in their home countries. Many of them, in time-honored immigrant tradition, sent money home to support families.

But their lot in Hong Kong was destined to be lowly, no matter how long they stayed or how smart they were or how well they did their jobs. The law denied them the right to abode: the right to stay in the country without restrictions from the immigration department. We ran many stories in the *South China Morning Post* over protests and court cases testing the law. I was endlessly amazed at Hongkongers' vehemence in wanting to keep the foreigners from rising any higher on the social ladder. The usual rationale was that the immigrants would demand too much in social services. What the better-off didn't say was how much they benefitted from the immigrants' labor.

The domestic helpers kept losing in court. But they always had their Sundays on the sidewalks, their daylong picnics in the parks.

BEN DIDN'T really want to come to Hong Kong. He thought it would be too Western a place to count as a foreign experience. But we insisted. He should come and visit us for a few weeks in the summer. He could go to school and practice his Chinese. We could do some travel as a family.

It worked out better than any of us hoped. We took a trip to Thailand together, maybe our best vacation ever. Then Ben enrolled in a course in international business at the Chinese University of Hong Kong, which, its name notwithstanding, conducted its classes in English. Ben had never taken a business course and doubted he'd like it. His first day or two were not promising. His classmates came from everywhere: Korea, Australia, Russia, Hong Kong itself. They made fun of him for talking with his hands. He felt self-conscious about looking scruffy — the home uniform of New College of Florida — when they were all clean-cut. So he got a haircut, shaved his whiskers and bought a couple of shirts with collars. And before long, when they heard what he was saying, those kids didn't care if he talked with his hands. He could talk with his toes so far as they were concerned. Because what he said made sense. And that mattered, because the course was set up on the team principle.

The professor, a visiting lecturer from America, divided the class into groups and assigned them problems to solve as a unit. Ben's group was supposed to analyze Toyota's stumbles in Japan. He knew how to do research and how to explain a position to the whole class. His teammates promptly named him their captain, and soon he was assigning tasks to the others and enforcing deadlines.

He got an A, which he wanted to turn down in favor of pass/fail, explaining that the course was graded on a curve and some of the other students needed the good grade more than he did.

"No, no, no," we said. "This is no time to be generous. You earned that grade. Take it."

He did, reluctantly.

Ben's own New College of Florida, in Sarasota, did not issue grades. Students got written evaluations from their instructors. The college also required each senior to produce a lengthy thesis. Ben, combining his double-major in anthropology and Mandarin, decided to write about Chinese practitioners of a quasi-religious movement that was banned in the mainland. Many of its members had fled to Hong Kong, where they frequently demonstrated for their cause. The demonstrations were stirring — thousands of Chinese men and women marching for freedom and dignity, marches that wouldn't be tolerated on the Chinese government's home soil.

Ben met a few of their leaders, who soon took him to the apartments of refugees with rich stories to tell, sometimes speaking in Mandarin which he could pretty well understand with the help of his go-betweens. He plunged into the project, a real researcher, working with material so sensitive that he had to disguise his sources' names when he published his thesis.

In a scant few weeks, he got under the surface of things in Hong Kong.

THE BEST part of being in Hong Kong was very possibly the Foreign Correspondents Club, a glorious anachronism that held the romantic intrigue of an old Somerset Maugham movie. The club in fact did appear as a setting in John Le Carre's "The Honourable Schoolboy" — although then it was in a different building, closer to the harbor, and an important gathering point for media covering the Vietnam War. In the early 1980s the old colonial waterfront gave way to a modern Wall Street-like sea wall of gleaming financial towers, and the club moved inland and uphill into a handsome old pile on Ice House Street that was once one of the city's first places to buy ice cream and refrigerated milk.

Dominating the present-day club was a high-ceilinged room with an immense British-style bar, the stately wood posts holding racks of glasses overhead which never stayed empty long. Shelves and shelves of bottles stood behind quite-proper bartenders who started serving libations before noon and kept going until late at night. You could browse newspapers and magazines from around the world and meet friends for lunch or dinner. Sooner or later, you met everyone you knew in journalism at the FCC. I went there to hear a lecture on the supposedly insatiable sexual appetites of the last Empress Dowager. I went to watch the Super Bowl, which took place on a Monday morning, Hong Kong time, and for which the club laid out an American breakfast of bacon and eggs. We met friends in the club's Chinese restaurant for a feast of hairy crabs, an annual delicacy.

Once upon a time, the club truly was a journalists' place, a home away from home for itinerant European and American reporters and photographers; it still had a small shower, exercise room and workspace for correspondents on the go. For years, the only Chinese allowed were the cooks and waiters. But now it was a social club that welcomed the prestigious across all professions and races. We journalists were mainly on hand to assure the proper atmosphere, like Mickey and Minnie walking around Disney World.

Here was one place in the world where being a journalist still gave some social advantage. Instead of months, your application, submitted as an honored member of the working press, was acted upon within days, and you were charged a hell of lot less than the bankers, traders, lawyers and doctors whom you bypassed as you were waved in.

It was a club that would have me as a member, yet I was glad to join.

IF YOU made good money in Hong Kong, you could live well. Very well, indeed.

We became friends with one couple, Catherine and Guillaume, who lived in a spacious apartment on the quiet side of the island. Their living-room picture window looked onto an idyllic Pacific harbor. Pleasure boats bobbed peacefully before a watery horizon dotted with green hillocks. For this life of ease, the apartment rent was US$13,000. Per month.

They didn't pay it personally. Guillaume's company did. He was in shipping logistics, matching up cargoes with boats. He had plied the trade for years in France, but found he could do much better business in Asia.

"We're never going back," Catherine said. Although they loved France — a former lawyer, Catherine had started a business in Hong Kong to teach French manners and wine-and-cheese connoisseurship to the Asian nouveau-riche— they couldn't hope for the same high standard of living in Bordeaux.

Their neighborhood, it turned out, was filled with French people, and one evening the Barons invited us to a party. It was held outside, on the patio of their high-rise's swimming pools. All the women seemed casually elegant, the men relaxed and jovial, and the conversation always seemed to pull back, as if by magnetic force, to the topics of food and sex. It seemed very Gallic.

Oh, we had a fine time, Ellen and I, the token Yankees. We talked and laughed and charmed our way through the evening. One of the guests appointed himself refiller-at-large. He glided along with an open wine bottle in hand, and when he saw your glass reach the three-quarters-empty stage, he'd materialize to fill it up again. Soon I was tipsy. A little later I was drunk. After a couple of hours I could barely stand up to make my goodbyes. I was unconscious during the cab ride home. And still groggy the next day when Catherine called to check in on us.

"Are you all right?" she said, laughing. "My friends kept saying, 'Those American friends of yours. They don't know how to drink, do they?'"

To which I wanted to say: You weren't making fun of us, yo, when we were liberating your Parisian asses, were you? But my head hurt too much.

Lei Yue Mun: The Hong Kong that used to be

TOO LATE in our stay, we met Geoff and Angie. They were fellow journalists. Angie was a TV reporter who had been best pals with a dear friend from the States named Tomoeh. Once upon a time, Tomoeh and

Angie had been the most dynamic pair of Asian reporters in Cleveland. Then Tomoeh went on to the *Washington Post* and Angie to Bloomberg TV. In the summer of 2011, Bloomberg sent Angie to Hong Kong. Her husband, Geoff, put his own career as a TV news producer on hold to go with her.

They were Canadians, Geoff of good ol' Scottish extraction, Angie of Chinese, and had most recently been living in Chicago, my home town. She was beautiful and smart and funny and spoke Cantonese, and Geoff was hugely good natured and loved to talk about politics. We'd get together and crack each other up laughing all night.

On one night of high adventure, we boarded a ferry boat near their immense waterfront high-rise and took it across the harbor to a neighborhood called Lei Yue Mun. It was a ramshackle row along the water that still looked like the fishing village Hong Kong used to be, long before the British grabbed it and made it a node of the modern world. It was a still evening, a warm, pink sunset glow tinting the smog, night lights casting a romantic gauze.

We strolled along, and then went into one of the many stalls to pick our dinner. It was more aquarium than store, lined with tanks of live fish, crabs and sea creatures I'd never seen. Angie used her Cantonese to bargain with the proprietor. One by one, various choices went into plastic bags with water, as though to take home a goldfish for a pet. We paid, a cellphone call was made, and soon a boy of about 10 showed up. He took the bags and gestured for us to follow him. He led us through a maze of shops and store counters and restaurant, taking us all the way to the end of the walkway, which turned out to be the end of the promontory itself. He led us into a restaurant and we sat down at a table overlooking the harbor while our catches were sent into the kitchen.

And while we were on our second drinks of wine, the dishes started to appear, one recipe after another of seafood that was utterly fresh, delicious beyond description. The lobster was best. In a land where dairy foods are rare, it was served in a hot plate of baked spaghetti and cheese.

We were sated.

FRANK HAD been our landlord back in Shanghai, and he was also our host when we visited Hong Kong for the first time while we were still living in Shanghai. We hadn't meant for him to be our host. But when we told him that we'd made plane and hotel reservations for a long July weekend in his home city, he acted insulted. "I am a bit surprised that you've got your tickets as we should have arranged and taken care of everything as told you earlier over the phone call since you're certainly my great guests and good friends (if you allow me to say so!)," he said by email.

We wouldn't let Frank buy our plane tickets. We were adamant. But we were unsure what to do about the hotel. In a string of phone calls and emails, he kept insisting on paying our way. I worried that we were denying him face by turning him down. I did not have a solid understanding of face.

So I asked JJ, my boss in Shanghai, whether we should let our landlord pay for every bit of this trip as he seemed bent on doing.

"Yes, let him pay," she said briskly. Then she shrugged. "He's been charging you too much for the apartment. Let him pay in Hong Kong. You'll get some of your money back." With JJ, we were always overpaying.

And so our first visit to Hong Kong was practically wallet-free. Frank paid for the hotel, for tour-bus fares, for a string of luxurious meals. He smothered us with kindness. Smothered us, period, actually. We could hardly spend a minute without him and his wife, Eva, a lovely woman who seemed at times overwhelmed by Frank's mania for control.

Frank reveled in the role of host, showing us the best views of Hong Kong, the best egg tarts in Hong Kong, the best dim sum in Hong Kong, the best ferry ride in Hong Kong.

Simultaneously, he acted as if we Americans possessed super powers. His daughter had just graduated from Penn State University with a business degree. Could I help her get a job? I made a few inquiries with friends, which led to a job interview somewhere but not a job offer. All through our Hong Kong trip, he kept talking about a health problem he was having. He even showed us x-rays and doctor's notes.

What did we think?

"Frank, we're not doctors," we told him more than once. "You have to take these records to a medical person for a second opinion."

He looked at us, wounded, like we'd let him down.

When we decided to move to Hong Kong, we worried a bit about Frank. We wondered if he would take us by the hand the moment we landed and insist on taking the lead while we looked for an apartment, or choose restaurants for Saturday night dinner, or meet all his relatives during Golden Week. We worried that he'd suffocate us with kindness.

But we didn't hear from Frank when we arrived in Hong Kong. We didn't hear for him for the first month. Or the next month, or the month after.

We sent him a couple of emails, gave him our new local phone numbers. But neither Frank nor Eva got back in touch.

We wondered what we'd done to turn him off.

Eight or nine months went by, and we had pretty much forgotten about Frank, when one day Ellen and I stepped off a tram on Hennessy Street in Central, at the corner of Giorgio Armani and Louis Vuitton, one of the busiest spots in Hong Kong, and there on the sidewalk, facing the other way, were the unmistakable figures of Frank and Eva.

"Hello!" we called. "Frank! Eva! How in the world are you?"

They turned around and saw us. Their eyes widened. For a second they looked embarrassed. Then they opened up with smiles, as if we were the closest of long-lost friends.

How are you? Oh, we've just been so busy! It's so good to see you again! How is Ben? We've been thinking about you! We have to get together!

This went on for five minutes or so, a whole routine of feigned enthusiasm and nervous laughter, exchanges of phone numbers and promises to call.

We never did hear from Frank or Eva again. Every now and then, we'd think of them and wonder, what the hell was that all about? We weren't Frank's tenant anymore. We had failed to find his daughter a job in America. We seemed capable of getting around Hong Kong unguided. I guess we just weren't of any use to Frank anymore.

Maybe we should have given him an opinion on his x-rays.

54
Teaching Way Off the Beaten Track

Ellen:

WHAT'S THE worst time of the year to look for a teaching job in China?

Answer: Between Thanksgiving and Chinese New Year.

And that, of course, is when I started my search.

We landed in Hong Kong the week before Thanksgiving and I was optimistic about finding work right away. After all, it had been easy to find teaching positions in Shanghai: All I'd had to do was check the internet and look for "English Teacher Wanted."

I was exactly what mainland-Chinese were looking for. I'd see ads saying, "English Language Tutor Wanted. Experienced teachers with English, Canadian, or Northeastern USA accents only." And here I was, a New Yorker with a degree in English and years of teaching experience, the perfect candidate.

But there was one ad I definitely didn't like:

"English Tutor Wanted. Blacks need not apply."

It made me furious. Immediately, I shot off an email.

"How dare you discriminate by skin color! Don't you realize that there are some excellent teachers with dark skin? You are being ignorant."

The guy quickly replied that, yes, I was right, he agreed with me — it was wrong to discriminate. But he knew his customers: they would never hire a dark person to teach their children. So he felt it best to be right up front about it to avoid any wasted time. A practical attitude, he supposed, but thoroughly offensive to American sensibilities. It was a moment that showed me just how far from home I was.

285

I began my job search in Hong Kong by checking the Internet. There wasn't a single teaching offer worth pursuing. I wasn't worried. I figured I'd find tons of positions in the Sunday classified section of the newspaper. That was naive. The first Sunday was a revelation— most of the ads in the paper were for classroom positions available in August. It was now November. What was I supposed to do for almost a year?

I doubled down on my efforts and answered every ad that looked remotely promising. Hong Kong has a huge number of "tutor mills" offering classes in business English to the upwardly striving. Some jobs were being offered, but with a huge drawback — I'd have to teach on weekends. When would I spend time with Howie and explore the city? When I ruled those out, I was left with a big fat zero of teaching possibilities until after Chinese New Year.

I alternated between being frightened and depressed. Frightened, because I was looking at the likelihood of living on just one income in one of the most expensive cities in the world. What fun would it be to be in Asia without any money to travel and explore? Depressed, because I had nothing to do while Howie went off to work every day.

I spent my days on the bus or the tram, taking long rides around the city. I talked to strangers in coffee shops. I went to the park and watched children play. With no friends and no work I was a lonely mess. I fantasized hitting the "reset" button and going home. Then I remembered that I didn't really have a home to go back to.

I couldn't give up my job search. Every day I checked the classified section. Finally my luck changed. Po Leung Kuk, or PLK, the Hong Kong equivalent of the United Way, was looking for teachers. I called and arranged to speak with Michelle McEwan, the director of the English teaching program. PLK's main headquarters was near my apartment. I had passed it many times, impressed with its unique architecture: a series of buildings attached to what appeared to be a Buddhist temple, complete with a carved and ornately painted archway. I had never expected to enter that archway.

Michelle explained that Po Leung Kuk was a large philanthropy, active in lots of different areas, including aiding at-risk children by setting them up in group homes in housing projects on the city's outskirts. These were kids who were removed from their families because of some kind of turmoil — drugs, alcohol, a parent in jail. PLK wanted to give them not just a stable environment, but help in education so that the cycle of poverty wouldn't preclude them from becoming successful citizens.

Michelle was a lovely lady with a heavy Scottish burr. She'd call the youngest students "the wee ones." It was like listening to somebody in a fairy tale. She told me how much she believed in PLK's work. She had even adopted a Chinese orphan from PLK. We hit it off right away.

The job she had to offer was very exciting. She wanted me to go to the housing projects where the PLK students lived and teach them English in the evenings. I would be going to Kowloon, across the harbor from Hong Kong island. It would be like traveling to South Bronx from Manhattan.

I wouldn't work from an actual curriculum. I'd have to improvise.

"Your goal is to make them feel comfortable speaking English," Michelle explained. "They're good at reading and writing it, but their speaking skills are poor. You'll find that a lot of the kids are shy, and they won't be comfortable talking to a teacher from the West."

This brought me back. I thought of my first teaching assignment, in 1970 when I was fresh out of college. I had graduated with a degree in English and taken some teaching courses, but didn't have a teaching certificate. I heard that the Chicago School District needed teachers so badly that you could get a job with just an undergraduate degree. So I applied.

Before I knew it, I was sitting down with a placement counselor for an interview. The interview took five minutes. It consisted of being handed three index cards, each bearing the name of a school and a grade level. One card was for a high school class, one was for a fourth grade, and one for first grade. All were in rough neighborhoods, where I would never want to be after dark. The interviewer told me that all three assignments were open and I should choose one.

This was a no-brainer. I picked the first-grade card, figuring that as a petite, young, white teacher with no experience in the classroom, I'd have the best chance of success and the least amount of trouble with the youngest and smallest children. It was a decision based on survival.

And so my teaching career began, unplanned, with my working in one of the roughest parts of Chicago, teaching children from the ghetto — and I loved it! I was the first white person my kids had ever spoken to and we learned so much from each other that year. It was one of my favorite years of teaching. And now it looked like I had the chance to recreate it – in China.

I quickly accepted Michelle's offer, even though it meant I would have to take the subway.

Growing up in New York, I'd had bad experiences on the subway. When I was about five years old, I once was almost crushed when the train doors started to close on me during a rush hour trip with my mother. We'd gotten separated and she exited first, and there I was, surrounded by a tightly packed crowd of very tall adults, trying to get to her, while the door was closing – a childhood nightmare come to life. Other times I came close to getting knocked down the steep stairways when I tried navigating them with my polio-braced leg. Walking up and down subway stairs felt like mountain-climbing to me. It was petrifying.

I never lost my fear of subways after that. I made a point of avoiding them whenever I could.

My attitude changed in Shanghai. With taxis expensive for long distances and buses impossible to navigate if you couldn't read Chinese, I had to reconsider the subways. I was not a happy camper my first times out. But I soon got over my phobia, realizing that Shanghai subways weren't anywhere near as foul or scary as the ones I'd known in New York, Philadelphia and Chicago. Subway travel in Shanghai was a really cool way to get from Point A to Point B: inexpensive, efficient, safe and not too uncomfortable.

But Hong Kong subways were more stressful. The system was incredibly efficient, possibly the world's best, and the stations were gleaming clean and bright. You'd walk past dozens of advertising posters and lovely little shops underground — bakers, tea- and herb-sellers, fast food places. But the over-air-conditioned stations made it feel like entering a cave. You'd come in from the hot and humid sidewalk and hit a wall of freezing air. You'd glide down a very full escalator, and there you'd be with hundreds and hundreds of other people, all lined up very politely, everyone trying to be orderly. Except in rush hour.

Rush hour had a very desperate feel to it. If you behaved with any kind of decorum, you'd never get on the freaking car. There were just too many people who were going to push and shove to get on. So you had to push a little and squeeze, too.

I was small — a tactical advantage. I could squeeze around armpits and get to a place that felt safe on the car: a strap to hold, a wall or pole to lean on.

One section of Kowloon was dominated by people from India and Pakistan, wearing traditional long-shirted clothes, and I was only tall enough to reach their armpits, placing my nose in a terrible proximity. The lack of deodorant would sometimes almost make me swoon. But I learned to adjust. I ratcheted down my expectations for hygiene and absorbed myself in books on Kindle. I would read with my left hand, holding the subway strap in my right, looking up every few minutes to see where I was. The subway was great at flashing the minutes to the next stop. I got to where I could stretch my reading to the last 15 seconds, the point I knew I had to pack away the Kindle and scoot. I was very proud of my timing.

Subway rider

The subway would drop me into the pulsing heart of Kowloon. Emerging from the station I'd walk through a street market teeming with Chinese people buying anything from a live chicken to the latest high-tech cell phone, one jammed stall next to the other. Then I'd cross under a busy street by way of a pedestrian tunnel. Westerners were rare in this section of Hong Kong. I was often the only *guailo* — Cantonese for "honky" – but I never felt worried for my safety. I always felt safe in China, even in the public housing projects.

Sometimes I took the bus. The Hong Kong bus system was amazingly elaborate and thanks to my Chinese neighbor, Jon, I found a great route that started just half a block from the apartment, took me all the way through the tunnel under Victoria Harbour into Kowloon and dropped me off about five blocks from one of the group homes where I did my teaching.

But I was always a little anxious on the bus. I had a hard time anticipating when my stop was coming, even when listening intensely to the recorded announcements, straining to make out the Chinese sounds. Many of the intersections in Kowloon looked alike. I was afraid I'd miss my stop and not know how to get back. This actually happened once — the second time I took the bus. Instead of relying on a map, I asked the bus driver to let me know when I reached my stop, and he said OK. After a while, I spotted a stop that looked familiar.

"Isn't that it?"

"Oh no, oh no," he waved dismissively.

Ten minutes later, we were at the terminal, three stops too far. I was so angry with the driver, the know-it-all pretending to know more English than he really did. I had to really hustle to get to class on time that night.

The Hong Kong projects weren't like the Chicago projects I'd seen years ago, their stairwells reeking of urine, bullet holes in the windows, people always watching out for rats and cockroaches. Hong Kong public housing was clean and well-lit. The elevators were unthreatening. People on board didn't speak English but always gave me a smile.

Mothers would tell their little kids, "Say hallo," trying to get them to practice their English. The kids were shy, so I'd start the communication by looking right at them and smiling.

"I'll say hello first OK? Hello!"

And they'd laugh and then they'd say, "Hallo." Then everyone in the elevator would smile and laugh like it was the best joke they had ever heard. I felt like a stand-up comic who'd just killed.

The projects were large concrete buildings without many windows. Unlike the subways, the projects were un-air conditioned with just floor fans to move the warm, humid air around. I'd ring a bell or knock on the door, and wait and hear, "Just a minute, just a minute," and there'd be the rattle of keys and locks. It sounded like a prison guard welcoming you to Alcatraz. I got the feeling that security was important not because crime was rampant – on the contrary, the projects felt very safe – but because the adults in the home were responsible for the kids and couldn't risk any runaways.

In each home I visited lived a house-mother and her husband — foster parents to nine or 10 kids – along with an assistant who would cook and help with the cleaning and laundry. I met four sets of parents in the different homes, and they all seemed very sweet and caring. Even when the kids acted up or tried to cause trouble, the house parents handled the disturbances calmly. I was there often enough, for three hours a night in some places, to truly believe that the kids were in good hands.

The home in which I spent the most time was filled with teenaged girls — a cross between a sorority and a juvenile detention center. One of the girls would be screaming "She took my hair bow!" while another darted around the apartment holding the bow high in the air. The fight would end with the girls dissolving in laughter and the house mother shaking her head and smiling.

No one seemed to stay mad for long, but a few of the girls could be genuinely unpleasant. One, named Joyfield, was an extremely bright 17-year-old. At my first class session I had asked each girl to tell me three things about themselves. When it was Joyfield's turn she told me she hated living in the group home and that she was much smarter than the other girls. She was such a snob about her intelligence that she even talked down to me. I decided the best way to handle this was to put her down in a way she might appreciate.

During a conversation on "English adjectives that best describe us," I suggested to Joyfield that she look up "snide" and "obnoxious."

"I looked them up," she said the next time I saw her. "Point taken."

Without a set teaching curriculum, I was constantly on the lookout for interesting ways to get my students to converse with me. One day I brought in a Chinese celebrity magazine and played a version of "Who's Hot, Who's Not?"

I asked the girls to say who they thought was handsome and why. They pointed to the pictures of Asian pop stars, all bare faces and soft features: effeminate, to my eyes. They asked me if I agreed that the guys they had chosen were good looking.

Uh, no, I said. I preferred a different look.

Who? they asked.

"Brad Pitt," I said.

They looked at me quizzically. Had they actually never heard of Brad Pitt? We raced to the computer and quickly found several beefcake photos of the actor.

"Eww!" they cried and pointed to his strong jaw and rippled biceps.

I suddenly had an "ah ha" moment. None of the guys they liked had strong jaws. The girls didn't like muscles and six-packs. They looked for nice smiles and dreamy eyes and I suddenly understood why Michael Jackson was so popular in Asia.

One of the girls that Joyfield looked down on was Kiki, a quiet girl who, when I first started coming to teach, would never talk, but would hang back in a slouch, letting me know through her body language that she was there only because she had to be. She warmed to me after I tried to say a few words in Chinese. That made her laugh. She saw how I struggled and that I understood how hard it was to speak a foreign language.

Kiki wanted to talk, but was afraid she'd appear foolish. We had a breakthrough the evening we played "Who's Hot, Who's Not?"

Kiki pointed to a guy and said, "He's pretty."

"No," I corrected her, "he's handsome."

"OK, he's handsome."

She was getting animated by the conversation. Suddenly she stopped and said, "Can you believe this? I'm talking to you in English." And a huge grin spread on her face.

I smiled. "I knew you could do it," I said. "You just needed to know it."

One of the best conversation starters I found was a series of educational card games. The favorite was called "Sleeping Queens." You could learn a lot about the kids from the way they played it. The girls would pair up and play as teams, though no one said they had to. They'd be holding their cards and whispering. Joyfield, of course, always felt she had to win. She got really prickly if the game didn't go her way and berated the other girls who weren't as bright about the strategies they were using.

At another home, I played "Sleeping Queens" with boisterous teen age boys. You could almost feel the testosterone in the air. They played the game aggressively and felt no compulsion to play honestly. In one game a 14-year- old boy said, "Excuse me, I have to go to the toilet." From the twinkle in his eyes and the smiles from the other payers I figured something was up. I turned around and sure enough, instead of going to the bathroom he had climbed onto the sofa behind me to look at my cards and tell his partner what I was holding! To this day, I'm still not sure if I was more angry or amused at his chutzpah.

Some of the kids were stinkers. Like the girl who talked about my skin.

She was very attractive and self-possessed, a real rebel who would come in late and start talking just to disrupt the class. She made it clear she didn't care what my agenda was. The second or third time I met her, it was a warm night and I was wearing a sleeveless shirt. She sat down and stared at me.

Finally she asked me a question. "What is wrong with you?"

"What are you talking about?" I asked.

"You know." She touched her own forearm. "What's wrong with your skin?"

"There's nothing wrong," I told her. "They're called freckles."

"You know," she said, all superior. "There's something you can do for that."

She was referring to the creams that Asian girls use to whiten their skin. That's a beauty obsession, looking as white as possible. No stylish woman in China would ever intentionally get a tan.

"Yes, I understand," I said. "But these are called freckles. They're very common for Western people. You may not believe this, but some people think it looks nice."

"Oh, no, really?!" she said.

I started laughing. "Yes, really. In fact, my husband actually thinks I'm attractive."

"Really." Her tone was total disbelief.

At which point, the other girls jumped in. They knew she'd stepped over a line. "Don't listen to her," they pleaded, "She doesn't know what she's talking about"

I looked past them, and just laughed at her.

"Yes, really."

Ellen and Wing

OF ALL my students, my favorite was named Wing.

Michelle had told me ahead of time that Wing was special, that everybody who meets her wants to keep her in their life. And it was that way for me too.

At our very first meeting, she gave me a great smile, looked directly in my eyes, put her hand out, and said, "Hi, I'm Wing, really nice to meet you."

It was so not Chinese — or teenage, for that matter. All the other students I taught acted shy and elusive for the first few classes, and then they'd allow themselves to warm up. It was as if being shy was a form of good etiquette. But Wing didn't buy that, not at all.

At only 17, she had a great poise about her. Here she was, living in a foster home to escape a troubled family, but she never acted bitter or angry. She was very enthusiastic, and she talked with lots of hand gestures, which is very much not the Chinese way. Wing appreciated my time and valued it, and saw how I might be able to

295

help her. For instance, she was filling out an application for a college prep class and asked me to look at what she had written. One question that seemed to stump her was, "Write about what motivates you."

"I don't really know what they mean by motivation," she said.

So I talked to her about different motivators — like, how some people are motivated by pride to do well in order to get into a good school, or by the fear that their family would put shame on them if they didn't get good grades. I asked her, "What is it that makes you stay up at night and work for hours on the weekend, when you'd rather go out and have some fun?"

She thought for a minute and then said, "Oh, gosh" — she invited you into her thought process — "OK, I think my motivation is that I'm not happy or satisfied unless I do my best. It just doesn't feel right to me."

"Wow, that's the purist form of motivation," I told her. "It's not like you'll get money or a treat: those are external things. You have internalized the learning process, and you want to do your best for yourself, not to please anyone else. And that's fabulous."

I exchanged emails with her a year later, so I know that when she turned 18, she aged out of the foster care system and had to go back home and live with her family.

There was always a lot of yelling and arguing and she wished for a place of her own. She said she'd done pretty well on all the tests needed to go college. She'd needed a 4 on all subjects to get into a four-year college. She'd received a 4 on most things, and one 5, in English — but ironically, had only scored a 3 in written Chinese. She said that had always been her hardest subject. Now, because of one grade in one subject on one day, this brilliant girl was only eligible to go to a junior college. It seemed so unfair, but Wing was undaunted. She told me she would try her best at the junior college, and planned to go on to a full-fledged college when she graduated. I wish her the best.

I didn't realize how attached I had become to my students until it was time to leave them. Saying goodbye turned out to be much harder than I'd thought.

Almost every child gave me a small present or a handwritten note.

In one of the houses I visited, two sisters wrote:

> Miss Ellen
> Thanks you teach we English
> You is very nice, we very like you
> Sorry, Im English very bad, hope you understand my English.
> — Sally and OnOn

And there was this, from Kiki (reprinted just the way she wrote it):

> Thank you for you teach me. And you are the good teacher since you born in the moon. (Not in this world.) You teach me a lot of English word so my knowledge will be morn than before. I think it is international language so I am very hard to study it. I am so happy to meet you.
>
> Although you can't be my teacher we can be the friend. When you free, or nothing to do, you can email to me. Do you remember when first lesson — I am so cool — and now I am always smile at you and speak a lot of thing.
>
> Can I ask you a question? Why do you be my teacher and appeared in my live?

People have so much more in common than I'd ever thought. On paper, it looked like those kids and I shouldn't have had anything to talk about, We were so different in socio-economic backgrounds, in language, in age, in appearance, in life experience. But I totally related to them. We shared a lot. Which is amazing, when you think about it.

Although, for reasons I will never understand, they weren't into chocolate.

55
Stories in a Diaspora's Stones

Howard:

HAPPY VALLEY owed its name to the morbid sense of humor of long-ago colonials. The once-marshy neighborhood was originally a site for grave yards and "happy valley" was a Victorian-age euphemism for burial grounds.

A conspicuous cluster of cemeteries still sits there, just west of the historic race track, and I'd ride past them on the tram every day on my way to work. There was a Protestant cemetery dating back to the First Opium War, 1839 to 1841, the world-changing event that forced China to cede Hong Kong to Queen Victoria and to open four ports, including Shanghai, to Britain.   Adjoining that hilly resting place, where the first to lie was a British lieutenant named Benjamin Fox, killed by a cannonball in Guangzhou in 1841, were cemeteries for Catholics, Muslims and Parsees.

And off by itself was the Jewish cemetery.

It was a block and a half from our apartment on Shan Kwong Road, up a steep hill about halfway to the top, where the big apartment buildings would give way to the majestic Hong Kong Jockey Club. It was easy to miss it. Its gates were tucked between two much larger buildings, a Buddhist school trimmed in bright red paint and a Buddhist temple that hummed with the soft sound of chanting. But there we'd find it, the Star of David carved into its stone gateposts, a metal sign proclaiming "The Jewish Cemetery."

It dates from 1855, when the Sassoon family — prominent Jews from Iraq — bought the land from Queen Victoria. Jews began arriving in Hong Kong soon after the British took it over. By 1872, 40 Jews lived in the colony. Some of their remains are in the cemetery. A few sparsely worded sarcophagi went back to the 1850s.

In those days the cemetery must have been surrounded by farmlands. Now it was circled by high rises. But the cemetery remained a quiet place.

The surprising thing was, it was still in use, some 160 years later. We saw some graves that were only a few months old. We saw others where fresh stones had been laid. Souls here were still loved, missed and cared for.

The cemetery was larger than we suspected, with terraced plots that wound up a picturesque hillside studded with palm trees. Some 360 people are buried in the cemetery, according to a recent issue of Hadassah Magazine, which also estimated that about 5,000 Jews live among Hong Kong's 7 million.

The headstones were evidence not only of Jews' long history in Hong Kong, but of the incredible geographic diversity that had preceded them there:

Montague Levien Salamon, 40, from Sydney, Australia. Died 1887.
Pinchas Moses Papier, 56, born in Berdicheff, Ukraine. Died 1900.
Mayer Nachem Weinberg, 35, born in Alexandria, Egypt. Died 1901.
Pepi Eidelstein, 67, born in Brody, Austria. Died 1899.
Amalie Herzberg, 8 months old, born in Chemulbo, Korea. Died 1890.

Albert Weill, 48, born in Soultz-sur-Forets, Alsace, France. Died 1921.

Harry Landau, 26, born in Shanghai. Died in Saigon, 1931.

Dina David, 80, born in Harbin, China. Died in Hong Kong 1990.

Leon Weill, 38, who "died 27th April 1944 at Shamshuipo Camp" — a casualty of the World War II invasion of Hong Kong by Japan.

Some headstones told of devotion:

In memory of my dear husband Zeev (Vladimir) Shannon (Zubitsky), who taught me what real love is. Born in Kunalei, Siberia, May 25, 1905. Died in Hong Kong, January 4, 1973.

Some spoke of isolation:

Anatoly Livshitz. Passed away in Shenzhen, alone in this world, on 18 Tishrei 5766, 21 October 2005.

And there was this inscription, which truly haunted us:

You may be gone yet linger near
At the dawn of every day
And at every moment thought brings tear
For the son that we did slay

Sassoon Elias David Sykes
Born 2nd May 1937
Died 2nd May 1938

A child related to the famous Sassoon family … dying on the very first birthday, his parents seeming to confess a responsibility for his death.

What kind of tragedy was this?

It was a mystery, every bit as mysterious as the insistent survival of the Jewish people, who, though small in number and often despised, were scattered all over the world, yet managed to keep alive their identity and traditions and to prosper, one generation upon another, even in so remote a place as colonial Hong Kong.

56
Lessons From a Student

Kids at Mudpies: After school, more school

Ellen:
IT WAS the beginning of March, the Chinese New Year finally over, and at last I began to get more teaching assignments.

I got some work at an English-language private school named Mudpies, a short tram ride from our apartment.

It was a complete 180 from Po Leung Kuki

The Mudpies kids were aged 4 to 7. They were affluent Hong Kong children who were often brought to class by their nannies. Their supplemental English instruction was just one of many after-school obligations to go with their music lessons, organized sports and homework.

These children were expected to live very busy, scheduled lives, just like their parents. The curriculum was orderly and systematic. The students expected to complete chapters and take tests. Teachers were expected to keep detailed notes to prove to parents that their children were progressing. Since the classes were often taught after a full school day, we began the lessons with a 10- to 15-minute fun time – fun, meaning educational games.

Despite the regimentation, the school put great emphasis on creative writing and we were encouraged to help stretch the students' vocabulary.

If a child wrote, "The dog ran home fast," we would ask for alternate words until the new sentence might read, "The shaggy grey hound bounded through the park to reach his destination."

One of my students, a seven-year-old tycoon-in-training, found these exercises difficult. "Why is this 'being creative' so important?" he demanded. None of my explanations ever seemed to satisfy him.

THEN CAME a teaching assignment that was a complete surprise — giving lessons to a neighbor in my building.

Several weeks earlier, Howie and I had gone to the opening of Classified, a new branch of Western-style café around the corner from our apartment. We had been watching its progress for months. The "Coming Soon" sign promising a coffee/wine bar with gourmet pastries and cheeses sounded delicious, but expensive.

As with so many restaurants in our part of Hong Kong, there was an assumption that expats had large disposable incomes and could easily pay for Western treats like croissants and cappuccinos. A new luxury high-rise was being built down Yuk Sau Street from the café so they were certain to have a strong customer base. The thunderous pounding of the pile-driver and the incessant rat-tat-tat-tat of jackhammers usually had us avoiding the street during construction hours, but a promotional post card offering two-for-one coffees persuaded us to brave the dust and noise to try it.

Classified had an inviting indoor-outdoor feeling. The front wall opened to the sidewalk. The décor was contemporary, with an exposed brick wall and a large chalk board with the day's specials at the entrance. Patrons sat themselves at big dark wood tables with benches. Most of the customers were the wealthy-looking expats we expected, but next to us sat a young, well-dressed Asian couple with an adorable little boy.

This baby was cute even by my very high standards of cuteness for Asian babies — so I started to smile and talk to him. His parents seemed glad I was admiring their son, and we began a conversation. Their names were Mary and John and it turned out that they lived in our building. Both were native Hong Kongers and spoke English fairly well.

Mary said she'd had a corporate job before she had her baby and was now a stay-at-home mom. I told her I was a teacher, loved children and would be happy to babysit if she ever wanted some "mommy time." We exchanged phone numbers before they had to leave to put their son down for a nap.

I didn't hear from Mary, but that didn't surprise me. After living in Hong Kong for several months, I knew that people often said they would call and never did. And since the couple lived on the first floor, a chance meeting at the elevator was out of the question. And so I was surprised when one day Mary phoned and, instead of needing a sitter, asked me if I would consider tutoring her husband, John, in Business English.

Well, sure. We arranged for the first meeting to be at our apartment the next Saturday morning at 10.

On the day, John called a few minutes ahead to say that he was having trouble feeding the baby and that he would come as soon as he could. Strange, I thought. Why is he doing that when Mary is at home? But I didn't say anything.

About a half hour later, he arrived, looking very upset. And as he stood in the doorway of our tiny apartment, his eyes grew large.

"Oh, your flat is so big!" he said.

"Isn't your place the same size as this one?"

I gestured for him to sit on the sofa.

"Well, I guess so." he said. "It's just that the baby's things take up so much room that there's no space to walk."

He told he me he'd almost cancelled because of a problem at home. He said he had been feeding the baby when the baby food spilled all over the room, sparking a huge argument with his wife. She always insisted on his taking care of the baby on Saturday mornings. But she never seemed satisfied with how he did it.

I got the feeling that John had more on his mind than Business English.

Our class began with John explaining that he was one of four Chinese men working in an office owned and run by Australians. He said his job required that he give progress reports to his supervisors in Australia.

"I need to be able to talk on the phone to them and I feel nervous and don't know what to say. I'm afraid I may say the wrong thing because I don't understand what they are asking me. The office is very competitive and the boss is always comparing my work to the others. Sometimes they laugh at me.

"Do you think you can help me?"

He looked so nervous and unhappy. I could tell his stress at work was just the tip of the iceberg. I didn't know how much I could help him, but I had to try.

I began by saying that Australian English is very difficult to understand even for native English speakers. That seemed to make him feel better right away. He asked that I speak to him as I would to any English speaker: "Speak as quickly as you do to anyone. Don't slow down for me. I need to be able to understand English at a fast pace."

"I'm from New York. We talk faster than any other Americans," I said. "If you want to hear fast English, you've come to the right place."

John smiled for the first time.

We agreed to meet for two hours every other Saturday. I gave him articles from The New Yorker as reading assignments that we would discuss. To help him at work, I suggested he write himself some scripts that he could look at when he had to speak with his supervisors over the phone. I also suggested that when asked a question, he repeat it back to the person. That would allow him to make sure he understood what he was being asked and also give him some extra time to formulate his answer. We practiced, I asking him questions and he rehearsing answers.

John left our first meeting looking much happier than when he arrived.

Our second meeting began right on time — sort of. At exactly 10 o'clock John rang the doorbell. He was holding his son and smiling.

"Oh, will I have two students today?" I asked with a smile. "You know I love children. I'm glad you brought him."

"Oh, no. I was just on my way back from taking the baby for a walk and I wanted to explain that I would be coming to you as soon as I put him down for his nap."

A half hour later, John returned looking very different. He explained that Mary had the baby on a very strict nap schedule and she was furious that John had brought their son home a few minutes late. Again, an argument.

John wanted to know if I thought she was right to be so angry.

"Oh God," I thought. "I didn't sign up to be a Chinese marriage counselor!"

I told him that raising a young child could be very stressful and that it was common for couples to fight.

"We argue so much that the police have come," he confided. "We have a social worker that is assigned to help us and I can see a psychiatrist if I want to."

I was wondering what I had gotten myself into and thinking how happy I was to have Howie sitting in the next room.

Once John calmed down, the lesson went smoothly. He loved reading The New Yorker and wanted to talk about the advertisements in the magazine. He was particularly interested in the ads for high-end watches. He wanted to know what brand of watch Howie wore.

"I'm not really sure what brand he wears. Is that important?"

"In Hong Kong it is very important," he said. "You are judged by what you wear and your watch lets people know your status. If you get a promotion, you are expected to go out and buy a complete new wardrobe. Including a new watch. People expect it."

Aha! Since moving to China I had been struck by the prevalence of advertisements for luxury watches. The huge billboards for expensive timepieces were so prominent, I used them as landmarks to help me navigate my way around town. When I saw Nicole Kidman in a sexy white gown with her diamond studded watch sparkling on her wrist, I knew I was near my bus stop. Nicholas Cage was near the Times Square shopping center. Roger Federer and Megan Fox stood watch near our bank branch on Hennessy Road.

Watch advertisements, and jewelry stores showcasing watches were everywhere, and now I finally understood. It was a status thing. And for Hongkongers and newly prosperous mainland Chinese who came shopping in Hong Kong, status was all-important.

When I shared the watch story with my friend, Angie Lau, a Canadian expat with ties to Hong Kong, she told me an amazing thing. A friend of hers, a single career woman, had saved up her money to buy a designer purse. This friend went to the flagship Louis Vuitton store in central Hong Kong ready to spend about $3,000 for the purse. When she entered the store she was the only customer there. She looked around for a few minutes on her own. Then she was ready to speak to a clerk. But as hard as she tried, she couldn't make eye contact with either of the women behind the counter. They seemed to be avoiding her, acting like she wasn't there, looking at the store clock, peering out the window.

Finally a bus pulled up in front of the store and a group of Chinese women ran in. The clerks sprang to attention. One of this group went right up to the counter and studied the shelves. In less than a minute, she pointed to the purses on the top shelf.

"I want them," she said. Meaning, the entire shelf of purses.

She bought them all.

She was one of thousands of nouveau riche Chinese who flooded into Hong Kong every day from the mainland on special shopping junkets to buy things they couldn't get in their own towns. Money was no object to her. She was there to purchase status.

My neighbor John taught me a lot about what it is like to be a native Hong Konger. He was under terrible pressure to be financially successful.

He told me of visiting an old school acquaintance who invited him up to see his new apartment. John said the apartment was luxurious, with a huge window looking out on the city and a flat screen TV larger than John's own living room. He left his friend's home feeling like a failure. He could have had a larger, more comfortable apartment in another area of Hong Kong, he said, but he lived in our building because it was a prestigious location.

"People always smile and nod their head when I tell them I live in Happy Valley," he said.

John's wife Mary also felt the pressure. I would often see her walking with the baby stroller looking in the shop windows. She wasn't just window shopping, she was studying the window displays to know what she should look like to bolster her status.

I never saw her with any friends, so I invited her to go on an outing with me to Stanley, a village on the other side of the island. I had taken the half-hour bus ride there by myself several times and I thought it would be fun to have some company. I was wrong. Mary spent the time complaining about John and how much work she had with the baby. As she told it, John couldn't do anything right. He didn't help enough at home, and when he did, he did a bad job of it. When she wasn't complaining about John, she talked about how disappointed her mother was with her. I offered to hold her son and she looked surprised. She said her mother never visited or helped babysit. I guess she didn't think I would find holding a baby enjoyable. Now I understood why she had never asked me to help her with the baby.

The trip to Stanley was a short one. I had expected to have a leisurely stroll through the picturesque seaside village, taking our time browsing through the many shopping stalls in the market place. I thought we would end up at a café by the beach sipping something cold. But Mary seemed anxious to return home almost as soon as we got there. She kept looking at her watch. The baby would need his nap, she said.

A few weeks later John told me we would have to postpone any further lessons. He had been laid off and wouldn't have any money for lessons. I sent him off with my best wishes and several issues of The New Yorker.

Occasionally I would see John and Mary walking downtown with their little boy. Window shopping.

57
A Chuppa in Tianshan Park

Howard:

ONE THING we truly loved about Hong Kong: its value as a stepping-off place. People were always coming or going to some other country. Holidays in Europe. Long weekends in Laos. Visits home to New Zealand.

And so we traveled as much as we could, though less than we would have liked.

In Guilin Province in mainland China, we found the unworldly landscapes that were so haunting in the movie Crouching Tiger, Hidden Dragon, mound-like mountains that stand like fingers and blur in the mist. We were surrounded by them as we rode a boat on the Li River. They were in the near distance as we pedaled 10 kilometers on bicycle. And then we climbed intricately terraced slopes to Longsheng, an ancient town high up in the hills, where the "ethnic minority people" wear clothing that looks almost exactly like that of the South American Indians of the Andes.

In Bangkok, we sat stuck in some of the world's worst traffic jams and gawked at the astounding splendor of the old royal palaces and Buddhist temples. In Chiang Mai in Thailand's north, we flew through a jungle from a zipline, rode elephants through a lush countryside, got happily lost in a massive outdoor market. And everywhere in Thailand we met the world's sweetest, most accommodating people.

A wedding took us back to Shanghai. Our friend Rebecca Kanthor, a fearless young woman from Rochester who freelanced for CNN.com and Public Radio's "The World," was marrying Liu Jian, an artistic man with kind eyes who wrote novels and folk songs and played guitar; he was the guy who organized the club date at which Ben performed a year before.

We'd been to their house for a break-the-fast on Yom Kippur the previous fall. It was a strange setting: a ramshackle flat in a Chinese lane, where men in undershirts played mahjong under a bare light bulb till late at

309

night, laundry hanging overhead. Rebecca's parents had arrived for a visit and she had invited some American friends. Liu Jian smiled at everyone and said barely a word, his English consisting of little more than "hello" and "bye bye." A *b'racha* over the wine wafted over the lane off Wuyan Lu in the Xuhui district of Shanghai.

Now they were getting married. It would be their third ceremony. The first was a certification at city hall. The bored clerk stamped their papers without even interrupting her cell-phone call. The second was in Liu Jian's small home town in Henan Province, in central China. The whole town turned out. There were costumes and parades and the groom rode in on a horse. A photojournalist friend of Rebecca's produced a spread that went out over the internet — one photo, I was startled to see, making it into the *South China Morning Post*.

This celebration would be in a public park for the couple's Shanghai friends. Ellen and I flew into the city. Immediately, we felt at home. We knew these streets, the bicycle-lane railings alongside them, the architectural styles of the buildings that lined them, the food stalls, the convenience-store logos.

We visited the *Shanghai Daily*, where nothing had appeared to change, and had warm visits with JJ, Adam and old polisher colleagues. Ellen and I revisited our favorite restaurant with American friends, the dark and beautiful Yunnan-styled Lost Heaven. We had late drinks with two sharp young reporters for the *Daily*, the brash and funny Jessie Dong, and Xu Chi, who had picked for himself the very cool English name of Saladin.

Rebecca and Liu Jian and their friends rode to the park on bicycles. Rebecca's parents had arrived from Rochester, her brother and sister-in-law from Philadelphia; Liu Jian's parents had traveled from central China. One set of relatives didn't know how to talk to the other, so lots of smiles and nods sufficed for conversation.

We gathered in a green clearing, several dozen friends and relatives. The bride held a bouquet of yellow flowers and Liu Jian wore a simple checkered shirt. The couple stood under a *chuppah* made of a Chinese textile as a Mandarin-speaking American friend explained that the Jewish symbol represented the new home they were forming. Liu Jian and Rebecca exchanged vows they had composed in Mandarin and English.

Liu Jian's words were so heartfelt and guileless. He looked squarely at Rebecca's parents and said, "Don't worry. I will love her just as much as you do."

It might have been the first time that a man from Dong'an, Henan Province, stomped on a glass to mark his marriage.

We were happy for them. But we were also happy for ourselves and for the journey we'd taken. We couldn't believe that a place that had been so foreign 18 months before could now be so familiar.

We felt we now owned this place, in the way that one possesses new stretches of the world once you internalize them.

Shanghai was now part of us, and probably always would be — a city we could claim as a former home town, no longer half a world away, but as immediate as our thoughts and feelings.

Liu Jian and Rebecca Kantor, exchanging vows

Ellen:

ON THE day of the wedding we went for breakfast at an Israeli restaurant in downtown Shanghai, something we hadn't found in Hong Kong. I even bought four bagels to bring home. Howie had a small triumph — he was able to use his old ICBC bank card, the very card that that had taken him six days and three trips to the bank to get after he lost the previous one in an ATM machine. He remembered his pin code, found that we had about $20 left in the account, and used it to buy a wedding card to accompany our gift. We felt a small victory using that hard-won card.

We asked our old friends, Jacky and Michelle to meet us at the park. Michelle had told us that she had a surprise for us and it was the one I had hoped. She was pregnant.

She was quick to tell us that the baby was a Rabbit, a very good sign for both boys and girls. She didn't know the sex of the baby because even though she'd had ultrasounds, her doctor was not allowed to tell her the gender for fear that a woman would schedule an abortion if she found out that the only child she'd be allowed to have was a girl.

"Would you consider having a second child sometime?" we asked.

Michelle and Jacky looked a little uncomfortable. We'd said something sensitive. Michele immediately explained that under the current law you couldn't have a second child unless both the husband and wife were only children. Michelle was an only child but Jacky had a sister, so they didn't qualify to have a second child — yet.

There was talk the policy might loosen up in certain areas, including Shanghai. Couples like Michele and Jacky, with one parent being an only, would be allowed to have a second child. But it wasn't the policy yet. They would have to wait and see.

"Have you chosen a name yet?" we asked.

They looked confused. "How can you choose a name without knowing the sex?" they asked us.

We said that in America it was the custom to choose both a boy's name and a girl's before the baby was born.

"A good name can take some time to find," I said.

Michelle said that a trend with her friends was to choose a part of the baby's name based on *feng shui*. The idea was that the time of day you were born determined which of the five Chinese elements — earth, metal, fire, water or wood — you were weak in. You add a name that will add to the weaker element, helping you keep in *feng shui* balance. Right after the baby's birth, parents go to a website in the hospital and type in the time of birth and a computer tells them what element is missing and some names that might help.

Jacky didn't look as though he was totally behind the idea.

So now we had two set of friends expecting babies in the near future and both were very aware of how the government regulations can affect their lives. Our Canadian friend, Marc, was expecting a second child with his Chinese wife, and the second child may not have the same citizenship perks as their first born.

And Michelle and Jacky might not be able to have a second at all.

58
Breathing Badly in Hong Kong

Howard:

EVERY NOW and then, when working at my desk in the SCMP newsroom, I would become aware of the smell of exhaust, the kind you get when you're around an outboard motor, and feel the inklings of a headache. It was diesel fumes, seeping through the office's closed window panes from the heavy traffic that flew by on the overpass on double-decked Canal Street, just outside. We were on the third floor, but that was no escape from Hong Kong's constant traffic, which seemed to roll past our shoulders. I had never before worked in an office that felt like an occupational hazard, but there I was. Even sitting at my desk in the civilized setting of a newspaper office, there was very little I could do to avoid the city's pollution.

The bad air blew in from Shenzhen, mainland China's manufacturing capital, just 20 miles or so away, and it blew in from the enormous cargo ships that left the city's ports every day, filling the sea like an armada. Each ship was like a skyscraper tilted on its side, loaded with scores of truck-size containers stuffed with the goods for Europe and North and South America — the clothes, furniture, electronics, toys that feed our Walmarts, Targets and Costcos.

Most of all, the pollution came from Hong Kong's own vehicles. Any resident making decent money bought a car or had use of a driver — and the whole point of Hong Kong was to make money. Hong Kong was an island of hills that jutted quickly from the shoreline, leaving little land for building. Seven million residents managed to squeeze in by building up. The city had more 50-plus-story residential towers than any other place on Earth. From street level, this meant you were almost always walking in canyons of concrete, steel and glass. Car exhaust had nowhere to go. It just floated there, graying the streets and sidewalks, dimming the skies, entering lungs.

Everyone knew about the problem. City hospitals recorded 400,000 documented cases of asthma. The newspaper routinely published the pollution levels at street level as well as in the air above — and the street-level readings were always much worse. Surveys of expats showed that the single most important factor that might cause them to depart Hong Kong wasn't the high prices or the tough competition for apartments. It was the pollution.

Yet there was little to be done about it. A bill to ban vehicles from idling when at a stop had itself been idled by lobbies for truckers and cabbies, who claimed that shutting off their engines would hurt their incomes.

It hurt to breathe. I would step outside our apartment building and instantly my lungs would seem to seize up, punctured by a hundred little daggers. Ellen and I began using inhalers just to start the day, coating our lungs with a steroid to widen their breathing capacity. The spraying kept us going, but we knew it was inadequate as a solution. Too many particulates per million were making their way into our bronchial tubes, microscopic time bombs that would surely choke our health, or even shorten our life, if we kept it up.

We'd try to escape by heading up Hong Kong's mountains. We could take a bus or a cab to a high point and find hiking trails that would lead us for hours through forested thatches and swooping meadows. We could get glimpses of the sea from all directions. We could see the towers of Central Hong Kong. And from high up there, we could also see the gray-black cloud that hovered over the streets and buildings of the streets we'd left behind.

It was very peaceful in those hills. We could be alone with trees and sky and stone steps beneath our feet. We'd frequently find old pillboxes and bunkers, the defenses of British Empire soldiers hoping to stave off the Japanese invaders of December 1941. The Japanese won that time, turning Hong Kong into another outpost in their short-lived Pacific empire and forcing many Hongkongers into prison camps in Stanley on the island's south side. All these events seemed recent up in the hills, where the geography looked just as it did in the 70-year-old photographs on the visitor displays. Now the invaders were joggers and backpackers and people like us, desperate for a patch of serenity and the scent of plants and earth.

For the moment, we would feel the relief of having escaped the smog. But even up in Hong Kong's pastoral heights, where the curving hilltops met the sky and we'd want to inhale deeply, deeply, the air was not pristine.

315

It was fresh only by comparison.

From the hills above, we could see the smog of the city we below. In the foreground, our neighborhood, Happy Valley

THE JOB, back downtown, was just fine. I'd rarely worked with a smarter bunch of people, and the finished product, the paper that people held in their hands every day — spread wide and filled with clean graphics, bold photos and smart headlines — was a thing of beauty. But my position felt a little tenuous. Some days, my editing to make a story read smoother and faster would be undone by the next editor. I found it hard to make friends with the Aussies and Brits who shared my hours. They took smoking breaks, standing on the sidewalk on Leighton Road outside our offices' front door amid the diesel fuel of endless double-decker buses and delivery vans. I didn't know how they could breathe at all. We were polite with each other, but I wasn't one of them.

Reg recommended me to the University of Hong Kong to help teach an introductory course to graduate journalism students. I met with the director of the reporting and writing program, Gene Mustain, an American who was returning home to Seattle after many years in Asia to give his son a high school education in the U.S. and a chance to play American football. He liked me. I got the job, and soon I was meeting with one of the other three instructors, a *New York Times* correspondent named Kevin Drew, to bone up on the curriculum and to select students for the sections each of us would teach. I'd have about 30 students and teach for four hours every Saturday morning, from late September till mid-December. I loved the idea, even though it meant spending hours grading papers. I had never taught journalism, but always had thought I someday should. Here at last I could gain the credential I most lacked when seeking teaching jobs in the United States. Every potential employer had wanted to see previous teaching experience. I didn't have any. Now I could fill that blank spot on the resume.

I spent several mornings at the university, poring through the admissions statements of the incoming students, trying to group the class by general skill level. The campus was built on a steep hillside, unlike any I'd ever seen. I'd get out of a taxi at a main gate at the base, climb some steps to the nearest building and take an elevator to the top floor. I'd leave that building and find another building to walk into, take an escalator to the top of that building, get out and find another building and another escalator — until I was about three-quarters to the top of this vertical campus. There it was, the Journalism and Media Studies Centre: a stately Georgian colonial building that smacked of British Empire, surrounded by trees and looking out from the heights onto a gray-blue distance and Victoria Harbour.

I tore through binders of applications. I noted students' ages, places of origin. They came from all over the world, a surprising number from mainland China.

I read the essays. One young woman from Hunan said she was inspired to become a journalist by visiting the Newseum in Washington, D.C. She wanted to dispel Americans' "ignorance about China."

The statements of purpose were inspiring.

"I want to bring a better picture of my country to the West." (Female, 22, Kowloon)
"I want to give voice to ordinary people in China." (Female, 23, Guangzhou)
"I truly appreciate freedom of speech after working in Beijing." (Male, 23, Hong Kong)

"I always want to write for the right." (Female, 22, Chongqing)

Reading these, I reconnected with the reasons I'd become a journalist in the first place, reasons that had gained some rust over time. What I did as a journalist had become a routine, a set of skills, a barrage of tasks to be managed, an identity, a salary. But when I was in my 20s, I too had believed that journalism had the power to change the world. I had seen it happen. Woodward and Bernstein had brought down a lawbreaking president just a year before I entered journalism school. After 35 years in the field, though, it was no longer so easy to believe that the mere act of bringing facts to light would bring justice. I'd spent a lifetime of getting words into print, and now my goals were much more modest: It would be enough to instill in these students the ability to discern truth from lies. It would be great if I could teach them to avoid adding to the world's store of bullshit.

I would love to do that, I thought.

As long as Hong Kong didn't kill us first.

I WASN'T so sure that wouldn't happen.

And so even as I planned on teaching in the fall, Ellen and I began, almost accidentally, to plot a return to the States.

Robert Strauss, a freelance-writer friend, tipped me to a job opening up in the Philadelphia area. Swarthmore College would soon be looking for an editor for its alumni magazine, its long-time editor Jeff Lott stepping down after almost 25 years. They'd be needing a replacement around January. What a beautiful gig. I could picture it: Returning to Philly, where I had many friends. Only a two-hour ride to New York, where I had more friends. Working at a college, a setting made to order for a former higher-education reporter, filled with interesting subjects, smart people to write about and a noble cause to promote, the advancement of the beleaguered liberal arts. A job sure to provide the security I wanted — steady employment for the next few years and good health insurance.

I wrote to Lott, introducing myself and looking for guidance, and he told me the search for his replacement wouldn't officially begin until the fall and advised me to contact a vice president for communications named Nancy Nicely. I sent her a letter by email. A reply came back within hours: Nancy knew me! We had worked together at the *Inquirer* 25 years ago, when she'd been Nancy Nowicki before she got married. One day, she reminded me, we had stood in line all morning on Philadelphia's South

Street for Springsteen tickets. She was thrilled to hear from me. And yes, even though the job formally wouldn't be posted until autumn, she was sure it could be arranged for Swarthmore to interview me in August, when I'd be returning home for a three-week visit.

I shot Ellen an email, telling her the news.

"OMG, this sounds really good, *kinehora*." Ellen emailed back.

"*Kinehora*" is Yiddish for "without the evil eye." It's what you say to keep bad luck from destroying the good thing you are talking about. Ellen was convinced that if you didn't utter "kinehora" as soon as you said some piece of good news, you were inviting its destruction. It was a silly superstition, but after spending half a lifetime with her and seeing how often fortune can reverse itself, I had learned to take no chances.

"Right!"

We needed our luck to hold. Escape was getting more urgent. Ellen wasn't well. She'd started feeling dizzy within weeks of our landing in Hong Kong. It was a kind of vertigo. She would rise from bed, or stand up after sitting in a chair, or simply turn her head, and her vision would blur, her surroundings taking their time to catch up with her like a slower moving pan shot in a movie. I knew the feeling because I'd had surgeries years before that tampered with my inner ear. It was a dizziness that, like motion sickness, brought you almost to nausea. You didn't want to move too much. Sometimes you didn't want to eat. The only real comfort was to sit as still as you could.

But immobility was not an option while we lived in Hong Kong. We had to walk places to shop, to eat, to work. We developed a routine whenever we walked up or down stairs or took an escalator — and we were always taking stairs or elevators, going down to the subway or up to one of the city's mazes of walkways that connected you from building to building above the streets. On the way up, I would take the step behind El and place my hand on her waist to steady her. Going down, I'd stand in front of her and she would place her hand on my shoulder for bracing. She rarely told me how lousy she felt. She simply bore it, leaving it to me to notice at times how much slower she was walking, or how all of a sudden she had gone pale.

We didn't know the cause. Maybe the pollution. Maybe the height of our apartment. Maybe the constant rattling of truck motors vibrating through our walls. Maybe the click-click-click-click of the crosswalk lights, noisy aids for the blind that mostly succeeded in irritating the not-deaf.

Any way we analyzed it, the culprit was Hong Kong. In some way Hong Kong was making us sick.

That feeling was reinforced when we took a trip home in August. Ellen's vertigo seemed to lift — not entirely, but some. Ellen and I visited our respective mothers, whose poor state of health was noticeably worse and who practically begged us to come back. We breathed fresh air, hung out with people we loved in Chicago, Florida and Philadelphia.

And I had a terrific trip to Swarthmore. I met with Ms. Nicely and our hour flew by … nicely. The campus was gorgeous, all trees and flowers and stately Victorian buildings on wide rolling lawns. We flew back to Hong Kong amid weird conditions — an earthquake had rippled Philadelphia the day before; as we took off, a hurricane was bearing down, apparently confusing the City of Brotherly Love with Miami. We were in a strange mood. We had liked the familiarity of America. We didn't really want to return to the tumult of Hong Kong.

Back in Hong Kong, we were lamenting this one day over the phone with Ben, who was back in the States after spending the summer with us in Hong Kong. He had done well in his course at the Chinese University of Hong Kong. He'd done amazing research for his college thesis. He'd accompanied us to Thailand, a wonderful trip. Yet for all that, he hadn't liked money-mad Hong Kong very much at all.

To Ben, the answer was obvious.

"You should just get out of there."

Made sense. So much sense that I soon gave notice at the *South China Morning Post*. My last day with the paper would be the last day of my contract: November 15. It didn't feel like a radical move. Reg had already left the paper, all but pushed out by his struggles with the publisher. A couple of his favorite reporters were out the door as well, and a top assistant also would soon be leaving, all scooped up by Thomson Reuters. With my rabbi gone, my position at the paper seemed less secure.

Well, Reg never did promise me longevity at the SCMP. He hadn't been sure how long he would stay himself.

And I told the University of Hong Kong that I had better not get started with the class I was supposed to teach. The sessions wouldn't end till late December, and I wouldn't want to have to quit in the middle. I recommended Alex Lo as my replacement. And my career as a college instructor came to a close before it began.

Little by little, we began telling our friends we'd be leaving in

November. And always, we got the same reaction.

It didn't matter where they were from: Hong Kong or mainland China, Australia, Canada, Singapore, France, England, Scotland, Ireland. They all looked at us with the same mixture of amazement and pity.

"What in the world would you go back to the U.S. for?" they would sputter.

"First of all, your government is a dysfunctional mess — hell, the Republicans nearly put you in default." This was after the House almost refused to lift the debt ceiling in their never-ending battle to stymie anything backed by Obama.

"Your economy still sucks. And you won't have health care."

It was all true. The United States stood alone in the world as the one advanced nation that lacked guaranteed, or even affordable, health care. Yes, Obamacare had been enacted in an historic victory, but its main provisions wouldn't kick in for three more years — that is, if the Supreme Court didn't overturn the law or a GOP majority repeal it. Even if enacted as scheduled, Ellen and I would be eligible for Medicare by then and wouldn't need it. In the meantime, El and I would be too young for national health coverage, yet too old to avoid falling apart. By going home, our finances would teeter, and probably so would our peace of mind.

Every now and then, one of our foreign pals would throw in a kicker. "You'll be lucky if you don't get shot."

I suppose this was the last great lesson we learned from living abroad. Around the world, people saw America as crazy — and very possibly, hopeless. Back home, I reflexively thought of America as the greatest nation on earth, the global beacon of liberty and opportunity. But to others, we were the loonies who held it sacred that every man, woman and child had the right to own a gun but not to be cared for when anyone gets sick. I saw a political system that, despite its abundant flaws, had set the template for self-governing republics worldwide; foreigners saw a country in the grip of billionaires, corporations and right-wing crazies who held the power to rig the tax system, allow Wall Street to run wild and block any sensible action on, say, global warming. They saw our armed forces not as the needed global policeman, but as cowboys with high-tech weaponry. We lectured nations about human rights. They saw Guantanamo and Abu Ghraib. And this was the view of our friends.

Our foreign friends all admired Barack Obama and couldn't understand the animosity of his Republican opponents. They had seen the parade of batshit crazies competing in the Republican primaries: Rick Perry, Newt Gingrich, Herman Cain, Rick Santorum, Ron Paul, Michele Bachmann... and shuddered that one of these yahoos could actually become president in 2012.

"It's all true," I said when I heard their rants, "everything you say. But what can I tell you? It's home. It's the only home we've got."

Ellen and I had sat out the U.S. recession for two years, and by now, we'd hoped, the economy would right itself. It hadn't.

Nevertheless, we realized we weren't cut out to be expats indefinitely. We'd been gone long enough. Maybe we'd have to taste our country's bitterness, to borrow a Chinese saying, but we had to do it. Dodging the bad times by perching ourselves in Asia had been a great idea, but with our health at issue and our parents struggling, it had a time limit. And time was up.

One day in late September, I spent an hour on the phone via Skype with two members of the Swarthmore search committee. It was a nice talk. They sounded intrigued by my experiences: as a journalist who'd covered many subjects, but especially higher education for the *Philadelphia Inquirer*; as college student in the Sixties, a period that meant a lot to the liberal, activist-minded college; as an expat who had widened his intellectual horizons by stepping outside the United States. They were friendly. I was beginning to think of them as future colleagues. They thanked me for my time and told me to sit tight. It might take weeks for the committee to take the next step and get back to me.

And so with some confidence we made airline reservations. We began selling off household goods, toted up the money we'd have to pay in Hong Kong taxes upon our exit, scheduled farewell parties.

One night after Ellen had gone to sleep, I was browsing my laptop around 3 a.m. when an email arrived from the States that jolted me fully awake. It was from Swarthmore.

Odd. Only four days had gone by since I'd spoken with the search committee. I wasn't supposed to hear from them for weeks.

I read the email. Then I woke up Ellen.

"I didn't get it," I said.

"What?"

"The job. Swarthmore just told me that I didn't make the next round of cuts."

"What? Are you kidding? But it went so well..."

"Yeah, I know, it did go well. They said that they were, quote, intrigued by me. But every other candidate they're still looking at has already been a college magazine editor. And that put me at a, quote, competitive disadvantage."

"Oh. Oh, no…"

"Yeah."

We sat there for a while, on the edge of our shelf-like bed in our tiny Hong Kong bedroom. My skills were not so transferrable to another field after all. With the job market so tight, employers could find the exact fit for whatever they needed. They wouldn't have to imagine whether a newspaper guy could edit a college magazine. They'd have a half-dozen college magazine editors to choose from. They were proven quantities.

So the Philadelphia dream was over. We'd return to Florida and camp out in Rachel's spare bedroom while we figured out our next move.

We were heading back to the States in the midst of a recession, and I didn't have a job. I had a lifetime of skills and experiences in an industry that wasn't hiring.

Oh, shit.

59
Epilogue

Ellen:
WE RETURNED to America in November 2011 feeling a bit beat up.

Howie came back with a bad back that required extensive visits to the chiropractor and some very weird ear infection that took a while to clear up. He called it his final "fuck you" from Hong Kong. I wasn't feeling much better. In addition to the almost constant vertigo, I had developed a problem with my foot that made walking painful.

And so we limped off the plane feeling more relief than exhilaration. We arrived just in time for Rachel's 35th birthday. She and Tal generously allowed us to move into their guest room in Hollywood, Florida. Us and our six bulging suitcases. Tal warned Rachel we might be there for a while before we could find an apartment. I hoped he was wrong. I was anxious to have my own place — but I had to admit it, living at my daughter's house was wonderful. After 450 square feet in Hong Kong, Rachel's house felt huge. I felt like an immigrant walking from room to room marveling at her modern appliances and swimming pool. I enjoyed helping with the laundry and having a clothes dryer again.

Most of all, I loved being so close to my grandchildren. One night, soon after our return, I was in Logan's room saying good night to him.

"Logey," I said, "I want you to know how much I missed you and how very glad I am to be back here with you."

Logan, who was just turning 8, solemnly nodded his head in agreement.

"GG, can you promise me something?" He and Sydney called me GG, short for Grandma Goodman.

"Anything I can, Logan. What do you want?"

"Well, I just want you to promise that you will stay here in Florida until you die and go to heaven. Can you do that for me?"

A knife to the heart. I hadn't realized how much he'd missed having his grandparents nearby.

"I promise to do my very best to stay here," I told him. And I meant it.

The first few weeks back were rough. Our plan was to stay at Rachel's house while we searched for an apartment. To do that, we needed to get a car. After two years without driving, I wanted something familiar, so I bought the same model Accord I had before we left. The drive away from the dealership was surreal. I was driving down I-95 in a Honda, listening to a familiar Latin radio station, passing familiar buildings. For a long moment I felt disoriented and confused — had anything changed at all? Had I just imagined the fantastic adventure of living in China?

Two years before, we had left optimistically. We were going to take advantage of our lives' unexpected turn, see the world and maybe find fame and fortune. We accomplished one out of three. Now we were paying the price for re-entry. After buying a car and two iPhones and putting down three months' rent, our savings were badly depleted. The cost of reclaiming a place in the American middle class was staggering. When a friend of ours years ago had moved to New York City, he said that he felt like he "hemorrhaged money." I knew the feeling.

We moved back to Delray Beach, where my real estate office, parents and friends all were. We were lucky in our house search, finding a wonderful two-bedroom apartment overlooking the Intracoastal Waterway at a rent we could handle. One month after arriving, we emptied our storage unit and moved in. It was fun settling in, reacquainting ourselves with our long-stored possessions. Howie quickly framed and displayed fabulous photos of our two years abroad.

Michelle, one of my American pals in Shanghai, had cautioned me about reentry. She said she'd been warned by a few of her expat friends that she might need counseling when she got back.

"I know I have to be careful not to brag about China," she said. "People in the U.S. don't really want to hear much about what your life was like there."

Was that right? I wondered. Erring on the side of caution, Howie and I followed her advice and made a conscious effort to tone down our conversations about living abroad. We didn't want to sound too much like China boosters, fearing that people would interpret our good feelings about China as some kind of disloyalty to our native country.

I wish I could say that we had a seamless transition back to our former lives, but that would not be true.

My life looks the same on the surface. I work at the same real estate office, spend time with my daughter and her family and try to give my mother the emotional support she needs as she struggles with my father's advanced Alzheimer's disease.

But it doesn't feel the same.

On the positive side, I love my home and remind myself daily how lucky I am to live in such a beautiful and pollution-free environment. But I miss the adventure. I loved that we were able to travel to exotic places I hadn't even know existed. It was great living with a "where to next?" mentality.

It's been five years since our life was upended, and I've learned many things.

I learned I am capable of great change.

I learned that my love for Howie only strengthens through adversity.

I have learned not plan too far in advance because things have a way of shifting and changing.

I have learned to try and live in the present moment and to enjoy it.

Will we get another chance to live an exotic life? Or are those days over? Am I destined to live out the rest of my days as a Florida grandmother?

I get anxious about this sometimes. I wish I knew what tomorrow is going to bring. But then I tell myself, You can't know.

I inhale deeply, hold the breath, put my fingers together Buddha-style, and tell myself: "Embrace the uncertainty."

Howard:
THE APARTMENT in Delray Beach overlooks the Intracoastal Waterway, a broad, peaceful canal. We have a roomy screened-in balcony and a view of a bridge that opens every half hour to let pleasure boats pass though. The sun

is bright, the air fresh and clean. For days after we first arrived, we just breathed the sea-scented oxygen. The two-bedroom two-bath rental felt like a steal at $1,400 per month, and it came with a community swimming pool, tennis court and exercise room. It was like a resort. A Publix grocery, drug store, restaurants and a movie theater were all within a 10-minute walk, and the beach and the Atlantic Ocean were 15 minutes by bike.

If we had moved here from our old house in Delray Beach, our mobility would have felt depressingly downward, but coming from Hong Kong, this 1,100-square foot apartment was downright roomy. With some adjustments, and a few book cases from Ikea, we found space for almost all the possessions that we wanted to hold onto.

Ellen slipped back into work right away. Her real-estate colleagues had kept her desk warm, and she began selling homes almost immediately. By being away for two years, she had missed the worst of the housing crash. Now the market was flickering to life. Her timing was perfect.

Her parents were thrilled to have her back and so were the grandkids.

Me, I had a harder time. Despite the dissatisfactions of Hong Kong, I hadn't really been ready to give up our life of travel and wasn't at all keen on settling back in Florida. I was torn for months, not knowing what I wanted to do, where I wanted to live. A newspaper editorship arose in Northern New Jersey that I could have taken. But I turned it down because it would have meant leaving Ellen much of the time, and we couldn't afford two residences nor the emotional cost of a separation. I interviewed for jobs in Montgomery, Ala., and Bradenton, Fla., telling myself that having health-care benefits would be worth relocating to a sleepy Southern city, living apart from El and conducting a long-distance marriage — until I snapped out of it and realized how unrealistic that was. I vowed to be content with my lot. But I couldn't stop obsessively scouring the journalism job websites.

Bobbey's powers of prediction, it turned out, had their limits. She had seen China as my doorway to a bigger future: books, lectures, articles, a bright next career as an Asia observer. It didn't happen.

For a while, I was able to keep working for the *South China Morning Post* via the Internet. I edited lengthy stories about industrial pollution in mainland China while overlooking the peaceful waters and Spanish-style mansions of South Florida. It was a sweet reversal: China outsourcing work to America!

I also started doing news reports online for the Florida Center for Investigative Reporting, a nonprofit news service that had sprung up in the void left by the collapse of newspapers. But the pay was low, even for a part-time job. Meanwhile, the SCMP named a new editor. New bosses came in whom I didn't know; the work from Hong Kong slowed to a trickle, then ended altogether. For a while I worked as a reporter covering Florida courts for a newswire for business lawyers. Then a better offer came along: to join a national nonprofit called Innovations for Learning. I became their staff writer, working from home in Florida, looking for stories to write about initiatives to improve public education. Money is tight, but we are getting by.

A year after we returned, my mother's long decline came to an end. We were nearby when she died, and for that alone we were glad we had returned.

I'm writing this with the view of the languid Intracoastal out the window. A sightseeing boat just floated by, disappearing beneath the drawbridge. Every now and then I go out into the humidity and swallow gobs of the fresh coastal air.

But I'm not planting roots. Something has happened to my idea of permanence. I think about all the other places in the world to possibly move to. I seek out the world news on TV, and when I see something on the BBC or anything about China, it's familiar with layers of understanding that were unknown to me before. My sense of belonging does not stop at our national borders.

I miss being out in the world, the feeling of being at the crossroads of cultures interacting, trading, borrowing from each other, in constant motion. It thrilled me that when Ben was in Shanghai, his college mates were from Ukraine and Kazakhstan, Saudi Arabia and Sweden, Korea and Los Angeles. In Hong Kong, his friends were Chinese and Russian and British. He never has to lose track with them. They're all on Facebook. This is the way the world is going: nationalities, like time zones, melting away. Cultures becoming more porous, opportunities more interconnected. It's an exciting time in history and exhilarating to be in the thick of it.

If our experience taught us anything, it's that there is a wide world out there, and no matter how old you are or how much your life has taken you in a single direction, you can change course. You can break your patterns. You can put yourself in places you never knew existed. You can see with fresher eyes.

You can hear something that sings to you in a language you never knew before.

River City, Guilin, mainland China.
(Photo: Jennie Parker)

Acknowledgments

OUR THANKS to the many people who helped us with this book.

Sue Hill's imagination and *guanxi* got us to Shanghai. Her editing tips and insights helped make the writing better. Barry Bearak and Conrad Grove offered invaluable editing advice and encouragement. Ben Goodman, who gave us such joy by being overseas with us, provided perfect suggestions on improving the book's tone and title. Belinda Long Ivey designed the brilliant cover. Jennie Parker, one of our traveling companions in Guilin, snuck a photo of us on a bike excursion through the region's small towns, and very kindly let us use it in the book.

We want to thank colleagues at the *Shanghai Daily* and *South China Morning Post* who looked over the manuscript. The *Shanghai Daily*'s main editors Jiang Jianjun and Peter Zhang declined to comment on the book and took no part in its production. We hope they see in it in the admiring spirit that was always intended.

And we want to thank our loved ones who helped us on our adventure. Our daughter, Rachel, and her family bore the brunt of our absence from Florida. Howard's sisters Susan and Barbara sent us books and other hard-to-find essentials when we were in Shanghai, unflaggingly cheered us on and gave us some terrific editorial advice. Howard's brother-in-law Seth Weinberger provided work and sustenance while this book was being written. We'll be ever sorry that our time in China kept us removed from our son, Mike, and his bride, Kate, as they embarked on their own adventures in Seattle.

Special thanks to our parents, the late Miriam Goodman and Gert and Martin Rubin, who gave us their love and support despite their own hardships. And to Howard's late father, Carol, our model in creating a life after a layoff, and whose personal motto — "Be of good cheer" — was never far from our minds.

Made in the USA
San Bernardino, CA
01 July 2014